ANIMAL SPY

Animal Welfare Behind Enemy Lines

TERRY SPAMER AND
GORDON THORBURN

THISTLE
PUBLISHING

First published 2007 by Vision

This edition published in 2015 by:

Thistle Publishing
36 Great Smith Street
London
SW1P 3BU

www.thistlepublishing.co.uk

ISBN-13: 9781910198827

To Denise

A Robin Redbreast in a cage
Puts all Heaven in a rage.
A dog starv'd at his master's gate
Predicts the ruin of the State.
A horse misus'd upon the road
Calls to Heaven for human blood.
Each outcry of the hunted hare
A fibre from the brain does tear.
A skylark wounded in the wing,
A cherubim does cease to sing.
The gamecock clipp'd and arm'd for fight
Does the rising sun affright.

He who shall hurt the little wren
Shall never be belov'd by men.
He who the ox to wrath has mov'd
Shall never be by woman lov'd.

Lines from 'Auguries of Innocence' by William Blake

CONTENTS

ACKNOWLEDGEMENTS

Loyalty and integrity are unusual qualities and I have been fortunate in being supported and inspired by some very unusual people. Denise has never doubted, Gordon and Andrew have never wavered, and Billy has given me his unconditional friendship over many years. I also thank Jim for taking risks and working with me, Ken for all his help with Ruadan, Faye for teaching me all that fieldcraft, and Lesley, Iris, Twyla and Sonja of Christa's marvellous Animals' Angels. Thanks also to Ken Lees of KGL Estates.

Terry Spamer.

INTRODUCTION

Imagine a little boy of four, perched on the settee between his dad and his dad's brother. The men are drinking beer. Dad is listening to his brother tell a story. The boy is eavesdropping, not realising that the story is being told for his benefit.

'There's a lonely zebra, see, got separated from the herd, and it's a hot sunny morning by the banks of the Ubangi river which, as every schoolboy knows, flows into the Congo. Poor zebra. All alone. In that heat. He munches a few blades of grass, flicks his tail at the flies, munches a few more blades of grass, and decides he really needs a drink. Which can be a very good idea at certain times of the day. Oh, thank you. Yes. Double Diamond will do well.

'Now, the zebra knows that drinking from the cool, cool waters of the Ubangi carries with it a risk, and that risk is called crocodile. Nine times out of ten, or even ninety-nine times out of a hundred, you can go and drink from the cool, cool waters and never see a crocodile. They only eat twice a year anyway. So you'd be unlucky to meet one that was hungry, one that fancied a bite, wouldn't you?'

The little boy sat, transfixed. His dad often said he was so hungry he could eat a horse, but the boy had never thought there was an animal in the world which actually did that as a matter of routine.

'If there is a crocodile, he – or it might just as well be she – will be lurking in the sand and mud by the edge of the river,' continued the dad's brother, Tony. 'Lurking. That's what he'll be doing. And you won't see him, lurking, because he blends in with the sand and the mud of the Ubangi shore.

'So, along trots the zebra. The sun is high in the sky. Must have a drink. That zebra is cautious. And so he should be. Over there is the pool of lovely cool water, so he just has to step across this little sandbank, so he steps across it, and dips his fine zebra head towards the water, and CRACK!' Tony slapped his hand on the boy's bare knee and the boy leaped a foot in the air.

'And this is where we see the cunning of that crocodile. His jaws are for snatching and crushing. He can catch the zebra, and hold it no matter how much it kicks and wriggles, but when it's dead, can he chew it? No, he can't. And he can't swallow it whole. Too big. So, he drags that zebra out of the Ubangi river and off to a little spot he knows where there's a particular arrangement of tree roots. He pushes his dinner in among the roots so it's secure, then he takes a bite at the rump and holds on. Then, he twists himself around and around like a spinning top until the meat comes away and he can swallow it. Lovely. Very nice, a bit of zebra. Rump steak. Has to be fresh, mind. Yes, aye, just the one more bottle then I'll have to be away.'

The little boy was me, that was my Uncle Tony, and my whole life from that second onwards was decided. At first that meant as much wildlife as could be found and watched and studied by a small boy in east Yorkshire. I collected everything that could be collected, kept frogs and newts and stone loaches in the outhouse sink, kept pigeons in a loft. I even kept a young tawny owl, which was quite an experience. Being a surrogate owl parent makes you learn a great deal about the habits and habitat of shrews, voles and field mice.

I became the wild boy of the woods, a combination of Tarzan, Crocodile Dundee, Just William and David Attenborough, and one day I shot a singing thrush with my air rifle. Its song had been the only sound in the wood that early Spring morning, and the silence of its death, and the touch of its warm body where it fell, and the blood oozing from its beak where before there had been music, filled me with despair at the callous depravity of the human race, membership of which I could not deny. I had been a wildlife enthusiast, or nut, to that point. Now I became an animal crusader, protector of all creatures which could not protect themselves against their worst enemy, mankind.

After several false starts I got a job with animals. I was the first male kennel maid in Hull, at the RSPCA rescue centre. I drove the animal ambulance for a while, met my first RSPCA Inspector, decided that without any question that was what I wanted to be and, eventually, I became one. The hardest part was persuading my girlfriend Denise to marry me and move to Doncaster.

It's not just a job, investigating animal abuse. You don't do it for the prestige, the power, the status in your street, the prospects of promotion, the glory, and you certainly don't do it for the money. You do it for the never failing challenge and the potential for satisfaction in achievement, and because you have strong feelings, impossible to resist, about the rights and wrongs of our treatment of animals.

It's the 'impossible to resist' part that can ruin your social life and make things difficult for your nearest and dearest. If you are that way inclined, you are so in all waking moments. For example, you could be phutt-phutting your way through the streets of Bangkok on a motorbike with your N&D on the back, enjoying a rare and well-deserved holiday, when you notice a dog with demodectic mange. This is caused by a mite of the demodex family, which lives in the follicles of all sorts of animals, including humans, mostly doing no harm at all. In certain circumstances, such as a dog having a weakened immune system, the mites go mad, cause dreadful itching, which makes the dog go crackers trying to scratch and bite itself, which causes wounds that become infected. Result: dog covered in pus and bloody sores, suffering terribly.

You stop the motorbike and work out what to do. In a Buddhist country, most vets will not put animals down but there must be one in Bangkok who will. Your N&D might point out, gently, that carrying a filthy, pus-matted, terminally mange-ridden dog on the back of a Siamese hired motorbike is not the accepted thing to do while on holiday (rare and well deserved). You, however, cannot leave the dog to suffer. A calm and reasoned discussion might ensue, attracting the admiring attention of passers by. The N&D in question, having heard this song many times before, will probably give in eventually.

Finding a Muslim or Christian vet in Bangkok is difficult under normal conditions but, with the encouragement of a N&D behind you on the bike, not so much carrying as wrestling with an agitated mangy dog, the task becomes urgent and may be accomplished. Failing that, you could try persuading a Buddhist vet to sort out the equipment, raise the vein and insert the needle, while you do the actual pushing of the plunger to put the poor animal out of its appalling misery.

Family outings to restaurants, family weekends camping, inviting friends and neighbours round for a barbecue, all such normal activities can be disrupted by an inability to leave alone when a sick or distressed animal comes into range. You can also find yourself easily upset by people who do not entirely share your priorities. In my own case, when I have to spend so much of my working time with people making money out of animal cruelty, I don't see why I should spend any of my precious leisure time with unsympathetic materialists who will argue that it's not worth paying the extra for free range, or that the fox enjoys the chase.

Years ago, when I was a uniformed RSPCA inspector in Bridlington, I knew about badger diggers, the men who send terriers down the setts to find and confront the badgers so they can be dug up and beaten to death for sport. I used to be called often to the aftermaths of badger digs.

There would be blood, and soil, and dead badgers, usually discovered by a walker or a member of a badger group, or a farmer. Nobody seemed to be doing anything about the digs or the diggers. The police, the RSPCA, everybody was looking the other way while the badger population of the East Riding was being reduced to nil by a dozen or so bloodthirsty cretins. The reason for the inaction was straightforward: it was impossible to catch the bastards at it.

I moved to the RSPCA Special Operations Unit (SOU), a small, dedicated taskforce looking at animal cruelty outside the normal run of things dealt with by uniformed RSPCA inspectors. We did well but we were facing exactly the same problem. We were reacting after the event. Thinking long and hard about this, it came to me that the methods routinely used against terrorists and 'ordinary' criminals could be the answer. As we were, we reacted after the event or just swept up after it. So I approached Ken Connor, long-time SAS man who was, as it happened, very sympathetic to the cause. Here was our ideal source of knowledge on fieldcraft, surveillance, concealment; all the things you have to do and the ways you have to behave when behind enemy lines. I went to Special Branch too, to find out more about mobile surveillance, urban surveillance, covert filming and sound recording.

Next I thought about informants. Anything we did in SOU that came out successfully was to do with an informant. How could we go about recruiting such people, and running them, rather than just waiting for the phone to ring? I went to see a top CID man, who began by inviting me to an international conference on the subject to be attended by the FBI, MI5, MI6 and all manner of police forces. I listened to a very senior officer lecture on the use of informants against the Provisional IRA and the Protestant paramilitaries. He emphasised how informants tended to be disreputables with hidden agendas, but of overwhelming usefulness despite being as pleasant to handle as a wet bag of giant millipedes. Here, I thought, was another way forward.

In SOU we began to feel ready to have a go. Up to this time, in the UK there had been not one case brought against a badger digger except where he had been stumbled upon by accident. Nobody had ever tried to catch one in the act, yet one dedicated digger could kill 3,000 badgers in a lifetime. No badger digger ever expects to get caught, nor did his father before him nor does his son after him – and this is the way they are, bred and brought up to it. Nobody thinks at the age of 18, 'I wonder what badger digging is like as a fun alternative to internet porn or PlayStation'. They are all introduced to it or some other form of hunting at an early age. They are immersed in it and it becomes a way of life. It's not explicable in rational terms, any more than free-fall parachuting can be explained to an airline pilot. I don't think a sane, balanced person with freedom of choice and full information would voluntarily inject heroin, or start smoking even, but in the right circumstances some people do it.

We tried our new strengths on the Isle of Wight, after word had come from an informant about a local professional huntsman and a terrier man from Essex. We hid in the bushes, secretly filmed and photographed, and prosecuted. In the days before a prison sentence could be handed down, they got stiff fines and painful contributions to costs. A series of operations followed; some had poor results, some had good. Our actions against illegal taxidermists were also made possible by this new knowledge and expertise, and on to dangerous wild animals being kept illegally, and endangered species, dog fights, abuse of food animals – all a direct consequence of informant handling and covert techniques.

When man plays animal for money or fun, animal will generally lose, and when that happens it's a game of three thirds. First we have the providers: the poachers, dealers, breeders, transporters, slaughterers, all those who supply a market for pay, regardless of any suffering they may cause to the 'product' and/or regardless of damage to habitat.

Secondly, we have the people who are the market being supplied. Those keeping a member of an endangered wild species as a pet, for instance, know perfectly well that it is endangered. Indeed, that's why they want it and are prepared to pay so much money for it, and why they can disregard the cruelty implicit in keeping a wild animal in unnatural confinement. Someone using powdered rhino horn as a medicine also knows the score. The directors of research laboratories who deny using wild-caught primates know they are lying. Anyone buying some cheap chicken drumsticks knows they came from caged birds reared in gross discomfort. You could argue that gourmets eating reindeer paté don't know how it got into the tin and what tortures the reindeer went through; well, they will when they've read this book.

Thirdly, where it's for fun rather than money, we have the unspeakable 'sportsmen' who supply their own requirements, and it is men. 'Sportswomen' are rarely involved except in hunting on horseback. Bear baiting is gone; otter hunting has been illegal for years and isn't done any more in the UK. Illegal or no, we still have dog fighting, cock fighting, quail fighting, badger-baiting and digging and, if you look hard enough, fox and stag hunting, fox cubbing, and hare coursing.

Wherever national and international law or popular opinion intervene, all these cruel people, from wild-monkey dealers in Ghana, to Mafiosi making salami out of Polish horses in Italy, to the man down the street who has an alligator in his bath, to a fellowship of gypsies and gamekeepers betting on the outcome of a cock fight – all of them rely on a combination of secrecy, invisibility and apathy.

So, we have two options. One is the traditional method: leave it to somebody else. Let's sit here and hope that a uniformed police officer will happen to walk in on a badger-baiting and come out of it able to testify. Let's hope that the bird represented in that dish of tikka masala led a happy life.

Two is my method: get out there, pretend to be the criminal or the market, infiltrate, gather evidence and expose the bastards.

There is a philosophy behind my action. These tenets are not anything deep or new; they're basic. Rule one is that our own interests as people should never take automatic precedence over an animal's interests. Our own interests are generally connected in some way with money, sometimes with science, religion or tradition; none of these give us slave-owner's rights over an animal.

Rule Two is that we should not apply value judgements to animals. People judge each other's value in all sorts of ways – beauty, intellect, prowess, size and shape, age, health and so on. As George Orwell didn't say, all animals are equal and none are more equal than others.

Back in 1965, after an outcry over methods being used in factory farming, the UK Parliament set up the Brambell Committee, which studied the problem and came up with the five freedoms (now often called 'the five needs' in the USA) to which a farm animal should be entitled. These were: freedom from hunger or thirst, from disease, from excessive heat or excessive cold; freedom of movement; freedom to act out most normal behaviours. These freedoms have been developed to apply beyond farming, to all animals, and they are my creed, and to a large extent are enshrined in European law. Humans should not impose on an animal hunger or thirst, distress, pain, injury or disease, or restrictions on natural behaviour. It's not difficult to understand. So why don't we all do it, always? Why are other countries so slow to legislate?

Because we like money, of course. Radix malorum est cupiditas, the root of evils is the love of money, and it has been the root of most of the evils I've met in my career.

Chapter One

SEE NO EVIL, HEAR NO EVIL

There are 300 and more species of primate in the world and another 300 sub-species. Of all these many and different primates, only one is not threatened with extinction in the short or medium term: us. Perhaps one day another animal will perform experiments on us, hunt us for food, keep us as pets and exhibit us in amusement parks. Meanwhile, it's only the other 600 we need to worry about, which is why I went to Ghana to meet Ernie and Albert.

These two characters could tell you all about the world-wide laws to which Ghana and every other United Nations country has signed up. The Convention on International Trade in Endangered Species (CITES) regulates or prohibits trade in all the primate species (except us) depending on how immediate their danger is. Then there are the national laws; it's illegal to keep primates as pets in Israel and Holland, and in the UK there is the Dangerous Wild Animals Act and a licensing system. It's against US law to import wild-caught primates to be sold as 'companion animals'; such imports and the offspring from US-based breeders can only be sold for 'scientific, educational or exhibition purposes'. So that's all right, then.

Such official good intentions Ernie and Albert need to know about because their livings depend on getting around them. Also ranged against Ernie and Albert are the international campaigns, sanctuaries and charities, and there's public opinion. For instance, most people in the UK disagree with keeping primates as pets. Yet, there is a market. The estimate for the UK is anything from 1,500 to 3,000 primates, mostly small monkeys, being kept in private ownership at any one time and it's anybody's guess how many of these are wild-caught and how many are from reputable and disreputable breeders. In the USA, pet monkeys are more popular and estimates go up to 15,000 'companion animals'.

For many private owners it will be a first-time, once-only experience because the pet monkey usually dies quite soon. Primates are not like dogs and cats and hamsters. They are nearly human. They're born with the spirit of freedom in their very blood and bones, and their sense of species identity is every bit as strong as ours. In the wild, they live long lives in highly developed, single-species societies; only in fiction are humans adopted. How can such creatures be suitable as pets? How long would you last and how happy would you be if you, on your own, depended for everything on a tribe of baboons?

In the wild, food is often very specific, environment likewise. Those companion animals pine unless they're with their own family, being able to do what they were born to do. Even if, for a tenth of a moment, you sanctioned the idea of keeping a pet monkey, or chimp, or gorilla, lemur or bush baby, where can they come from? If they're bred in captivity it might make them legal but it costs something like three times as much to breed a typical pet primate as it does to catch one in the wild. Which method do you think Ernie and Albert will go for, out in Ghana? And if they can shoot the mother and sell her for bushmeat while catching the baby for a laboratory or the pet trade, well, it's no contest, is it?

There are no proper figures, only estimates, but we can say that about 25,000 wild-caught primates are sold alive, legally, on the international market each year, some for pets but mostly for experimentation at universities, pharmaceuticals companies and commercial research contractors. They, the 25,000, are the survivors; we have no idea how many more primates are caught and crated but die before they get to market. Some die right at the start of the process, killed for food or for no reason other than not being young and female, which are the animals the trapper knows fetch the premium price. Many more die or contract diseases at the miserable, overcrowded collecting centres in their countries of origin, where the attitude is that it's easier to catch another monkey than take a lot of care to keep a caught one alive and well. Still more die in transit, in the holds of aircraft. By the time of delivery, we can be sure that the survivors are the minority of the catch.

American dealers and animal-broking companies buy more than everybody else put together, about a third of the legal trade, with the UK next in line. That's the open side, with its regulations, veterinary certificates, expense, species preferences, form filling and so on, and the open side shelters and shades the parallel universe of the illegal trappers and dealers who don't give a damn about anything except getting paid.

The official government position in the UK and African countries is that there is virtually no illegal trade in wild primates. Such trade does not occur and has not occurred, not for sale as pets and absolutely certainly not for research. In any year, British customs officers might pick up 10 or 15 primates illegally trafficked. On the other hand, if hundreds, possibly thousands of people in the UK have a primate pet, and I know from my long experience as an RSPCA inspector that they do, where do they get them? If the number of primates used in experiments is much greater than the number produced legally, and I am sure it is, where do they come from?

With more effort, resources, education and will, the small but significant trade in primates as pets could be stopped. It's visible. You know if your neighbour keeps a monkey. There should be a law against it. What you don't know is what goes on in research laboratories, by far the biggest type of customer. They want primates in 20s and 30s, 50s even.

In the UK the animal experimentation industry is more or less self-policing. There is no independent inspectorate to go unannounced into the labs, just a few Home Office people who have no incentive to stir things up. Occasionally an animal rights activist will find a job in a laboratory, take some pictures and cause an incident in the media. One such campaigner was Zoe Broughton, whose covert videotapes of two lab technicians abusing beagles, bashing them about and causing them a lot of unnecessary pain, shocked the nation when shown on TV. I got involved and, with a Cambridgeshire police detective sergeant, brought a case against the two men. They were convicted and given community service orders. This is what happens. Their employers, the best-known animal research establishment in the UK, could not be held responsible for the behaviour of two employees, so everybody got away with it, apart from the publicity. If that's the best we can do, if we have to rely on the Zoe Broughtons of this world, it's like doing away with the Independent Police Complaints Commission and relying instead on public-spirited burglars robbing the police stations to get evidence of malpractice.

It's also something the RSPCA is not involved in, not as a matter of routine, anyway. If there is evidence produced somehow and a case to answer, then the RSPCA will act, and that was how I first came across the secret world of animal experimentation. I was a young uniformed RSPCA inspector in Doncaster and I had a regular client called Ellis Raife Fox, a notorious animal dealer from a notorious animal-dealing family. I must have taken him to court five or six times for cruelty to farm animals. He'd get a fine and be barred from keeping whichever species it was for a few years, and we'd both look forward to the next time, with me hoping he'd eventually be barred altogether.

After yet another complaint from an informant, I was up on his smallholding and was surprised to find, in a shed, about 20 adult cats, all colours and kinds. 'What are these for, Raife?' I said. 'They're worth nothing to a pet shop.' Raife's response was to take me into his kitchen, pour me a cup of tea and offer me a bribe. With my connections, he suggested, and his connections, we should pool our resources and make a fortune.

I didn't say no, so he kept talking. These cats, he told me, were picked up off the street and were destined for Sheffield University. Raife was paid quite well for them. I must come across loads of stray animals in my line of work. If I could channel them his way, we'd both be on an earner.

This time, his court case really hit the headlines and the national media were right in there. While the newspapers concentrated on pictures of happy owners reunited with their cats, Sheffield University vigorously denied being Raife's customer, saying that no experiment could produce academically sound results without complete knowledge of the animal's provenance. Any research animal had to come from a properly regulated breeder. Domestic animals, collected willy-nilly, possibly diseased, could be of no use whatever.

Such a response was expected, and respected. Nobody bothered to ask, if that were the case, why a man like Raife Fox, who saw animals only as a source of income, who never kept a cow for milk or a pig for bacon but only dealt in them, would want 20 cats in a shed. Raife Fox told me a thousand lies and maybe this was one of them. Maybe Raife had had his Damascene moment and was setting up a free cat sanctuary. All things are possible.

Thoughts of Raife returned at SOU as I began looking into the activities of the Ghanaian I knew only as Ernie. I'd had word passed to me from an informant in the exotic reptile trade. It seemed that some pretty swanky animals could be ordered from dealers who knew Ernie. The man himself came to the UK once a year to make a tour of his contacts and call in his commissions in cash, which he took back home in his suitcase. In the UK, people ask questions when someone lives in a style way beyond any visible means; not so in Ghana, apparently.

Coincidentally, the BBC's Panorama team were working on ideas for a programme about the illegal import of wild animals and came to me to see if I had any leads. I told them about Ernie, saying he was definitely in the wild-caught snake business and I believed he was also in primates. In fact, Ernie would be willing and able to get virtually any animal anybody might want. Panorama asked me to set up a meeting, a lunch preferably, so they could film me having a chat with Ernie. I thought, if they're paying for lunch, I might as well get some film too, so I set two RSPCA colleagues ready to join the BBC at the restaurant table. That was my plan: take Ernie to a posh joint and have the covert camera operators noshing near by.

I put out some feelers and found out that Ernie was shortly due in town for his annual debt collection. I set up a bogus company with email, phone, fax and address, the business of my company being the import of small primates. I phoned him, told him I'd got his name from a dealer I knew, and invited him to meet me in the foyer of a certain five-star hotel in central London. I needed to show him that he was dealing at the top end of the market now. In future, he must feel he could look forward to this sort of lavishness whenever he was with me.

My colleagues and the BBC were already installed, enjoying their haute cuisine, and were able to film me turning up in the restaurant with a man of about 60, average height and quite stocky. Some of his stockiness was due to the precautions he'd taken against the English weather. Beneath his long black overcoat he had two jackets and a jumper, as well as his shirt and tie. He was affable, a smiley guy you might say, very easy to talk to and, as we settled ourselves with the menu and an aperitif and I turned on my hidden audio recorder, pleased to tell me all about his long experience and huge success in bringing wild-caught primates for laboratory experimentation to dealers in the UK and the USA. He didn't know what sort of experiments or which laboratories; that was not his business. All he did was fulfil the dealers' orders and, whatever orders I might have, he was the fellow to come to.

He would have the fillet steak, he decided. Yes, a bottle of Nuits-St-Georges would be just the job. Out in Ghana, he had an excellent system. His wife was a customs officer at Accra airport and his PO box address was there too. Everybody in the animal trade in Ghana knew Ernie and where to find him. People knew that, for a consideration, Ernie could arrange for the export of any wild animal. So many people had taken advantage of that interesting fact that he had bought his fine house, one of the finest in Accra, entirely from those considerations received from grateful exporting customers, and those from equally grateful USA and the UK importers. He was the middleman par excellence, the centre pin of the trade.

'Do you have many customers in the UK?' I asked.

'Many, many,' he said. 'All sorts of customers, for everything.'

'What about primates?'

'Also many, but all primates are sent to one place for distribution. In Northamptonshire.'

'Northamptonshire?' I enquired, as innocently as I could, hoping he hadn't noticed my ears prick and my nose twitch. 'Whereabouts?'

'It's a zoo,' he said, and started giving me directions, up the A6, left at the roundabout. If I had wanted any proof of Ernie's credentials as an illegal animal trader, he had just given me the very best of references. I knew how to get there all right, although I'd have called it a fortified farmstead and animal clearing house rather than a zoo. Certainly no member of the public ever paid to go in and nobody else could get in either, past the CCTV cameras, barbed wire, security gates and automatic lights. This organisation had cropped up time and time again in my investigations and I'd never been able to pin anything on them.

As a case in point there was a fellow we knew very well, a Belgian called Bienvenue, who had been caught on so many occasions, smuggling prohibited species into the UK, that the customs people used to phone us at the RSPCA when he was on the ferry. This time we had been asked by a wildlife police officer, who had a mole in the 'zoo', to follow Bienvenue off the boat and file a surveillance report.

The wily Monsieur B travelled across with an empty van while two unknown pals were in a car with an animal in a box. Once through Dover customs, with me following, the men met in a car park and transferred the mystery box. Bienvenue drove to the place where he was indeed welcomed but I could only watch and turn away, and wait for another day.

The police had him, though, and he featured in the papers. It turned out he had been supplying an order from a private collector for a bearcat, Arctictis binturong, which is a tree-dwelling, mainly fruit-eating kind of civet from the high forest canopies of South-East Asia. Unfortunately for this slow moving, rather graceful creature, looking something like a teddy bear crossed with a hairy, speckled, black-and-brown raccoon with a long bushy tail, the forests are being felled by loggers. This would be bad enough but people also like to eat binturongs, use their fur for clothing and body parts for medicine, and to keep them as pets. In the wild they tend to be solitary and nocturnal and occasionally vocal; in captivity they make a lot of chuckly and wailing noises, which people like. So far they have progressed from plentiful World Conservation Union Red List/vulnerable and CITES III, but it won't end there. Bienvenue got a small fine, nobody at the 'zoo' was charged; situation normal.

Back at lunch, I was becoming increasingly anxious about the BBC researcher. I thought he stuck out a mile, while my two colleagues acted their parts with professional ease. If our lunch went on much longer, I thought Ernie might smell a little rat on the table next door. I needn't have worried. Ernie was enjoying himself too much. He ate most of his fillet steak then decided it was overdone. He'd hardly got his complaint out before the waiter rushed off and, a few minutes later, came back with a fresh one, bigger than the first. I didn't want to spend the entire afternoon with Ernie so I told him I was a mild diabetic and couldn't eat sweet things, hoping I would not have to watch him eat pudding and cheese and biscuits followed by a double Irish coffee, but he gave his tummy a rub, explained that his wife had told him he must lose weight and, regretfully, he would have to cut short his lunch.

I was feeling quite perky after this episode and decided to progress it further. With one colleague in a suit – the supposed money-bags – and another who was introduced as my company's logistics manager, we picked Ernie up in a Mercedes with smoked glass windows and took him to Chinatown. Watching our expenses this time, we went to one of those all-you-can-eat places and Ernie was a very happy chap. We talked about numbers, times, funding, methods of payment, and I was delighted to tell Panorama that we were ready to go. It came as a bit of a blow when the BBC said they had decided to follow up some different ideas. I had to tell Ernie that my investor, the man in the suit, had been forced to keep a low profile for a while but I would be back in touch as soon as possible. I didn't have long to wait.

The RSPCA mounted an abortive mission to Mauritius, seeking illegal primate traders but using untrained personnel who went there without a cover story or any clue as to how to go about a covert sting, and no false ID. They could have been in serious danger through no fault of their own. They were keen, but new. They were sent by their unit manager on the grounds that it was their turn for a trip abroad.

Said manager, faced with a disaster, had no choice. With gritted teeth he had to turn to me, that smart-arse who had been around since the grass grew and knew everything. I was asked if I could rescue the Mauritius job somehow and the only way I could think of was by using Ernie. I told him my company had been trying to establish a new source of supply for a new client and it had all gone wrong. Perhaps Ernie, with his great experience and reputation, could put himself in the middle and see if he couldn't get the wheels turning again. He reluctantly agreed but got nowhere. Whatever the Mauritius traders had picked up from their contact with the RSPCA's novice agents, it had set them firmly against any fresh avenues of business with the UK.

In which case, said the RSPCA unit manager, how about going to Ghana and reinstalling my original plan? At first, Ernie wouldn't talk to me. I'd led him up two garden paths already and he wasn't interested in wasting more time. After I told him how much money was involved in this new venture, featuring me and the same logistics man but a different financial backer, plus the fact that we would come out to Ghana so he'd be on his home territory, he did say he would meet us.

We made a date for me and my great friend and colleague over many years, Bryn. Bryn is one of those people who looks nothing like his personality. Shaven headed, ugly as sin or incredibly handsome depending on whether he's listening at the time, not tall but the proverbial brick nettie, if he told you he was a martial arts instructor to the army and currently a bouncer in a mob-owned casino, you would believe him without hesitation. If he told you the truth – Guardian-reading leftie vegetarian RSPCA inspector – you would think he was trying to be funny.

Ernie rang to offer to usher us through customs and immigration without any delay or questions of any kind, so would we please supply our flight details. Whether this was a gesture of good will or a detective check on our real identities, I didn't know. Whatever it was, supplying the information would blow our cover before we'd started, so we switched our flights to the day before, intending to give him a story about mistaken days, crossed lines, sorry and all that. We were not the police or Customs and Excise. We were not automatically issued with false passports. We had to use our real names for the airline but we made sure we booked our hotel under our company name. If Ernie phoned us there, he'd be put through to an executive of Interfauna, suppliers of exotic animals and pets.

We duly arrived unannounced in Accra and took a taxi to our hotel, the Labadi Beach, which is indeed right on the beach with the ceaseless crashing of great Atlantic rollers to soothe you to sleep. It's the only five-star in Accra and, at €100 per night, quite ridiculously pricey in Ghanaian terms. The hotel was done out in what they called African style, and it was a kind of interpretation of ethnic Africa but according to the requirements and tastes of the international traveller who would never have dreamt of setting foot in anything authentic. My colleague Bryn and I wanted to see the real Ghana. We expected the worst and got it.

Only a few minutes from our palatial quarters there were open sewers in the middle of the street, sick and crippled people begging for food, the most abject poverty. It was the poorest back alleys of medieval London, except for the fog of fumes caused by the horrendous crush of clapped-out motor vehicles and the fantastic number of plastic bags blowing about everywhere. These were from the water sellers, who provided what they classed as clean water to passers-by, bus passengers, car passengers, motorbike riders, who drank the water and chucked the bag. One day they will have to invite Hercules to come and perform his thirteenth labour: picking up a million plastic bags.

Next day, we needed careful preparation for our meeting with Ernie, scheduled for 7pm. The tapes of our previous conversations were with Panorama so we would have to get him to admit key issues all over again, in particular his involvement with primate capture and export. In any case, it's frequent practice for individuals under cover not to be wired up at the first meeting. We listen and make mental notes of the key points, then wear the gear next time when we're much less likely to be frisked.

We picked our table in the bar with great care, finding one out of the way, quiet, in a corner so we could see what was going on around us, but with good lighting. We worked out our camera angles and rehearsed our cover story and our parts in it. My colleague Bryn would be doing most of the talking, partly because that was his strong suit and partly because he, our logistics manager at Interfauna, not present at the first meeting, the posh lunch, could more realistically ask some of the same questions.

We took it in turns to keep a secret eye out for Ernie's arrival. We wanted to appear cool, settled and thoroughly acclimatised when he walked in, which he did on time in a cocksure manner wearing a lurid yellow-and-blue Hawaiian shirt. He was on his home ground now, and his swagger made it clear that he wanted us to know that. We welcomed him like an old friend, bought him a beer and talked about nothing for a while. This is always an important phase of the meeting, the pleasantries, the establishment of friendly relations and, if at all possible, the pouring of several drinks down the neck of the target, which was no problem with Ernie. He liked his beer a lot.

We finished telling him about the shortcomings of the hotel, compared to what we were used to, and were about to move on to serious business when I had visual confirmation of the accuracy of Robert Burns' lines about the best laid schemes of mice and men. Not many yards away from us, a jazz band was assembling. It was just one of those things. They didn't do us a favour by playing so loudly that we couldn't hear ourselves speak and so were forced to move, but they were loud enough to jeopardise our sound recordings.

We ploughed on anyway. Ernie reaffirmed that he was a regular exporter of primates to the UK, to the zoo', and that these wild-caught animals were for research. He also made it plain that we were not to mention research during our negotiations with Ghanaian officials. A bribe would ensure that they didn't look at the paperwork and didn't ask any awkward questions, but we must not make matters more difficult by using words in their presence that they didn't want to hear.

The first official we were going to see was a senior guy in the management hierarchy of the Ghanaian government wildlife department. We were to go to his office the next day and we were to be as pleasant as could be. If our business was to progress, we had to get on with this very big cheese, Ernie said. I called the waiter over to order Ernie his ninth or tenth beer and went to the gents. The meeting was drawing to a close and I had to check the recorder. Equipment is always the weakest point in any covert operation. Faulty batteries, loose connections, malfunctions, they all happen, especially when you think you have some really good evidence in the can. Such kit I suppose isn't built for long-term regular use, or maybe the RSPCA was buying it from the cheapest supplier. Anyway, if we hadn't got what we wanted, I would somehow have to get Ernie to summarise it yet one more time. Apart from the unexpected addition of a jazz backing track, it was fine, and we could get Ernie his last beer and watch him reel cheerfully into the street.

Our big cheese, we anticipated, would be no pushover. Whatever his record, he was a senior government official whom we were asking to take a massive risk. A mistake leading to public exposure would mean losing his job at the least and possibly some more swingeing punishment, as often happens when a corrupt organisation turns on one of its own and puts the scapegoat out in the desert. In our favour we had Ernie, fully convinced of our bona fides, well known to all, a most reassuring influence. We thought we probably also had human nature on our side. A corrupt official loves a bung, and the promise of one often suspends wise judgement and common sense. I knew this from my long history of dealing with villains, toerags, scallywags and shysters so, on balance, I believed we would get what we wanted. After a swim in the pool and a self-congratulatory chat over a last beer, Bryn and I retired feeling well satisfied with the story so far.

Ernie picked us up next morning and he seemed a different man from the cocky, hail-fellow-well-met we'd been with the night before. Decidedly on edge, he was, and dressed in collar and tie. His reputation was at stake on this meeting, as well as a lifelong supply of cash. With him he had his protégé Albert, a tall, slim, well-mannered man in his late 30s, who was learning the trade. He'd already succeeded in establishing an export route to the UK via the Czech Republic and was sending primates for research every other month in lots of 20 or more. He'd tried it the direct way but had run into trouble with the customs at Heathrow. They'd wanted to know where these monkeys were going, for heaven's sake, so Albert set up his diversion. Apparently the customs at Prague didn't ask so many awkward questions and, with the cargo once through a European airport, neither did Heathrow.

Ernie was proud of his apprentice but retained his clear position as top banana. Albert would come with us to the government building but not into the meeting. Ernie briefed us again, emphasising that we must not mention research. Here was the narrow gateway through which all our business must pass. Without our man and his official approval, we could not do a thing.

We already had pressures of our own. With the failed Mauritius job and the money being spent on the Ghanaian expedition, we had better not cock it up, and I was beginning to feel RSPCA politics turning against me anyway. After such small beginnings – me on my own against badger diggers – the RSPCA SOU had attracted management procedures, executive reviews, memoranda in triplicate, all those trappings that the front liners hate and find frustrating. I was for action with the minimum of admin, which had been perfect when we were a small team doing more or less what we wanted. Now I was a troublemaker, forever trying to push the boundaries, someone who didn't understand the importance of office meetings lasting an hour and a half in which animals were not mentioned once. If the Ghana job turned into porridge, I could see Chief Inspector Spamer being posted to the IT department.

All this seemed suddenly irrelevant as we almost died a hundred times in the ten minutes it took Ernie to drive us from hotel to office building. Such an ordeal would easily account for any nervousness Bryn and I might have been showing, but not for the sweating brow and restless mien of Ernie. Ghanaian wildlife's Mr Bung had the jitters, which I was 80% sure was down to the perceived gravity and potential of the meeting. My 20% of doubt, that perhaps he was jumpy because he was about to try and stitch us up, was assuaged by the sight of the Ghana coat of arms of two eagles and the Forestry Commission Wildlife Department nameplate on the door of the building. Inside was a huge reception area furnished to the best governmental standards, with the biggest ceiling fan you've ever seen swishing away, assisted by a dozen smaller versions fitted in every nook. Their combined efforts did nothing to reduce the temperature which was building up rapidly, in the atmosphere and in our agitated minds.

When we reached the office, Ernie knocked and walked in, leaving Bryn and me outside. We exchanged glances. Confidence was the thing. We'd taken care with our dress – smart short-sleeved shirts, ties, polished shoes – and we'd taken the requisite number of deep breaths. We had no camera because, in the heat of day, it would have seemed suspicious wearing the more bulky clothes needed to conceal it, but we did have our audio recorder. We were ready.

Ernie just about walked out of the office backwards, as if he were leaving the presence of the Emperor of China, and left the way clear for us. I strode forward, hand outstretched as I believed would be expected from a British businessman, to find a middle-aged chap, in his 50s say, with greying hair, quite distinguished looking. He was at home in his big office, on the management top floor, and he was anyone's equal. With introductions made we took our seats facing him, but before we could start what amounted to our presentation, there was some cryptic talk between him and Ernie. This was to settle the government man's commission, a matter which could not yet be stated openly but which was apparently resolved to mutual satisfaction.

He turned to me with an eyebrow slightly raised. What did I want, he seemed to wonder. I showed him our business plan, our paperwork, a list of previous successful ventures, and explained that Interfauna was keen to open up some new routes of supply as we could not keep up with demand. We thought that an initial consignment of 30 monkeys, patas, mona and spot-nosed species mixed, would enable us to set up the system and prove it, ready for a regular throughput. This brought instant agreement, which had Ernie almost dancing in ecstasy. To make sure we understood the favours being bestowed on us Ernie, still mopping his brow every 30 seconds with half an acre of spotted handkerchief, explained again the supreme importance of our man. While not suggesting directly that we kneel before him and include him in our prayers, such gestures would not have been out of the way in Ernie's eyes. Ernie also explained that the noble official's commission, in this case US$50, a lot of money in Ghana, was by way of seed funding, a start-up payment which would ensure the smooth and swift accomplishment of all necessary formalities but could not be expected to maintain its lubricative properties beyond this one piece of business. Future trades would have to be similarly oiled.

Since we knew there would be no future trades, we immediately agreed to this and, with handshakes all round, spilled out of the office. Ernie's joy was unconfined. His perspiration dried and he slapped our backs as if we'd taken five wickets each against Australia. We were all going to be very wealthy and we would never regret the good fortune which had brought us together.

With Ernie in such a good mood, I decided to spring a little surprise. What about ivory, I asked him. I had a very promising side commission from a businessman in the UK who was keen to import carved ivory, a considerable market and very lucrative now the trade had been banned. This was no problem to Ernie. He was on a roll. He knew all the key people and all the best carvers. He just needed to make a few phone calls and tomorrow he would introduce me. He, Ernie, was my man. Meanwhile, he and Albert would take us to lunch, their treat.

The kind of people I find myself investigating are invariably of the unreconstructed carnivorous tendency, whereas people like Bryn and me, in and out of slaughterhouses all the time and constantly exposed to violence towards animals, tend to favour the vegetarian side of things. This is not something to admit when in the company of our villains, with whom we are supposedly at one in life. They regard vegetarianism as only slightly less peculiar than men wearing make-up while trainspotting. No amount of cover story could help you if you told a badger-baiter or someone like Ernie you were veggie. Bryn and I accepted the kind luncheon invitation with good cheer, but knowing we would have to sacrifice our dietary principles if we were not to jeopardise the job in hand.

The restaurant was like a typical small British city caff, with cheap metal and plastic chairs and Formica tables, except instead of a washroom there was a communal bowl of water in the corner. There didn't seem to be a menu, which didn't matter because Ernie insisted we have the house speciality. Orders were given in the local dialect, beers arrived, and Ernie was in festive mood. He positively beamed with pride when the food came, as if he'd spent the whole morning with Delia Smith and Gordon Ramsey, cooking the Ghanaian equivalent of lobster thermidor.

The waitress gave each of us two bowls, one with a sort of meat stew and one with a doughy substance something like Italian polenta, made out of maize flour. I'd seen this stuff before but the stew was a bit of a mystery. We watched Ernie and Albert to see how we were meant to deal with it, seeing as we'd been given no cutlery, and the method was simple. You tore off a piece of the maizey polenta and used it as Asians use a chapatti as a scoop. We were soon going at it, the constant supply of beer helping to subdue our aversion to meat-eating and the excellent flavour and tastiness of the stew helping to suspend any feelings of vegetarian guilt.

I was about halfway through mine when I noticed an ingredient that I hadn't expected and which I'm sure would not occur in anything Delia or Gordon would make. It was the front half of a small foot, with five toes and, not unnaturally, I stared at it long enough for Ernie to notice. He grabbed it from my bowl, put it in his, and called the waitress over. In between sucking this little foot, removing whatever meat and gristle there was from the bones in a noisy celebration of everything Ghanaian, he gave the waitress a terrific dressing-down for allowing such a thing into the lunch of someone so delicate and refined as myself, being from England and not educated in local stew lore. When he'd finished sucking I asked Ernie what it was.

'Grasscutter,' he said. 'Animal eats grass. Everybody eats it.' I thought this a fairly wide definition, and it was definitely a foot not a hoof, but Ernie would not be more precise. Back home, later, I researched the subject and found that grasscutter is their common name for the African cane rat, Thryonomys spp, which is an enormous rodent related to and looking like the South American coypu. I saw these animals in the Ghana countryside quite often, being carried over shoulders, no doubt heading for the pot. They're very numerous, trapped in the wild and farmed as livestock and, as a delicacy, make good money at the meat market.

There were no more toes or other recognisable body parts in my stew or Bryn's, so we got it down as politely and enthusiastically as we could, lubricated by more and more beers. The triumphant Ernie kept ordering whether we'd finished the last one or not, despite knowing something we didn't, which was that he was paying for the food, about 30p a man, and we were paying for the drinks, four or five times that. All right, beer is cheap in Ghana, and four times 30p wouldn't buy much beer in the pub at home, but it was the principle of the thing.

I could see an issue or two being raised back at the RSPCA. My phone would ring, my boss would call me in to his office and, in that special way he had, ask me to explain my expenses claim. 'Look at this,' he'd say. 'Five star hotel, and beer, beer, beer. And this lunch. More beer. Nothing but beer.' 'Ah well,' I'd say. 'That's because Ernie paid for the rat stew.' His face would be a picture worth framing.

We thought the beer might become free now as we were taken off to Ernie's uncle's place for more. The route was through an appalling shanty town where every dwelling was built of whatever the rubbish tip could provide and every alleyway had an open sewer running down both sides. Ernie's uncle's house was typical, with a tin roof and walls made from a mix of hardboard, second- or third-hand plywood, more tin, nails and pieces of string. The loo was a bucket in a shaky lean-to, the bucket being emptied in the street when full. The uncle was typical too, scrawny, grey-haired, straggly beard, not many teeth but also jolly, welcoming and genuinely happy to see us.

He showed us his shop, which was a 1960s kitchen unit with sliding doors and plastic handles containing a few miscellaneous tins of food, bottles of sauce, soft drinks, and beer. We were his first customers of the day.

He showed us into his backyard where there were wooden boxes for stools and an array of curious metal objects which looked familiar but not quite identifiable. The answer came with the nephew, a lad of about 18 with a physique which would have filled Mr Schwarzenegger with envy. I didn't bother asking him about his personal trainer, his dietician and his rolling road with heart monitor. I just looked in awe at what I now recognised as his gymnasium equipment, with weights made out of wagon wheels welded to axles and dumb-bells out of pieces of diesel engine. He was going to turn professional, the nephew confided, and compete internationally, after first winning

Mr Ghana. Good for you my lad, I thought. I hope the judges are honest.

This expedition was necessary because a friend of the uncle owned a Ghanaian restaurant in London and when we went to it we would obviously fare better if we had an introduction. Most definitely, we said, wondering idly if they used locally caught rats or the authentic type. It would our first stop after Heathrow. I did have the place checked out later, by a colleague who lived near it. It was mainly a fish restaurant - no bush meat, no grasscutter, all above board and hygienic and beer at £3 a bottle.

If anyone wants to produce the most terrifying, hair-raising computer game ever, they only have to recreate a drunken Ernie driving through downtown Accra. He was a terrible driver anyway but, newted on his uncle's entire stock of cheap lager, he reached new levels of risk-taking and near-missing which in a normal city could not have lasted more than ten seconds. Perhaps with everyone doing something similar they cancelled each other out in some way. Bryn and I had no choice but be there, right inside the game; we'd never have found our way through the hundreds of identical back alleys. On foot, we'd have surely been robbed and beaten at least. In Ernie's car, our fate looked equally certain but there was no 'at least' about it. With both hands off the wheel a large part of the time, cursing every pedestrian and other driver in the most crowded streets you could imagine, simultaneously blowing his car horn and his own trumpet, praising himself to the skies for his leading role in pulling off the most amazing business coup which would make us all rich,

Ernie somehow got us back to the hotel. Bryn had closed his eyes after the first minute and kept them closed. I half wished I'd done the same, but then I would never have come to know how the early Christians felt when the lions and tigers were let loose.

Ernie wanted to carry on drinking. We said, not unreasonably, that we were tired out, suffering from jet-lag partly beer induced, and we couldn't keep up with Ernie. Stories of his prodigious abilities as a beer-drinking man would be told around the dinner tables of England. He would become a legend in his own opening time, and we would see him on the morrow.

Chapter Two

A CARGO OF IVORY AND A CASE OF POISON

As well as exotic reptiles, primates and every other kind of live animal the world might want, Ernie said he could provide ivory, new ivory, in tusk. He could also introduce us to the best carver in Ghana who would turn our ivory into a Siamese pagoda, Blackpool Tower or Gypsy Rose Lee at any stage of her act. He told us all this and said what we should do was pay a visit to the souk, have a look at the raw and carved ivory there, see what we might fancy, then he'd come with us and do the deal on most favourable terms.

Initially, that was what we planned for the next day but, as we discussed it over a rat-free dinner, we changed our minds. If ivory was on open sale in the souk, on our doorstep, we could save that investigation for our last couple of days. Ernie had said that one of the reasons Accra was such an important hub of the ivory trade was the nearness of Mole, a game reserve reconstituted as Ghana's oldest and biggest national park. Here, most the few elephants remaining in Ghana were conveniently gathered together. This was where the middlemen operated and Ernie knew them all.

Mole seemed a logical place to start but enquiries revealed that nearness in the African sense meant no more than a day's journey in a cattle wagon and, as all internal flights had been cancelled indefinitely, our only option was the luxury coach leaving Accra National Bus Station at 7am. We'd been there long enough by now to know that 'luxury coach' would be another concept with a local definition, and sure enough it turned out to be a 30-seater single-decker bus, Leyland Motors circa 1958, of the type used long ago in the UK to ferry folk into town on market day. There had been no thought of air conditioning when the bus was built under grey skies in Lancashire, and there was no sign of it now as we left the city and headed north into the heat of high morning.

The countryside was mostly flat, semi-desert, rocky, with little vegetation, very few trees and the occasional village. We saw no wildlife at all but again a great many plastic bags, the by-product of the itinerant water sellers. A mother and three-year-old daughter were sitting behind us, the little girl restless, and soon the child was on our knees and staring in fascination and bewilderment at our white skin and the hairs on our arms. We had sweets with us and gave her some, which she stashed away in the folds of her dress. The mother seemed fascinated too and was keeping a close eye on me, to the point were I began to feel uncomfortable.

The matter was explained when I drank the last out of my water bottle. She came up to me immediately and, nervously, as if she'd had to screw up her courage to do it, asked if I would be kind and give her my empty water bottle. Her gratitude was embarrassing. A plastic bottle, thrown away by the million in the West, thrown away many times by me, was a valuable household article in the impoverished heartlands of this desperate country. Mother had been keeping me under surveillance so she could get to me before anybody else, the second the water was gone.

We'd taken no sandwiches with us on our journey and so ate whatever the roadside vendors supplied. Chickpeas in curry sauce with flat bread was our dish of the day, and jolly nice it was too. Our stops were brief, otherwise we could have taken time to seek out the man who surely would have been there with the grasscutter kebabs and rat casserole.

Everywhere we looked we saw people on the edge of survival. There were no signs of wealth in this hard land, no signs of ease. The cheerful folk, with their good natures bearing them up, had to scratch and scrape for every little thing. In my own country, people throw away half of what they buy. Here, there was hardly an item, no matter how trifling, which did not have a value.

As we reached what we thought was our destination and got off the bus, these thoughts ran through my mind. For the moment our purpose was pursuit of ivory dealers and, ultimately, elephant poachers, organised criminals who knew exactly what they were doing. But our general purpose was monkeys, caught and traded by innocent villagers trying to feed their families.

If ever I wavered, I wavered now. How on earth could I blame these poor people for turning a penny any way they could? Of course, I couldn't blame them. They would never understand why I thought it was wrong for them to take a monkey from the forest and sell it. They were on almost zero income without that trade and there were plenty of monkeys in the forest as far as they could tell. How could I, a relatively rich westerner, come piling in with my high principles, put a stop to local custom and practice and make people even poorer than they already were?

With such arguments spinning around my head I failed at first to take on what Bryn was saying about our current project. He had a map in his hand and was pointing into the distance, at about 90 degrees from the cloud of dust which was all we could see of our departing bus. Mole was that way, he said, and it was another 40 kilometres at least from where we'd been dropped, at Demango Junction.

Ever optimistic, we set off walking along the dirt road, hoping to thumb a lift from the next vehicle to happen by. Night was threatening and we were strangers in a very strange land where, to go by the reactions of the people on the bus, the white man was as rare as the unicorn and probably hadn't been seen since the last district commissioner left what was then the Gold Coast. I asked Bryn if his studies of Africa had included the Ghanaian populations of lions and hyenas. He thought they weren't all that common in these here parts, but in any case it was a well-known fact that lions preferred their game to be tall and dark-haired rather than short and bald. I was sure that they'd be much more likely to go for a barrel of meat like him rather than a stringy, bony number such as my good self and, in any case, it was also a well known fact that lions were lazy and so wouldn't bother chasing a thoroughbred long-distance runner like me when they could pick off the nearest short-legged Scouse midget.

After an hour of this and similar, it was pitch black and so the far-away headlights of a large-ish vehicle were easily spotted some way behind us. We stood in the middle of the road and waited, and began waving our arms probably long before the driver had any chance of seeing us. He did pull up and, walking behind the headlights' glare, we discovered the bus we'd seen in all the picture books and Hollywood films, painted in the gaudiest colours and patterns and absolutely packed solid. There was not a square inch of room inside and not very much outside, but we were able to climb onto the roof and find ourselves some space between the straw bales, the lorry tyres, the children, the vintage sea-going trunks, the boxes of vegetables and the two goats.

We'd already done 12 hours on a bus, admittedly in proper seats. Now we had another two hours of rocking and rolling at an average speed of 13 mph into a stiff breeze. This breeze proved to be exceptionally important and the instrument of a Heritage Moment. The goats were in front of us and more on Bryn's side than mine, which was why it was Bryn and not me who earned his place in the RSPCA Hall of Fame, with distinction. The billy goat decided he needed a leak, and whether he was on top of a bus or chewing thorn bushes on the plains of Africa made no difference to him. If you've got to go, you've got to go, and so he let out a very creditable amount of billy goat pee which flew along the breeze straight at Bryn.

He couldn't do much about it in terms of evasive action or he'd have fallen off the bus. It's a difficult choice to make on the spur of the moment: do I roll off a moving bus onto stony ground, or do I sit here and get drenched? Anyway, it was soon over and those within earshot could wonder what all those words meant that Bryn was saying so feelingly. Some of the words were said over and over again, and a future traveller in this region may puzzle over how these country tribesfolk learned to swear in English with a strong Liverpudlian accent.

I had almost stopped laughing by the time we got to Mole but started again when I saw the bemused expression of the man behind the counter at the chalet place we booked into, ambitiously called a motel. As Bryn was paying him, he caught a whiff of billy goat pee and couldn't reconcile that particular sensation with the circumstances.

Our chalet had running water but it didn't run at night. When we asked why, we were told that the water was pumped from a near-by pool, fed by waterfall, but the system was turned off during the hours of darkness which was when the elephants and other big game mostly came to drink. In which case, we thought, perhaps we could go for a swim there in the morning. This was considered inadvisable by the locals, due to the very high density of crocodiles. I said to Bryn that the crocs must congregate there in the hope of pulling in an unwary antelope or some such. Anything smelling of goat would surely have them in a frenzy.

We didn't sleep much that night, mostly because we had to keep running outside to what passed for the sanitary arrangements. The chickpeas had included a heavy dose of unfriendly bacteria. Food poisoning Ghana-style is a painful and exhausting business and there was nothing we could do except sit it out, and kneel it out. At least I'd given Bryn a good laugh with my soup at dinner. I'd told the waitress that I wasn't well enough to tackle any food so she said she would get me a special soup, very light, that would sort me out. She brought a bowl and I drank the contents spoonful by spoonful; then she brought another bowl with soup in it. 'What for you drink finger washing?' she said.

Next morning we discovered that the nearest telephone was 6 miles away; a taxi would be necessary if I was to call in to the SOU office. Bryn was slightly mystified by my sudden burst of professionalism.

'Why do we need to call in?' he wanted to know. 'Are they going to send out a search party otherwise? For goodness' sake, man, you've been missing for a week before now and they've never bothered.' Then the penny dropped. 'You want to tell them about the goat pee.'

I fiercely denied this and said that while I had gone missing before, we'd never had two of us poisoned and missing in deepest Ghana in pursuit of armed and ruthless elephant rustlers. No, I had to call in, and if I happened to mention goats it would be purely in the line of duty. In which case, he insisted, duty should include all matters connected with soup.

This was the only bright spot in an otherwise awful day. Ernie's so-called leads proved useless and we couldn't gather any information from the motel staff either. They expected guests who wanted to go on safari, which largely meant a guided walk to the water-hole. They knew nothing about ivory. We did chat to some of the park rangers, who told us that elephant poaching was common but they could do little about it. They had no training and no radios, a lack which they had sorely felt when one of their number was shot and killed by the poachers. Unable to radio for help, the dead man's companions had to hide his body from scavengers and walk back to base before they could get a vehicle to go and retrieve the corpse, an exercise which took them two days in sweltering heat. While these men were devoted to the cause, they had to cover about 1,900 square miles holding something like 500 elephants. They felt under-resourced compared to their enemy, and their enemy was ruthless.

On the bright side, we wouldn't have had the energy to do anything if we had found a hot trail. Forswearing sustenance except water of known origin to try to calm our insides, by the early afternoon we were utterly fed up with being baked and desiccated while going nowhere. Any option seemed preferable, even a 12-hour bus ride back to Accra arriving at three in the morning, particularly when it was followed by a five-star luxury kip, followed by a high quality breakfast, followed by poolside ice-cold drinks.

We were feeling altogether better and fully functional by the time Ernie phoned. He suggested another lunch, which we refused – we weren't quite as functional as that yet – in which case Albert, would take us to meet another uncle, in another part of town with no identifying features. It was Albert's uncle who had the features: a shock of white hair, no teeth and the skin and bent frame of someone who'd lived for a hundred years, although in reality he was probably no more than 50. In his small, plain flat, which would have been immediately condemned by any British housing department, he earned a little money from Albert by keeping monkeys awaiting export.

He had two there that we could see, one a red patas in a tiny wire-mesh cage and the other a mona in slightly more spacious accommodation. Both were obviously wild-caught, both exhibiting the characteristics we'd expect – panic as we approached, frantic attempts at escape quite heedless of injury, bared teeth, noise, incontinence – and the patas in its cramped bit of space managed to get its tethering cord wrapped around itself like a tourniquet. The more it panicked, the tighter it pulled the cord, like a rabbit caught in a snare. We could all see this, it was Albert's uncle's job to do something, but nobody moved. I had to point out that they were about to have a dead monkey, or at least one useless for trade, before the uncle, grumbling in the local language, presumably about the annoying little habits of wild monkeys and the irritating concerns of British businessmen, got the poor thing untangled. I had hoped the monkey might bite the old sod but he was too wily for that, damn it.

Albert was keen to show us another aspect of his business and drove us out to a much better area, a pleasant suburb where people had nice bungalows with gardens. We were able to observe this because closing the eyes was not necessary with Albert driving. Although he had some of Ernie's style and was clearly a graduate of the same driving school, it was obvious that he'd had more than one lesson.

Albert's bungalow was one of the larger ones, set in its own grounds, and we arrived simultaneously with three trappers back from some days in the wild. They were a sorry looking, undernourished lot, dressed in rags and flip-flops made from old car tyres but they had a valuable cargo. They all had sacks, and in the sacks each had two gravid (pregnant) royal pythons, Python regius. These boys would be getting pennies for their work and going home to their grass huts and cornmeal dampers for dinner, while Albert reviewed his many-sided businesses and laid the dining table ready for chicken and wine.

In the UK, a baby royal python about a foot long will fetch between £90 and £150; the more unusual striped ones £250. They don't grow to a very large size, 3 or 4 feet, but people who buy them may not realise they can live for 30 years or more. When alarmed they coil up into a ball, head tucked in the centre, which is a demonstrable selling proposition in the pet trade. Some pythons will lay about a hundred leathery eggs; the female royal only has between four and ten to incubate. She tidies her eggs into a heap and coils herself around them for three months, which is no problem to her since she can go without food for much longer than that, even a year. Like all snakes she is cold-blooded, yet in a mechanism not properly understood the egg-laying pythons can raise the temperature of the eggs above the ambient.

Such a low reproductive rate and great popularity as pets – they are gentle-natured beasts – are putting the species in danger and export permits are required in most of the countries which have them in the wild, including Ghana. Permits were no problem to Albert; he could get them by the hundred but, recognising this decline in the population while appreciating the foreign currency to be made, the Ghanaian wildlife department struck an official deal. In a process sometimes called ranching, the trappers went to the same place annually to catch the same female pythons. The deal was that, once the snakelets had hatched, the mother and a majority of her young would be released back into their own environment, while the dealer could keep a few babies for trading. As you might expect, Albert and his fellow ranchers didn't release any of the young, just the cash-cow females, which is what they would have done had there been no deal with the wildlife department. As it was, government officials got a rake-off, the trappers and dealers could go about their business with official impunity, and the only sufferers were the pythons.

Albert took Bryn, me and the gravid pythons to his warehouse, a unit on an industrial estate. Inside on shelves were rows of large plastic washing-up bowls, and in the bowls were pythons coiled up, incubating eggs. He had baby Gaboon vipers there too, and rhino vipers. If snakes are the acme of reptiles to dealers and illegal keepers, vipers are the acme of snakes. Their fangs are fixed on a moveable upper jaw, in effect a hinged mechanism which has the fangs lying flat in their mouths when not required but instantly swinging forward and locking when they are. The fangs are backed up by a reserve supply, growing but hidden in the mouth, so that if one is broken another moves into place and welds to the jawbone. Most viper species do not lay eggs but give birth to live young. The Gaboon can produce 50 or 60 pencil-sized viperlings, although more usually a couple of dozen, and the rhino viper has a smaller number of slightly larger babies.

The Gaboon viper, Bitis gabonica, can reach 7 feet and has the biggest fangs of any snake, 2 inches long. The Gaboon and its close relative the rhinoceros or nose-horned viper, Bitis nasicornis, live in the woods, the rhino near water. They are extra attractive to reptile enthusiasts because they have a bite which can kill you and they are pretty with it, in forest-floor camouflage geometric patterns of primary colours, rather than the dull greys and browns of the rock and desert dwellers. Also, they have a slow and lazy way of life and tend not to attack humans unless, taking a walk in the woods over the colourful carpet of leaves, you happen to tread on one.

Your viper would be lying in wait for its prey rather than chasing it. Usually dinner is a rodent although they are partial to the smallest antelope, the royal, Neotragus pygmaeus, which, at about 10 inches high at the shoulder and about 7 pounds in weight, makes a very nice meal, swallowed whole, naturally, head first. Rodents too can bite and, to avoid an injury which might turn septic, the viper strikes the prey, injects enough venom to paralyse and kill it, then leaves it to struggle on as far as it can before it expires. The viper follows the scent trail and finds its meal safely dead. The Gaboon, much the bigger snake, relies on quantity of venom and may, despite the risk, hold on to its prey until it dies. The rhino has neurotoxic as well as haemotoxic venom and a small dose is enough. Both strike faster than the eye can follow even though their normal state is the peaceful snooze and, not surprisingly, they have few natural enemies.

In more washing-up bowls Albert had female scorpions, many of them, each with 50 or so tiny young holding on to the mother's back. The mother doesn't feed her babies – they have a supply of egg yolk inside them – but carries them about until the yolk is all gone and they have to drop off to pursue their lives solo. The rule with scorpions is, the bigger the claws, the less they rely on their sting to catch prey, and so the less poisonous they are likely to be. Albert's scorpions were emperors, Pandinus imperator, which are big, 6 inches long, and have huge claws.

Some people would argue that scorpions make the perfect pet. They don't eat much, just the occasional insect, and they don't need the company of other scorpions. Indeed, two scorpions kept close together may fight, not stinging each other so much as bare-knuckle boxing to death, whereupon the victor eats the vanquished. In the mating season, the male courts the female with a kind of pincer-holding, tail-rubbing dance and, in some species, as a reward for a successful joining is killed and eaten unless he skips off quickly.

Emperors are the giants of the family and rarely go in for such vicious behaviour. They hardly ever sting and so are popular in the pet trade. A baby will cost you £5 retail, and an adult fully grown £15 or £20. They are, as one pet shop put it, 'your ideal first scorpion', which is why over-collection has put them into CITES Appendix II, one of only three scorpion species out of 500 to be so listed.

Scorpions, and Gaboon vipers for that matter, do not have big brown eyes and are unsuitable models for pink furry nightdress cases. Even on a professional level, people find it hard to relate to such animals. While it's relatively easy to get government departments and the general public much exercised about chimps and seal pups, you won't find many folk going to the barricades for creepy-crawlies and snakes, some of which would thank you for your trouble by putting you in the chapel of rest.

I couldn't see my bosses at the RSPCA getting excited either, not even if we did what Albert wanted, which was to take some baby vipers back with us in our hand luggage. He tipped some of the little rhino vipers out of a bowl into the palm of his hand to show us how harmless they were, and told us that no customs officer was going to search through a collection of snakes like this to make sure there wasn't a CITES endangered species among them. This was how he got the rarer snakes into the USA he said, by shipping them with the more common and deadly types.

That was all very well, I said, but we had a different system in the UK and if we were discovered bringing in venomous snakes we'd be put in prison for two months. Albert was disappointed but had to be satisfied with our refusal and offered to drive us back to the hotel. I told him a true story about two dealers I said I knew – except they weren't dealers, they were Scottish SPCA (SSPCA) – who wrongly identified a small green snake as a young emerald tree boa, a South American species harmless to humans. They handled this snake without any precautions until a third man came along and told them that immature emerald tree boas are not normally green. They are usually red, orange or brown at birth, gradually turning a vivid golden yellow at around six months, and only later wearing their brilliant green skin. What these men had was Trimeresurus trigonocephalus, a bright green pit viper from Sri Lanka.

Albert didn't know about pit vipers from Sri Lanka. Before he could have a genuine laugh, I had to explain that they belong to the same family as rattlesnakes, water moccasins and the fer-de-lance, and that they are absolutely deadly. With this extra education Albert thought it a most amusing story so I told him another, just to show what these snakes can do. A friend was moving a baby puff adder, which is a desert-dwelling viper known for its aggression, using a wooden ruler. It was a 12-inch ruler and a 6-inch snake, which fell off the ruler and, as it fell, twisted in mid air and bit my friend on the thumb. This man was a tough character, an ex professional wrestler, but he told me that, in the hospital, the pain he suffered from this little snake had made him wish himself dead.

Albert thought this was very funny also. With promises to work out a system for importing and distributing his reptiles in the UK, we said cheerio and told him we would be taking a look at the ivory in the market next morning. Albert said we'd have no trouble finding people to deal with; plenty of stalls sold carved ivory for the tourist trade. I said we also wanted raw ivory, whole tusks, and Albert thought we'd have no difficulty with that either.

We found three market stalls straight away in the grandly titled Cultural Centre, selling ivory carved into all kinds of ornate shapes with the highest degree of skill. They are real artists, these carvers, literally scratching a frugal existence like so many of their kind. Perhaps a western artist could pickle a couple of the dead elephants, sell them for millions and give the money to these carvers so they wouldn't have to work any more. We asked if it was old ivory or new. Of course it was all old. New ivory was not permitted. This would be the story all the tourists were told and I was sure that few if any would wonder where the continuous supply of old ivory was coming from.

We needed to make a friend of somebody, so I had a chat with the brightest-looking lad selling the carvings and enquired if he had an ostrich egg. I wanted it to make a bedside lamp, I explained. Well, no, he didn't have one but he knew someone who did. We followed him through a network of back alleys. He was called John, he was 18, and he led us to another, much bigger market, mostly selling food but also skins and animal bits and pieces. The stall he took us to had dried animals, huge heaps of them, dried chameleons, bats, lizards, rats, all sorts, and behind the display was a dried stall-holder, a frightening old woman who must have been the witch doctor's grandmother.

Bryn began humming that Nina Simone song, 'I'll put a spell on you', while our guide asked her something in Ghanaian. Every bit as skinny and leathery as one of her specimens, she nevertheless had plenty of energy. Possibly fortified by a breakfast of dried bats' gonads she trotted off to a store room where we heard her crashing about and moving things around, obviously looking for something. There was a small gurgle of triumph and she emerged with a paper bag. John made sure we understood that this was the only one she had, that it had taken her a lot of time and effort to find it, and so she would expect a decent price. We had no worries about that. The last thing we wanted to do was upset the witch doctor's grandma when she had all her ingredients so close to hand.

What we did wonder about was the size of the paper bag. It was too small and when she opened it we saw why. Inside was not an ostrich egg but an ostrich head, wizened and mummified, rather like the woman selling it. She was quite offended when it was explained to her that dried ostrich heads made terrible bedside lamps. Seeing as he was laughing so much, I extracted 50 pence worth of Ghanaian money out of Bryn and grandma seemed happy with that, happy enough anyway we hoped not to change herself into a vulture and perch on our hotel window sill.

Our guide, like all such in any bazaar or souk in the world, was not put off in the slightest by this failure but pressed cheerfully on, taking us further and further into the market, which seemed to go on for ever. The nature of the goods for sale changed as we progressed. An old gypsy friend of mine has a motto, 'Everything's for sale', but I don't think he could have imagined the range of things on sale here and, as in other souks, you could not see how they made a living. There might be 30 stalls selling sheep's heads but only one woman buying. Another 30 traders each had mountains of tomatoes and gourds and green bananas; how could they all sell them by the end of the day? In the most remote and unregarded corners, poverty-stricken individuals sold old instant coffee jars and cola bottles.

Certainly none of the traders were expecting tourists. Bryn and I had everyone's attention as great curiosities; no westerners ever wandered as far as this into the real Ghana. Every time we turned a corner and passed from one trading area to the next, we picked up more and more of an entourage until we had a queue behind us longer than the conga on New Year's Eve. Our guide was most reluctant to give up his quest but eventually we persuaded him that an ostrich egg didn't matter all that much in the great scheme of things and what we really would like was to see some raw ivory.

He took us back to the Cultural Centre, leaving our crowd of fans disappointed behind, and from the back of his own carved-ivory stall and the two of his neighbours he produced 18 tusks, the smallest 18 inches, the largest 3 feet. These mostly looked very fresh, still dirty and in their natural state. We said this was good but really we needed larger quantities to make the project worthwhile. Our friend John was not at all disappointed; he could see a much bigger earner coming up. He was a lad in shorts and car-tyre flip flops. One day he wanted to possess a suit, a car with a full set of tyres and a lawn-fringed bungalow, and we could help him on his way. He asked us to come back to the Cultural Centre next morning, when he would have arranged for one of the very big dealers to be there to meet us.

Ernie had disappeared for the moment. Perhaps he'd heard that we'd taken him at his word and gone in search of invisible ivory middlemen in the far, far bushlands and so we might not be in the best of moods. We would soon find out where the real dealers were, right here in the city, and the real reason why Ghana was so important to the trade. Meanwhile a leisurely afternoon by the pool seemed in order; tomorrow we would be going into uncharted territory, where large sums of money were at stake and where, consequently, the personal risks were high. Not that we had any great fears yet; our quarry believed they had everything to gain from our continued good health. Only if we blundered would suspicion be followed by danger.

Yet another blazing day in Accra saw us meeting John. We carried stills and video cameras, took a taxi and tried our best to memorise the route but it was hopeless with no street names, no numbers, nothing to tell one dreary, run-down alley with open sewers from another. Even the taxi driver would never have found it without John. It was just another cheap breeze-block shed, run down and seedy, but here we were going to meet the man who supplied all the shops in Accra with ivory and was a master carver himself.

John disappeared for a few minutes and came back with Hallaji, a shortish chap with a grey beard and moustache late 50s or early 60s and, like almost everyone we met in Ghana, a smiley, chirrupy chap, very friendly, eager to please. After much handshaking and a glass of orange juice he took us into his best room to show us his carving. It was very impressive, stunning even, starting with a beautifully made rhino next to a hunter carrying his bow and arrow and the other tools of his trade. You could not help but admire the craftsmanship and feel sympathy for such an artist who would never get proper financial recompense for his talents and the work he put in.

If he didn't understand the true market value of his art, neither did he appreciate how difficult it is to import ivory into the UK, and he easily swallowed our story about wanting to fill a container with it and ship it into Felixstowe. A container-load would be no problem, he told us, and popped out for a minute, returning with a massive 4-foot tusk, raw as could be, wrapped in brown paper. Six more appeared, almost as big, and one question occurred to me. If Hallaji was such a big wheel in the ivory trade, why did he live and work where he did? Why didn't he at least have a bungalow like Albert's?

My unspoken query was answered when another man appeared but was not introduced to us, perhaps because he was so important he should need no introduction. He was dressed in a Savile Row suit, fine cotton shirt, silk tie, Italian hand-made shoes. He beckoned us into the room where Hallaji had been to get the tusks. It was stacked to the ceiling with ivory, some worked, mostly raw. Here was half a container already in stock.

Mr Big explained that very little of what we could see was local in origin, because there were so few elephants in Ghana. No, it all came from the big elephant countries like Tanzania and South Africa, where the police and the world authorities concentrated their energies to suppress the trade and thought they were succeeding, while the smugglers quietly carried the ivory across into Ghana, where mostly the authorities weren't looking and any that did could be paid not to.

We exchanged business cards, took photographs, weighed a few sample tusks and parted full of promises. Bryn and I were in that state where you can't really believe what you have seen. Here, in the capital city of a United Nations country, people were willing and able to supply illegal, immoral ivory by the ton to a couple of western businessmen they had just met and, to judge by the blasé manner of Mr Big and his expensive suit, they were quite used to doing it. We were not anything special. We had not been treated with Ernie-type excitement at the fantastic prospects we offered. This was regular trade for our man and his associates. We had no idea how to get a container-load of ivory into the UK, or the USA or anywhere else, but quite obviously there were people who did know how to do it.

We were scheduled to go back to HQ. If we were to blow the lid on this trade we needed more expeditions and more resources which, with that sinking feeling, we rather thought we wouldn't get. I'd been told many times by my bosses that the RSPCA was a welfare organisation, not a conservation one. In my simple way I thought that killing elephants to get their tusks was not helpful to their welfare, but I knew that those whose offices have carpets would not see things from my point of view. We would file our report. It might be forwarded to the proper authorities and they might do something but somehow I doubted even that. The RSPCA was not known for good communications with others. I could suggest getting somebody like Greenpeace involved but anything with political undertones might have filled the high corridors with fright.

Ernie phoned offering to see us through customs and check-in with no fuss. We had to put him off again, saying we were thinking of taking another trip inland before we went home. Also, we didn't really see why he thought his offer was such a big deal - that is, we didn't see until we got to Kotoka Airport departures. Our flight arrival there had been chaotic, being faced with a quaint mixture of 1950s UK provincial aerodrome, tropical heat and their attempt at 21st-century systems and technology, but at least it was chaos in a quick dose. As soon as you were through the formalities and somehow found your luggage, you were in a taxi and away.

Departures was quite different. To check in, we needed a check-in helper, so we were told by a persistent young man whom eventually we paid to go away, only for him to be replaced by another, who expected payment for pushing our luggage trolley. He had a colleague, who offered to make sure our luggage was safe in return for a small fee. Bryn whispered something in his ear and both boys disappeared. Reaching the check-in desk we were told we had to clear customs first, so we queued for the nothing-to-declare route only to have our baggage searched very thoroughly. Moving along we had it searched again, and again.

'We should have paid the first guy,' said Bryn, as we rejoined the check-in queue, listened to the unintelligible announcements, took it in turns to visit the most disgusting toilets ever seen at an airport and congratulated ourselves on our foresight in allowing so much extra time. In fact, we proved overgenerous and ended up with an hour and a half to wait. There didn't seem to be a bar open so, spotting one of our check-in helpers, I asked where the nearest bar was. He led us to a certain taxi, which is one commodity they're not short of in Ghana, and told the driver to take us to the Shangri-La Hotel. After a very rapid ten-minute drive we wandered through a spotlessly clean air-conditioned reception area to a grass-roof shaded table by huge swimming pool, ordered some ice-cold beers and decided that this would be our most enjoyable hour of an otherwise exhausting day, including seven hours in the air.

Our friendly waiter told us that while customs officials expect gratuities from foreigners, they often rob the locals if they find anything they fancy in the luggage. The worst foreigner case he'd heard about was of an American girl leaving Katoka quite late at night, when the customs guy said that her passport photograph wasn't her, it was her sister. For US$50 he'd turn a blind eye to this fraudulent behaviour. The girl wouldn't have it. She produced other forms of ID and pointed out that the passport had been stamped on entry. In which case, said the customs man, that would be US$100 to correct two frauds.

We knew we would be back, for the monkeys if not for the ivory. Maybe next time we'd stay at the Shangri-La. Yes, let's do that, we said. Here's to the Shangri-La.

Chapter Three

OF YOUNG MONKEYS AND OLD DEVILS

After much haggling we managed to squeeze more funds for Bryn and me to go back to Ghana and finish our primate investigation. As predicted, my bosses had done nothing with my ivory report so I'd passed it on without official sanction to a friend who worked in conservation, and he'd taken it to high places and eventually to the Ghanaian government. With shock, horror, protestations, wailing and gnashing of teeth, the announcement was made that all ivory stocks would be seized and the guilty parties would be dealt with. Frankly, I didn't expect to see much difference when I got there. If they had indeed seized the ivory, some official would have sold it back into the market. Whether they had or they hadn't, I was quite prepared to see the same plentiful supplies on stalls in the souk and my man John plying his trade.

We flew into Kotoka well prepared, with a pack of 200 Lucky Strikes lying on top in each of our suitcases. At a nod from us, these were confiscated and we were through and heading for the Shangri-La. The rooms were grass-hut type chalets in the grounds but with rather better facilities than your typical native hut: air conditioning, TV, internet, mini bar, fridge, phone, safe, the lot, and the greatest of these was air conditioning. With efficient porters and waiters and uniformed security staff, it seemed a different world to the gimme-gimme crush and corruption at the airport only ten minutes away. The room information pack praised the casino and the restaurant, noted that the breakfast was famous throughout Ghana, and mentioned that pets were allowed. That might come in handy, we thought.

Bryn and I had debriefed very thoroughly and gone over everything that had been declared by all parties. In particular we were keen to check that there were no inconsistencies in what we'd said, no little lapses which might pop into Ernie's brain and give him cause to hesitate. Ernie was a jolly chap who liked his beer and was naïve in some ways, but he'd been in the business 30 years. He had networks organised in Britain and America. He was cunning, untrustworthy and no mug. Just how far his arm could reach we'd see later. Meantime, I had the easy task of buying Ernie beer in our hotel bar and fixing up an appointment through him with the top brass at Accra Zoo, who would certify my wild monkeys as bred in captivity, physically sound and free of disease.

We wanted to take video footage at the zoo but we had the same problem as before in the government office. In the heat of mid morning, nobody would wear the amount of clothing needed to conceal a camera, so we flew a kite. Our friends back home, we said, our financial backers, wanted to be sure that the product they were buying was looked after properly. These are City people, we said, bankers, accountants. They approach everything in the same businesslike way. They demand quality assurance, and they want to see pictures of the conditions in which their purchases are held. They want to see inside the warehouse, as it were.

Ernie could understand the sense of this and was sure there'd be no problem. I could bring my camera and take all the pictures I wanted. With Ernie in an agreeing sort of mood and happily on the beer, I thought I'd raise the issue of visiting the outback to see the trapping at first hand.

This, however, he could not understand. Why did I want to do this? He'd never been into the bush to see the trapping, nor had Albert, so why should I? It wasn't in any way necessary. The monkeys came in from the villages, he took delivery, paid up the monkey-catchers' pesawas and that was that. If you didn't need to do something, you didn't do it, full stop. That was Ernie's philosophy, along with buy cheap, sell dear. There are 100 pesawas to the cedi, and at that time £60 would buy you 1 million cedi, so now we knew what he was paying for his monkeys.

Without hard evidence of catching in the wild, that is, filming the trapping of monkeys which could then be traced through the system, we had no case, so I was very anxious indeed to persuade him. I'd started on the telephone from home; now I was at it again, to the point of Ernie becoming exasperated. I had to back off for the moment. He didn't like this sort of pressure on an issue which was totally beyond him, and I didn't like the funny look in his eye. More beer, Ernie.

All became sweetness and light again in the morning when we reached Accra Zoo. One of the senior management there was also a special veterinary adviser to the Ghanaian government wildlife department, an old friend of Ernie's, and well disposed towards a bung. Here we were with the second link in this very short chain. Ernie got the monkeys, the zoo authorities vetted and certified, our government man stamped and pushed the papers, Mrs Ernie made sure there were no little hitches at the airport, and Ernie collected the money from his clients. How many criminal set-ups would be envious of a tight organisation like that? It was smooth, efficient, leak-proof, profitable, self-contained and very compact. It was perfect, in fact, except for one flaw: the customers.

Ernie had already told us about one customer for poisonous snakes in London who'd disappeared owing £2,500 and reappeared doing business with another reptile exporter. 'It's a small world,' Ernie said. 'I have many friends in London. This man was very foolish.' It was almost impossible to feel the implicit threat from such a friendly, happy-go-lucky fellow who could surely not be the one to send the boys round, but £2,500 was a great deal of money in Ghana and Ernie made it plain that his response to the debt was not aimed simply at getting the cash.

Accra Zoo was a sad place. It reminded me of film I'd seen of London Zoo in the old days, Edwardian times, when wild animals were banged up in steel-barred cages and nobody gave a thought to what they might feel about that. The animals at Accra were in such cages, looked depressed, and were without any form of natural stimulation. Our observations had to be brief as we were marched to the director's modest quarters, a small room with a desk, a chair and a fan. He was another cheery chap, younger than the others, in his early 30s, tall, lean, with wavy hair, and a trim moustache, a man of the professions on his way up. He was pleased to tell us about his qualifications as a veterinary surgeon and his training in England; he came across as genial, urbane, quite old-school really, with never a hint of corruption. He led a double life. The bungs went in his pocket, the dirty work was done to earn them, but there was no need to mention anything about that.

He took us to see the holding area, a long bank of small, individual cages, many of them occupied by patas, mona, green and spot-nosed monkeys, exactly the species we'd been expecting to see. That these were wild specimens could not be doubted. As we approached, they flung themselves around their cages, frantically scrabbling at the bars, screaming and yelling as they leapt hopelessly from side to top to bottom of their prison cells, baring their teeth at us as we got closer, urinating, defecating, demanding to know which king of the animals it was who had sentenced them to this unbearable agony. It was a horrible sight and I kept the video short. There was no need to dwell on it. It was blindingly obvious to anyone with the slightest knowledge of primates that these had not been bred in captivity and were wild in more than one sense of the word.

These young monkeys, treated all the same and, if they survived, scheduled to meet the same fate in a research lab somewhere in Europe, are fascinatingly different from each other in nature. Green monkeys, also called vervet, Chlorocebus aethiops, are small ground-dwellers but, not being very fast in monkey-predator terms, tend not to stray far from woodland. They have a brown-grey coat speckled with green and yellow, they eat anything that's going and live in troops of 20 up to 50 based on the families of related females. The older females with the largest families are ranked highest; the males are rated by their fighting prowess and so can rise and fall in importance. Vervets are known to become particularly nervous and stressed in captivity and the juveniles even more so. Three-quarters of young wild-caught vervets are likely to die within a few days.

Patas monkeys, Erythrocebus patas, also ground-dwellers and omnivores, live in much smaller troops, of one male and maybe half a dozen females, with the dominant female in over-all charge. An adult male patas can run at sustained speeds of 35 mph; another primate called Roger Bannister ran at 15 mph when he broke the four-minute mile. Also called the hussar and sergeant-major monkey because of their Colonel Blimp-style moustaches, the patas see their habitat – savannah and semi-desert – being reduced by farming but increased by deforestation.

Spot-nosed monkeys, also called guenons, are the smallest of the Old World primates and there are three species, all tree-dwellers: greater, Cercopithecus nictitans, lesser, C. petaurista, and red-tailed, C. ascanius. They live in troops of a dozen up to 40 or so, with permanent female members but led by whichever male happens to be boss at the time, eat fruit and insects and prefer rainforest by rivers. Another guenon, the mona, Cercopithecus mona, is a colourful, noisy, highly social tree-dweller which also eats mainly fruit and insects, living in female-dominated troops usually with only one male although small troops can come together to form temporary, multi-male tribes of 50 animals. They seem to fly through the treetops, leaping from one thin, bending branch to another. If they miss and fall, they rarely seem to hurt themselves and just rocket up the next tree.

All these monkeys have a lifespan of about 20 years unless taken by one of their natural predators – the big cats, birds of prey, pythons – but it's not the leopards and the crowned eagles which have put them into CITES Appendix II, that is, expected to become threatened with extinction unless trade is controlled and permits applied. Doing his bit to get them into Appendix I, our man at Accra Zoo explained that each monkey would be blood-tested for contagious diseases, inoculated against rabies and wormed. Quite how he'd manage this with frantic, panic-stricken little monkeys with sharp teeth, I didn't like to ask. I did ask him about how and where the monkeys were trapped. He didn't really know and certainly didn't care. That had nothing to do with him. His attitude was the same as Ernie's. The monkeys came from the wild, yes, that was confirmed, but the only important matter was that they arrived, they got here. How they got here, well, why should he worry about that?

We shook hands and left. That evening we were due to meet Ernie and Albert again for another celebration, hopefully not involving rats' toes, and I would be forced to lay it on the line about the trapping. We had to see it. For the moment, another step in the sequence could be taken. Our financial backers, I said, our City types, wanted to know about Ernie's solidity as a trader. They would take my word for it but it would help me a lot if I could see some records, some invoices, receipts, that sort of thing. I raised this in the full and certain knowledge that the consequence for Bryn and me would be Ordeal by Driving, but we had to do what we had to do. At least Ernie's road-insanity was not amplified by alcohol this time. Our ride to his house would have been the preferred choice had we been offered the alternative of being locked in a wardrobe with a Gaboon viper.

Ernie's house was luxurious by local standards although in the UK we would have dismissed it as a Nissen hut in a very bad area, and it was certainly not one of the finest in Accra as he'd claimed at our five-star lunch in London. He had a TV and a fridge, a proper bed and a telephone but the bog was the standard bucket in the yard. It was a much more downmarket pad than Albert's, which was a surprise because we'd been given the impression that Ernie was the big cheese and Albert was just a Dairylea triangle by comparison. After our fool's errand to Mole, we were beginning to see Ernie as more of a con artist than we liked. We'd have to watch him even more carefully; not that we'd ever had any illusions about him as a person, but it would not be good for our case if he turned out to be a small-time crook after all. I was thinking about how excited he'd been about that government official, and how vainglorious, and how he took vulgar advantage of free fillet steak and beer. If Albert was sending 20 monkeys six times a year to Britain and lived in a smart bungalow in the local equivalent of, say, Barnes or Highgate, what level was Ernie dealing at if he could only afford to live in a crumbling flat in Accra Tower Hamlets?

Maybe he was an eccentric. Maybe he liked to count his money rather than spend it. In any case, he had mountains of official dockets stamped by his colleagues in the monkey-smuggling ring. This was all very well but it wasn't what I wanted, and we sifted through the pile of papers, and Ernie brought more, and we sifted again saying how impressed we were, and aha! There it was.

I nodded at Bryn, who asked Ernie if he had a cold beer or a cola anywhere, having already noted that there were tins of both in the fridge. While they went to the kitchen I pocketed my prize, a copy invoice from Ernie to a British buyer with a PO box in Cheshire, for 20 Mona monkeys: £1,600.

Ernie had told us about this deal before, in one of his expansive beer moments. The buyer had placed the order, paid up front with a banker's draft, taken delivery, and disappeared. Ernie had tried to find him again but he was gone. Most bizarre, Ernie thought. Later, back in the UK, we would find that the PO box was a mailing address for a firm describing itself as one of the world's leading pharmaceuticals companies.

With our paperwork proof we only had one more phase of play, the wild trapping. Ernie was still obdurate but we were getting desperate. If trapping was off the itinerary, we'd had it, so we resorted to the good offices of our old friends, Messrs Cock, Bull and Story. The British government, we said, was on the verge of banning imports of primates altogether, and of passing a law against keeping primates as pets. These moves were not publicly known yet, but we had a mole, a tame one, in the Cabinet Office and such matters had been discussed at the highest level. It was all part of seeming to be green. Concern for the environment. Experimentation on animals would be drastically reduced. All animals for UK research purposes would have to be bred locally. You'd be all right, Ernie, with your reptiles trade and your American business, but UK primates could become a dead duck.

'A dead duck?' said Ernie. He'd never heard the expression. Never mind that, we said. We have a chance here to turn this around. If we can show how well the monkeys are treated, from the trapping stage, to the proper blood testing and inoculations, to safe transport and arrival at Heathrow, this irritation might well go away. Our contacts suggest the government is perfectly balanced on the fence at the moment. The green/environment/animal-rights lobby is saying one thing; the pharmaceuticals companies are saying the opposite. A clandestine meeting with the right people, a little film show, well, it could swing it our way.

To Ernie, our desire to see the trapping had seemed illogical and downright idiotic. In undercover work, we often find ourselves asking for the unreasonable so that we can get at the evidence and, as here, the trick is to come up with something that, no matter how far-fetched, makes our position look believable if foreign to common sense.

Driving back to the Shangri-La, Ernie relented. We would go and see the trapping which, as it was a continuous, constant activity would need no special arrangements to be made. Ernie was busy the next day so he would pick us up at 8am on the day following, an arrangement sufficient to cause another celebration featuring beers on us in the hotel bar. While I went to get them in, Ernie told Bryn that he was expecting a very important business contact to visit him shortly from Cairo. This fellow, Ernie explained, was Egypt's number one man in exotic animals and he was coming to see Ernie, nobody else, looking to place orders worth lots of money. Perhaps Bryn had heard of this man. Amr Saad, he was called.

Turning up with the refreshments, I found Bryn in the middle of a coughing fit. It was a while before Ernie went to the gents and I could be told the reason. Amr Saad was an old adversary, a man I'd exposed in a sting only the year before, resulting in his entire collection of live animals, many of them rare and very rare species, being seized and his partner in crime, the director of Cairo Zoo, losing her job. If he saw me in Accra, it would be Bryn and me doing the losing and possibly being seized too.

Ernie, oblivious of the anxiety he was causing, went on and on about how marvellous was Mr Saad and how his choice of Ernie as his representative in Ghana bestowed enormous credit on them both. What astuteness Mr Saad displayed in his selection of Ernie, and what satisfaction Ernie felt in this confirmation of his status as a top-rank international operator. Soon we would meet Mr Saad and doubtless his regal introduction by Ernie would bring us all greater fortune.

The good news was that Saad didn't know Bryn, and that I was using a different alias and cover story. Provided Saad didn't actually clap eyes on me, we should be okay. If he did, then our project was blown and we might very well have trouble leaving Ghana. Ernie had all manner of contacts at the airport; we'd never get out that way. Our senior civil servant would have power and influence with the police. After Ernie had gone it didn't take us long to imagine ourselves planted with drugs and positioned as the evil white men trying to set up a crack-cocaine dealership in the innocent and beautiful country of Ghana. Or perhaps we were spies, the advance party of a secret liberation front trying to recruit respectable businessmen and government officials to the cause. After these flights of fancy, well, maybe not entirely fancy, we could seriously consider the consequences of being beaten to a pulp and dumped somewhere in the jungle to find our own way home. We looked at the map. Could we cross the border into Ivory Coast or Togo? How were things in Upper Volta?

Ernie was so pleased with himself over Amr Saad that anything could happen. He could turn up at our hotel with the man and expect me to get the first round in. He could bring Saad along on our wild trapping expedition. He could insist on a formal meeting, at his house perhaps. If he did that, at least I could contract gastro-enteritis and send my regrets with Bryn. Otherwise, we had no control of the situation at all and that made us very, very jumpy.

A further possibility was that Ernie had already boasted about me to Saad, and/or that Saad had become curious and asked about Ernie's new UK business colleague and what I was like. Come to think of it, that was more than possible. It was probable. Bryn and I talked it around and around and inside out. Any sensible person would cut and run. The risks were too high. We had a good deal of evidence to take home with us. But, the big but, we didn't have the clincher, the one sentence in the story that would make our happy ending inevitable. But, an equally big but, Ernie and Saad could well be leading us into a trap and, once we began going along with it, we'd had it. There would be no escape.

We had to take the chance, we decided. We couldn't get all this way along the project and give in. Having made the decision, all our nerves disappeared – temporarily, as it turned out – but for the moment we were the cucumbers of cool. Tomorrow, a visit to the Cultural Centre to check on the ivory situation would be followed by a light lunch and a relaxing day beside the pool reading the guide books to Upper Volta.

Our man John, in front of his magnificently stocked ivory stall, greeted us like his oldest and best friends. We apologised for the first deal falling through. Our money-bags had decided to invest instead in the Colombian coca industry, but we thought we might have found another way. Give our regards to Mr Big, we said, and we'll hope to see him next time.

So, that was how far the Ghana government's actions had reached; nowhere at all. They hadn't confiscated anything. They hadn't done anything, apart from writing a memo saying they had.

Came the morning, came the nerves again. The semi-condemned men ate a jittery breakfast. Our plan was for Bryn to wait in the hotel lobby while I hid in the bushes outside, so I could see if Saad was in the car. If he was, I'd radio Bryn and leg it, and Bryn would be ready with my apologies for being indisposed. The car was late. After half an hour Bryn telephoned Ernie's house. He'd been having problems with Albert and he'd be there at 9.30. He still hadn't arrived by 10am and the hotel staff were clearly curious about their guest who crouched in the shrubbery an hour at a time before dashing inside for a whispered conversation with his friend.

In such a situation you must keep your brain working along logical lines, considering the actual possibilities and trying to evolve reasonable courses of action for each. You remember your training, you remember what the SAS instructor told you about staying in focus on reality, while your mind wanders among filthy cells in Accra jail and watery grasscutter soup for the rest of your life. Or, there was the shorter-term alternative of being thrashed with baseball bats and thrown where the leopards might find you, or the crocodiles.

Ernie's next arrival time was 11am and he did drive up soon after, alone. I ducked around the side of the hotel and walked into the lobby just as he and Bryn were shaking hands. Still we were not at ease. It would have been better for our nerves if he had brought Saad along. We'd have known where we stood. Although Bryn would have been on his own with them, we thought it unlikely that they'd try anything dodgy with me still at large. Now we had to commit to the last stage of our project, hoping against hope that it was monkey trapping we were going to experience, not Bryn and Terry trapping.

Ernie was most apologetic. One of Albert's uncle's monkeys, due for export to the Czech Republic, had escaped and terrorised the neighbourhood, pulling down washing off the line and ransacking three apartments. I had a good picture in my mind of this because of an experience I'd had in my uniform days at Armthorpe, a mining village near Doncaster. A chap had ordered a squirrel monkey for a pet but, when he opened the crate, out jumped a three-quarters-grown baboon. It sank its teeth through the palm of his hand and leapt onto the table, sweeping everything to the floor. The man shut the door on it as it started on the kitchen cupboards, opening the coffee jar and pouring the powder out, which it mixed with a bag of sugar. In a few minutes it had emptied every cupboard, throwing tea bags about the place, cups, glasses, tins of spaghetti hoops, jars of jam, squeezy bottles of HP sauce, the lot.

The man rang us and I got there about two hours later, armed with my trusty dog-grasper. Never having dealt with a primate before, I thought in my greenness that this would be sufficient. The man showed me into the kitchen and there was the baboon, all 2 foot 6 inches of it, sitting happily on the floor, covered in flour and cocoa and enjoying the last finger-lickings of a jar of peanut butter while searching inside the wrapper for the Hovis crust. In the wild, baboons can be extremely fierce but this one seemed not to mind humans much. Another characteristic is that they'll eat pretty well anything that can be eaten, and it was illustrating that trait perfectly. Very shortly I expected it to work out how to open a tin of sardines.

I had a cunning plan involving some tranquillisers which were issued to us by the vet to help us subdue dangerous dogs. I put one of these tablets in a banana and gave it to the baboon, which munched it with obvious enjoyment until it reached the tranquilliser. It spat the tablet across the kitchen floor, finished the banana and looked at me as if to say 'What next, clever clogs?' I had no more ideas, just tranquillisers and bananas, so four bananas and spits later I had to try to think of something. Lowering the loop of the dog-grasper towards the baboon's head only produced a tired gesture, knocking it away. 'Can't you do better than that?' said the baboon in my imagination. He had the upper hand and knew it, so I decided to bore him into submission. For the next 30 minutes I pushed the dog-grasper at the baboon, which pushed it away until, fed up with this game, he turned his attention to a tomato which happened to be near-by. As he delicately began to peel this tomato I got the loop down and tight around his neck.

The worst fight I'd had with the grasper up to that point had been with a very large feral cat but that was nothing compared to an adolescent baboon bouncing around in every direction. I was bigger and stronger and had to win in the end, I told myself. There were no mobile phones nor any sort of small video camera in those days, otherwise my titanic struggle with a floured, seasoned and breadcrumbed wild baboon might have become a timeless classic. As it was, I got it back into its crate, which the owner secured with some extra pieces of wood nailed into the top.

The man thanked me for my help, promised to give up all ideas of keeping a monkey as a pet and said he'd have to think of something else for his wife's birthday. Gazing at the truly wonderful mess, surpassing anything a large and determined gang of three-year-old humans could do, I said that if he didn't look sharp and get it cleaned up he wouldn't need to worry any more about such matters as wives' birthdays.

My amusement at the same thing happening in three Accra apartments had to be hidden from Ernie as we began our two-hour drive into the country, still not relaxed although Ernie's story was plausible and his irritation at the delay seemed real enough. Heading generally north through the same countryside we'd seen from the bus on our Mole outing, we came to a small village of about 30 grass huts plus a few more favoured dwellings with stone and mud walls. These were raised a couple of feet off the ground on stone pillars, making a nice shady place for a nanny goat and her kids and some very tough-looking chickens. We could hear engine noise coming from one of the bigger huts, which we were told was a maize-threshing machine, the pride and joy of the village and its main source of income. If threshing your impoverished neighbours' maize paid better than monkey catching, that could only be a statement on the minuscule prices offered by Ernie and Albert.

The village children surrounded us excitedly, smiling and giggling, happy as only those can be who don't know what they're missing. Trying to think of some way I could respond to their welcome, I filmed them with my video camera and played back the tape. The effect was sensational. They pointed, laughed, put their hands over their eyes, laughed again. A few of the shyer ones looked, well, shy, and puzzled, and one or two even looked a little frightened by the white man's magic. I don't know who was more surprised, the children or Bryn and me that such everyday technology hadn't reached a village two hours' drive from Accra.

After a while a young man produced a cage made of wood and wire mesh, quite a big cage, about 2 feet square, with a simply sprung trap-door mechanism in its top. Food was put on the trap-door and the monkey's weight would operate it. I had to wonder how much weight was needed when I looked inside and saw one of the saddest things I have ever encountered. Two baby spot-nosed guenons, no more than six weeks old, sat there in a corner with their arms around each other, an expression of complete bewilderment in their eyes. On the floor of the cage were bits of rotten fruit, although these tiny monkeys were surely not weaned from their mother's milk. The mother must have been carrying these infants when all three fell through the trap. What had happened to her I didn't want to inquire. The baby prisoners' fur was matted with diarrhoea and there was more all over their prison. The only concession to a tree-dweller's life was a bit of copper pipe stuck across the cage roof.

While I filmed this nauseating scene, Ernie told me the monkeys were to be shipped by air to the Czech Republic, not an EU member at that time. From there they would probably go to the UK. Looking at them, I doubted very much they would reach halfway. Guenons are nursed by their mothers for six months, being gradually weaned onto fruit and insects from about nine weeks. They are obviously smarter and more aware of their surroundings than their human infant equivalent but what would that count for, in this horrific situation at six weeks old?

Whatever intellectual position a person might hold on animal experimentation, nothing could justify this. From the moment they had the gross misfortune to meet a human being, these little creatures were being put through a process of agony, at any point in which they might die from sheer misery and illnesses caused thereby. A human traps them in a cage, takes them from their mother who is probably killed, holds them captive for days or weeks, ships them in vehicles and aircraft, holds them again in cages, and finally gives them over to be sacrificed for the greater benefit of said humans. It makes you feel sick and ashamed. It would certainly be an astonishing thing if any research laboratory ever admitted to being a part of it.

Back in Accra, Ernie and Albert wanted a night out but we were not in the mood. Still Ernie kept banging on about his big Egyptian and how we should all form a happy crew, paint the town red and celebrate our lucrative future together. Eventually we bargained him down to a few final beers back at our hotel later on, when we would place our order, for ten each of mona, patas and spot-nosed monkeys a month, and dish out the necessary cash for wheel-oiling.

Wishing the while that we were about to expose the real villains, the pharmaceuticals companies, the research establishments and the do-nothing, behind-the-scenes politicians, we set up the meeting in our hotel room. We could hope that our report would cause a stir and force the issue into the important people's faces. To do that, we needed to summarise and reiterate all the various parts of the deal and the process, and record same on camera and audio. Being in our room meant we could avoid any passing jazz bands but also arrange our equipment to best advantage, which included a goodly supply of export-strength lager placed in the vital spot.

Sure enough, Ernie and Albert sat obligingly beneath the spotlight and Bryn did a first-class job of recapping. I counted out the bribes: US$50 for the government cheese, US$50 for the zoo guy, US$20 each for Ernie and Albert as a gesture of good will, and we got all that on the video. We shook hands on our deal, agreeing at Ernie's forceful insistence that the word 'research' would not appear on any paperwork. They would ship 30 primates 12 times a year, with half the money up front and half on delivery. Tired out, we said our goodbyes and turned our thoughts to getting out of Ghana.

We'd told Ernie we were going to have three days' holiday, doing what tourists do, so he arranged to pick us up after that to take us to the airport and usher us through, with or without supplies of ivory and Gaboon vipers. Instead, we paid our bill next morning, took a taxi from outside the hotel, and tried to pass unnoticed through a small airport where we were the only white men, Ernie's wife was a customs officer and most of the other officials knew Ernie and were on the take. The monkey god must have intervened on our behalf because we went through at the speed of a fairly athletic snail, which was very good by local standards and, weary but satisfied with a job well done, we were soon airborne and on our way to Manchester.

On the plane home I felt my anger rising. How could the British authorities be so easily conned? Anybody with half an eye could see that these monkeys were not what they were supposed to be. They showed every characteristic of being wild-caught, while a document from a Ghanaian government department said they were not. What do you believe, the evidence of the living creature or a piece of paper? My guess was that the two kinds of evidence were not being compared. Some lowly official in the British civil service was checking the paperwork against paperwork criteria. If it met requirements, fine. Through apathy or ignorance, or both, nobody was checking the monkeys. Surely, if they knew that these close relatives of ours were in the wild one week, in Accra zoo the next week and a UK research laboratory the week after, they'd do something? Wouldn't they?

I said it would be hard to get out of Ghana but I hadn't meant it the way it turned out. First, Bryn's luggage didn't arrive. It wasn't on our plane. We had taken great pains to share and secure our precious video and audio tapes about our persons so that no delving customs official might find them, but Bryn had left his car key in his suitcase. While I arranged for my wife Denise to come and get me, Bryn settled down to wait for the next flight in from Kotoka.

By the time I got home I was feeling queasy. By the morning I was down and out with the full-length, director's cut version of The Grasscutter's Revenge. For two days I was helpless. On day three, I forced myself back to the office to start compiling my report on the Ghana project. This, a complex and difficult investigation concluded successfully, was going to explode on the nation's front pages. No longer would the government or anybody else be able to deny that wild-caught primates were used in the UK for research. Bryn and I had done a very, very good job. What was a few days of Ghana Colon compared to that?

My report on the monkeys got nowhere. I don't think I've ever been so let down by people. The animal smugglers, catchers, baiters, misusers and abusers might be villains but at least you know where you are with them.

I had a debrief meeting with my boss and was surprised to find him seeming disappointed that we'd done so well. He was never a great supporter of my wilder projects and I was used to him and his glum receptions, but this was exceptional. We really believed we had the goods at last. Even he should have been pleased but he sounded as if we'd brought home a heap of trouble. I thought, if I came to your house with lobster, fillet steak, champagne, peaches and cream, you'd say 'Very nice, Terry, but who'll wash up?'

I should have realised something was going wrong when Bryn was checking out the PO box number on the invoice I'd lifted from Ernie's house. We had a good working relationship with the Post Office investigations unit, quite a long-standing relationship too, and if we wanted to trace a box number to help us find a criminal suspect, help would be forthcoming. Bryn rang; he'd have to ring back next day, which he did. This time the PO investigator said he couldn't discuss the issue, end of story, sorry.

We had never had such a response from a government agency before, so I rang our contact's boss. I got the same abrupt treatment. One explanation might have been that the police or customs were already on the case, but then the post office people would not have been so edgy and the police or whoever would have been in touch with us for any information we might have had. Experience said that wasn't it, so what was it? The refusal to help us must have meant orders from above, or some sort of coded protection afforded to the PO box. Possibly it arose from the threats of violence from animal rights extremists towards anyone involved in animal experimentation. Possibly it was something else.

Still confident that our work was going to knock down the walls of Jericho, we wrote out the full version of our report. Bryn took it to HQ personally and watched in disbelief as our manager put it in a desk drawer without looking at it. When he came back and told me this I was straight on the phone. Oh yes, he would read it soon, he was just rather busy at the moment. Six phone calls later, he had read it and was delighted to take the Mick out of me for a typing error, spelling Czech Republic wrongly.

Still we waited for the summons to the usual big debrief meeting, with our boss, other senior managers, and people from the media and campaigns department. Instead, I had a call from one of the special scientific officers who, he was quick to tell me, had regular meetings with the pharmaceutical companies and major research contractors. He was entirely dismissive of the work Bryn and I had done. Such trade in wild primates did not happen. It had not happened, nor would it happen. He was confident. He knew.

I said, what about the invoice? He would like to see that. With his many contacts he'd be able to find out all about it. I didn't much care for this man and his opinions, nor did I trust him, so I produced a dummy invoice, the same in every respect except I changed the year and the month. He rang me a few days later, to confirm that these monkeys had indeed arrived in UK as specified but had gone straight into zoos and private collections, and would I please not waste any more of his time.

I kept this episode to myself and did a little investigation of my own. It wasn't difficult. There aren't that many major pharmaceuticals companies admitting to animal experimentation. So I wondered what to do, and was still wondering when I got a fax from Ernie saying that my monkeys were on their way, ten each of patas, mona and spot-nosed as agreed. Talk about flap. I could have found out what spring is like on Jupiter and Mars. What was the reaction going to be when I came to work with 30 monkeys? I'd had no idea Ernie would work so quickly. I'd expected to have the thing exposed before he had a chance to collect his wild primates, never mind send them. I faxed Ernie back. Luckily, he had slightly exaggerated. He had the monkeys but he hadn't actually put them on a plane. Hold on, I said. Don't do anything until I say so. There is a strong rumour going around that the government is going to act against primate import.

And that was that. My report sat in my boss' desk drawer, never to surface. Although I never heard from them again, I have no doubt that Ernie, Albert and the rest carried on as normal and mysterious importers of primates found their usual ways around the law.

A year later I happened to be chatting to a couple of staff from the RSPCA press office, and I told them about Ghana. They'd never heard a word, never seen the report and, perhaps because they were not too high up in the management structure, were amazed that such a golden opportunity had been let slip. 'Ah well,' I said, 'you'll understand when your hair turns grey.' I summoned up my pet bit of Latin again. 'Radix malorum est cupiditas,' I declared, and they looked amazed at that, too.

CHAPTER FOUR

LOOK AWAY NOW

I think this case has to be the most disturbing and vile abuse of animals I have come across. After 27 years in the RSPCA I thought I'd seen everything – animals being tortured, hanged, burned alive, you name it, but this was something different. This was a kind of individual commercial torture for the perverted sex market. It was cruelty for financial gain but there's nothing unusual in that. No, this was creating a new dimension of sickening exploitation which I guess would be beyond the imaginings of most people. The resulting court case, the first of its kind in the UK, would reach the newspapers without any accompanying warning to readers. This is only a short chapter but let me recommend that, if you are in doubt about the strength of your stomach, you skip it.

So, there I was, believing I'd seen all a human could do to our fellow creatures in this world, when the telephone rang. The call was from our Stoke-on-Trent office. A uniformed inspector colleague, Julie and I had a rather strange conversation. Julie seemed to want to tell me something but couldn't. She'd rung me with a purpose, but she was being secretive about what that purpose was.

I gathered that the police were behind it and needed help from the SOU, so I thought perhaps I could try and to get some sense out of them.

No such luck. The police constable responsible, called Andy, was equally cryptic. All he would say was that he had a video which depicted a level of cruelty to animals completely outside his experience. He and some of his fellow officers at the station had been shocked and saddened enough to shed a few tears, and furious enough to vow that the maker of the film would be found, banged up and, if they had their way, taken out into the exercise yard and shot.

My colleague Ian and I jumped in the car and headed for Stoke where PC Andy told us that, during an investigation into what had appeared to be a routine domestic – young couple breaking up in acrimony, father of girl sure she had been mixing with undesirables – they had come into possession of a VHS cassette which he now proposed to play to us. Ian and I sat down, with Julie and another RSPCA inspector, Dawn.

The first scene was videoed from the passenger seat of a moving car, with the camera focusing on the footwell of the driver's position. The driver, from the shape of her legs below a mini miniskirt, was undoubtedly female. The viewer's eye naturally followed the line of her legs down to her high heeled shoes, shiny black stilettos, and from there to the brake pedal, and … what? What on earth was that? Taped to the pedal was a live brown mouse.

Every time the girl braked, the little mouse felt the force. We could hear instructions coming from the camera operator, a man, telling his star to brake as gently as she could so that the mouse lasted longer. After about ten minutes of this, the poor animal was a red-and-brown blob of pulp and the scene ended. A few seconds followed of welcome blank nothing, then we were off again, this time looking at the whole female, possibly the same one, possibly not, but we got a brief look at her face and she was certainly an attractive girl, one who would have turned heads walking down the street in Stoke-on-Trent in her tight top and very short skirt.

The camera went to her bare legs and now we could see it was not the same woman. This one had a tattoo of a dolphin on her right ankle. She had the same kind of shoes though, black stilettos, and was standing in a bathroom like the sort of smart set-up you see in expensive showrooms, with the best Italian tiles and fittings and a luxurious bath which just had to have the jacuzzi option. The woman held in her hand a length of white picture cord. On the other end of it was a ginger-and-white guinea pig, tied by the throat.

The girl seemed to want the guinea pig to pay more attention, or do a dance on its back legs maybe, because she kept pulling the cord to lift it partly off the ground. The man's voice from behind the camera, the same man's voice as before, warned her not to pull so hard or she'd strangle it. I deduced from this remark that dangling the guinea pig by its neck was not the main event but only the curtain raiser, and my eyes went to those stiletto heels.

Sure enough, she put a heel to the animal's body and pressed, gently. She did this slowly and several times, and then pressed harder. The guinea pig squealed. She placed her heel to another part and pressed again, and harder again. The guinea pig screamed, a high-pitched, heart-stopping, pitiful, piercing cry. In that room there was well over 50 years' collective experience of RSPCA work but this sound was being heard for the first time. In the north of England they call it a screak, the noise that metal makes on metal when there's no oil between.

The torture went on for several minutes, which seemed like hours. The animal was gradually giving in. It could still manage a loud, shrill screak when the heel was applied but obviously its frail life couldn't last much longer. Our lord of the camera and our lady of the stilettos were not to be denied their final triumph and so, before the cavy could expire from its repeated stabbings, Miss Piggy stood on its back with both feet, full weight, and cracked its spine in two.

Cut to black. I looked at my three colleagues. If Ian's jaw had dropped any further it would have come right off. Julie was as white as a sheet and there were tears rolling down Dawn's face. No one could leave, however. We knew there had to be more. PC Andy sat with a grim look. He'd seen it before and he wasn't moving until we'd had the same experience.

I made a note about guinea pigs. Cavies domesticated by the Incas. Food animal. And it was, too, and that's why the Spaniards brought it back, as a source of meat. Nobody in Europe eats it now. Clearly we've become more sophisticated in our use of guinea pigs than those primitive South Americans.

After a fuzzy few frames a new lady came into focus, long legged like the others but displaying her shapely pins below the shortest pair of shorts. I was beginning to cotton on by this time – perhaps the others were ahead of me – that here we had films made to stimulate some sort of foot fetishism. The camera hardly dwelt on the women's other attributes at all, just sufficient to establish that the legs, and more especially the stilettos, belonged to an attractive young example.

I knew what a fetish was: a means of sexual arousal displaced from the usual to the different. I knew that feet and shoes were very common fetishes among men. What I couldn't yet understand was where killing animals came into it, except as an extreme form of sadism mixed in with the shoes. In my innocence, I had thought that men with this kind of affliction liked to have the girl in the shoes sticking it directly to them, not to a proxy guinea pig.

In the middle of all these desperate thoughts I was trying to keep notes of what was happening on the tape, with a view to identifying the participants and formalising the evidence: timings, any little giveaways such as when the girl called out to her dog Sam in the next room, any hints from the film set, marks and skin blemishes on the women's legs. I'm afraid my note taking came to sudden stop as the next scene began to move on.

Beside the shorts-wearing female's feet was a piece of hardboard, flat on the carpet, and standing on the hardboard was a tabby kitten, about 12 weeks old I'd have said. It was mewing in the most pitiful way and we soon saw why as the creature tried to scrabble off its hardboard platform. One of its back legs, the right one, was fixed somehow, glued perhaps, but the leg was broken. We could only guess at what that cat was feeling as it turned itself around on its shattered limb, almost a full circle this way, and again that way, its front paws slipping on the shiny surface in its forlorn attempts to escape.

The woman put her foot gently against the kitten and stroked it with her shoe as it cried. The man's voice said something about hoping to make a 30-minute show of this but 15 minutes would probably have to do. Now, would she please put her heel on the kitten's head. She tried to do this but not very well, and her heel slid onto the kitten's neck. The kitten yelled its incomparable distress. The man behind the camera laughed.

My two lady colleagues ran from the room, shaking with rage and sorrow. I looked at Ian; he looked at me. If I had the same complexion as him at that moment, we both looked like death. Not only had we never seen anything like this before. At that point in our experience, we hadn't even known such things went on.

The woman strutted around her torture victim, deciding where to apply the next agony. She placed her heel on its backbone, near the neck, and pressed. Blood came out of the kitten's mouth along with its wail of pain. I could not believe this could carry on much longer but it did, and my watch said eight minutes had passed before the kitten died of its wounds. Our horrors were still not over even if the poor kitten was gone. Deliberately and precisely, the woman stabbed her heel again and again into the tiny body's neck until the head came right off.

End of part three. Part four was another mouse, stuck to a board this time like the kitten. Part five was a mouse taped to a glass-topped table, with the camera looking up from beneath. By the end of the tape, 20 small animals, mostly mice, several guinea pigs and the one kitten, had been reduced to mince.

Needless to say, we offered the police every possible assistance with the highest priority, shocked that such behaviour could occur without us ever having heard a hint or a whisper of it. Gathering and organising evidence to secure a conviction is a big part of an exercise like this and our first task was to get a veterinary surgeon to make a formal statement of his professional opinion on the suffering caused. It's not something you can easily measure, suffering, but that's the way the judiciary wants it: quantified and itemised. I called in Matt, an experienced vet and an old friend, and I sat through the tape again with him. I wish I could say it was easier the second time, but it was worse.

It turned out that there wasn't a great deal of detective work to do. The police had done a brilliant job at high speed and already knew who was who. The cameraman was called Craig Chapman, a fellow in his late twenties, an ex personnel manager who ran a secretarial recruitment agency in Stoke-on-Trent. It seemed that he had been applying specialised selection criteria to some of his more attractive applicants, spotting if they were especially hard up and potentially willing to do what he wanted for money. The average pay day for the stars was £200, while the producer was getting £200 each time he sold a tape of one incident, and we'd seen 20. The demand for new ones was so great that he couldn't keep up.

While his lucrative business burgeoned, Chapman had fallen out with his live-in girlfriend, who sent her dad round to the house to collect her belongings. He happened upon a video cassette. The label on it made him shiver but he sat and watched it at home. He demanded to know if his daughter knew anything about this. She did not, and insisted on taking the video to the police station herself.

Chapman and his accomplices were arrested and all confessed. Charges were brought and so now the job was to make sure they didn't get away with it lightly. Defence counsel would be producing all sorts of mitigating circumstances and reasons for leniency. We had to make our case hard, fast and lawyer-proof. Ian and I set about gathering as much supporting evidence as we could, and detailing every little thing in the 20 video shoots. One line of inquiry was the source of the animals, and they all came from the same place, a big pet shop and pet food retailer. The manager said he'd thought it a bit odd, that chap coming in to buy mice every week. He set up some safeguards to make sure it never happened again.

The court case was quite something. Nobody involved had ever imagined such a thing. Nobody had ever heard the word for it, squishing, also known as crush movies. Nobody had realised that otherwise quite normal young women could be persuaded for a few hundred quid to torture and kill small animals on camera.

For once I was absolutely certain that the accused were going down. Craig John Chapman, 27, pleaded guilty to conspiracy to publish obscene material and to various animal-cruelty offences. He got two years. Christine Louise Bestford, 26, Miss-Kitty-that-was and the only one of the three who would agree to do that, pleaded guilty to conspiracy and to cruelly terrifying, infuriating or torturing an animal, and got four months. Sarah Jane Cook, 21, Minnie Mouse who had known Chapman for years, trusted him, loved the cash and came up with her own ideas on novel ways to kill small rodents, also pleaded guilty: four months. Teresa Smallwood, 22, Miss Piggy, a single mother with money troubles, guilty: four months. All were banned for life from keeping animals.

We had also established that there was another man involved, called McCann, from London, and it was clear from Chapman's computer that here was another big name on the video scene. We got a search warrant, raided his house and found stacks of videos. Although some were imported from the USA, McCann was doing his bit for the balance of payments too, exporting his own home-produced stuff all over. Brian Patrick McCann, 47, of Islington, was found guilty of conspiring to produce and distribute obscene material and got nine months.

The shock waves from this investigation ran right through the RSPCA. Resources and top priorities were allocated and rewards were offered. Special training was given us in how to interrogate computer files and how to investigate internet crime, by computer experts and police who normally chased paedophiles. We went through Chapman's emails and McCann's, establishing the patterns, methods and tricks of the trade so that a strategy could be developed for future investigations. We were entirely sure that we were not dealing with an isolated incident. There was a network to uncover, trails to follow. While it was the only court case of its kind so far in the UK, there is nothing new under the sun. There would be hidden nests of poisonous people making this stuff at the very nadir of animal cruelty. Surely nobody could go any lower.

I went to see Chapman in jail. I thought, if I could turn him, he could lead me into the murky depths. Where there was a market somebody would be supplying it, and was there a market! My man said he had been inundated with requests from fellow inmates for copies of his videos, and word was getting around the entire British prison system. Alas for him, the judge had ordered all his back catalogue to be destroyed.

I came out of there quite encouraged. Chapman was willing to supply whatever information I wanted and would be active on my behalf as soon as he got out of jail. Now I needed to get full approval from my RSPCA bosses and the prison authorities. I should have known better.

Outside in the free world, the enemy was fighting a secret war and no matter what bits and pieces of evidence we gathered, in the short term we were unable to find sufficient to be confident of another successful prosecution. The judge in our one case had only allowed the video to be viewed in his own chambers and all copies had been burned by now. The media and the public never saw the show for themselves, otherwise we might have had rather more of a sensation generated.

The RSPCA is no different to any other large organisation operating on the public's behalf. It needs media coverage; its priorities are to some extent governed by such coverage and the pressure it generates. Without any public outcry, newspaper campaign or questions in the House, the whole squishing business became just too difficult for senior management to continue giving support. Despite the earlier furore, despite there being total unanimity in the RSPCA that this was the worst thing any of us, from top to bottom, had ever come across, it was quietly dropped. I was incredulous. What? The worst ever and it's too difficult? I wasn't allowed to follow up and so, as I write, to the everlasting shame of all concerned, the squishing continues but there have been no more cases brought in the UK.

Chapter Five

THE AVOCET MAN

The pied avocet, Recurvirostra avosetta, emblem of the RSPB, has been through some very hard times and has become the rallying standard for UK bird lovers. With its long upturned beak, finely sculptured stance and superb black and white plumage, it seems to come from a more formal, elegant and refined place than our noisy, dirty, clumsy world. Indeed, at one point our world became too much for the avocet altogether; the species suffered a disastrous decline to extinction in Britain between the wars.

A successful long-term conservation project, starting with breeding pairs in Suffolk, has helped the British avocet to a reasonably stable but precarious state. On the brackish, marshy margins of the Suffolk and Norfolk coasts there are perhaps 500 breeding pairs now and, if the weather is kind, their young survive and slowly increase the population. Similar numbers can be seen wintering in the south-western estuaries such as the Exe and Tamar. On mainland Europe there are many more but, thanks in large part to The Avocet Man and his associates, nowhere near as many as there used to be.

Required reading in the caged bird business is the weekly newspaper, established for over 100 years, Cage & Aviary Birds. Those of us in the free-the-birds business like to keep an eye on the classifieds, and we are used to seeing certain species for sale which are not your usual cage and aviary material. In among the canaries, cockatoos and budgerigars we might spot peregrine falcons and eagle owls, for instance, or lanner falcons. We commonly see finches – linnets, goldfinches, bramblings - but one day I saw something quite new being advertised: wading birds. Avocets, redshanks, curlews, offered for cash? What was all that about?

With habitat and breeding grounds disappearing under the civilising influence of mankind, redshanks and curlews are still reasonably abundant although RSPB amber status, meaning they have declined or are declining in numbers in Britain. They and the avocet are also noted for their extreme difficulty in breeding in captivity. You might say it's virtually impossible; certainly none of us had ever heard of it being done successfully.

Similarly new to us was the idea of a cash market for wading birds. Zoos and the major collections didn't buy their birds from the small ads, but we saw these ads appearing week after week, always with the same mobile telephone number. Then it would miss a week, then come back with something else obscure, such as dunlins. What was an individual buyer going to do with dunlins? They spend most of their time on the coast but breed on the high moorlands of Scotland and northern England. In winter you can see them feeding on the salt marshes in huge flocks, delicately ferreting in the mud before taking off to make 'wader smoke', swirling through the air like starlings. I could hardly think of anything less suitable for sale by classified ad.

Still the plot thickened. This same supplier offered some of the seedeaters – crossbills, which havethe tips of their beaks crossed so they can get at the seeds in pine cones, and hawfinches, the big beast of finches with the mighty huge beak which looks capable of cracking anything open. Then we saw blackcaps, a type of warbler.

An RSPCA inspector called Barbara joined the SOU and brought with her a story about jays. A woman had bought a pair of captive-bred jays through an ad in our favourite magazine and was horrified when the birds arrived. One was dead, the container was filthy having been used many times and never cleaned, and the surviving bird was very flighty and distressed, showing all the signs of having been wild-caught. Barbara had the case details and we recognised the phone number. It was the same one, the one to ring if you wanted avocets and dunlins. The police traced it for us and came up with a name, Redfern, and an address in a hamlet on the Welsh borders.

If ever a case demanded a CTR – close target reconnaissance – this did. We should have gone over there and found out what facilities he had, what his movements were and maybe even caught sight of some birds. Unfortunately, some people were losing sight of our organisation's purpose and allowing their common sense to be buried beneath cartloads of political correctness and fear of making a mistake. The Regulation of Investigative Powers Act

2000 was nothing to do with the RSPCA but some managers felt that we should conform to it. So, we went from routinely doing CTRs, looking before we leapt, to not doing any because we might infringe somebody's human rights or be accused of trespassing. The proper course might have been somewhere in between but we felt frustrated by overcaution, and it was this attitude from above that led to Barbara leaving the RSPCA and joining the police. We were also forbidden the infiltration and deception which are essential to some kinds of undercover work.

We still had one infiltrating deception, which was okay because it had been officially designated a test purchase. I was the nominated, experienced, not to mention only, undercover operator in the RSPCA so it was decided that I should ring Mr Redfern and see if I could buy a pair of avocets from him. Our choice of avocets was because this was the rarest bird so far on offer, and because none of us had ever seen an avocet close up. I rang from home on my mobile and recorded our conversation.

'I'm phoning about the ad in Cage & Aviary Birds, for avocets.'

'Yeh.'

'Er, well, do you think you could supply a pair, male and female?'

'No problem.'

'Oh, really, that's great. Excellent. Right, so, how do you tell them apart, the male and the female?'

'Males are bigger and darker.'

After another 20 minutes or so of non-stop chatter, we had established a price, £240 in cash, a place to meet, the Little Chef on the A5 near Oswestry, and a time, 10am the following day. He would be in a white Astra van with Grand Prix stickers on the doors. The birds would have to travel, I said, to the Algarve, to my friend's house. This would be no problem either. If I packed them in a nice big cardboard box with air holes, they would last 40 hours or more.

The plan was to have Ian and Phil, the RSPCA film crew, at the rendezvous ready to move in on the Astra van when it appeared. They would observe and video; I would tape the conversation on my hidden recorder. To give them plenty of time to set up with a good viewpoint, I would persuade our man to go into the Little Chef with me. I would be desperate for the loo, hadn't had time for breakfast, seriously needed a coffee and a Danish.

At ten past ten I saw the Astra turn in and park only a few spaces from me. I had to hope he wouldn't notice as I called the others on the radio, just to make sure they'd seen it too, and checked that my hidden voice-recording gear was working. The target got out and opened the back of the van. I could see a wooden crate. I felt the usual small tremor of stomach-dwelling butterflies as I left my car and walked towards him. We shook hands. He was happy to have me buy him a cappuccino so, locking the van again, off we went.

Redfern was a 6-footer, in his late 40s and, scruffy Herbert that he was with blond hair uncombed for weeks by the look of it, his chin unshaven for days, clothes grubby and tatty, I did wonder for a moment if we might be rejected by the Little Chef maître d' as not conforming to the house dress code, or perhaps their hygiene regulations. Scruff or not, he certainly knew his stuff about wading birds. He told me that my avocets had been hand-reared on chicken feed, little pellets meant for pullets which, if placed under water, they would take in their long curved beaks. He also knew how to feed and keep in good shape all manner of other waders and had recently supplied a well-known collection in southern England with avocets, oyster-catchers, redshanks, dunlins, curlews and others for a sea-shore extravaganza display, netting him a £20,000 profit. He also mentioned frequent travel to Holland and Belgium, where his major suppliers were.

Back in the car park, with my colleagues in good position, I fetched a cardboard box from my car while he opened up his van again. He gently lifted the lid of his wooden crate and inside was a sight to take the breath away, a most exquisite pair of the most exquisite species, two avocets in superb condition, seemingly unconcerned about their strange circumstances. If they were wild-caught, they were the most phlegmatic, sanguine, laid-back pair ever. They transferred easily to my box, my wad of cash was handed over and we took our leave, he doubtless to arrange his next deal, me to drive back to HQ convinced I'd just spent £240 of the RSPCA's money on something previously thought impossible: two legally bred, tame avocets. Scruffy Herbert had already impressed me deeply with his knowledge of feeding and keeping wading birds. Now I had to concede him the ability to breed them as well.

Back at HQ we all gathered excitedly around my cardboard box. My colleagues' reactions were as mine had been, whistles and head-shakings in awe at the beauty, grace and sheer style of these birds. We were in the presence of avian royalty, and well-fed royalty if the sheen on their feathers and brightness of eye was anything to go by. Whichever chemist formulated that chicken feed had had no idea what a satisfactory alternative it would make to the avocet's standard diet of small crustaceans and other underwater wrigglers.

I got on the phone to Roger Caton, a man I'd worked with many times before and the leading expert in trapping and every other aspect of wild-caught birds. The rings on our birds' legs seemed to be the proper thing and I wanted him to look at them. They were the DEFRA (British government Department for the Environment and Rural Affairs) -approved pattern, the right size and which ostensibly proved that these birds were bred in captivity. The standard procedure is to ring birds when very young, just a few days old; when the bird is fully grown the rings cannot be removed. I knew of finch trappers who would discover a nest, ring the hatchlings, let the parents feed them until almost fledged, then go to the nest and gather up the prize. Once they'd grown on a little it would be impossible to show that these were not captive bred finches.

Roger could cast no light on the matter. They looked kosher and their validity could not be disproved. Our only stimulus of continued suspicion was our belief that breeding avocets in captivity was not a workable proposition.

Whatever we were to do next, the avocets had to be dealt with. Our normal recourse in such cases, a marvellous lady called Megan Morris Jones, a wildlife rehabilitator of evangelical enthusiasm based in Wenlock, was already overwhelmed with burdens placed on her by the RSPCA and had no room for any more. No one to our knowledge had ever rehabilitated an avocet before nor released one back into the wild. These birds would be destined for the flocks and open spaces of Colchester Zoo, so what we wanted was a halfway house. Our next hope was a friend of Megan's, a very wealthy lady with a mansion in north Wales and similar enthusiasm, who had had large aviaries built to house Megan's overflow. She took the avocets and placed them in five-star accommodation with regular room service of the very finest chicken feed money could buy.

With all our thoughts on human predators we never gave a moment's consideration to natural ones, and the wealthy lady's aviary had a design fault waiting to be exploited by one of the craftiest. Madame came down one morning to find an avocet killed by a fox. The other died, probably of shock, shortly afterwards.

The poor woman rang to tell me, very distressed, it was all her fault, how could we ever trust her again. I had to work hard to reassure her. If there's a way to a kill, a fox will find it. If there's a tiny hole in the shed with goslings inside, the stoat will discover it. We create these unnatural situations and, if nature proves cleverer than us, we can only try again.

More determined than ever to catch our man, we consolidated the results of our advertising survey. If Redfern had sold all the birds he'd put up for sale in the few months we'd been monitoring, he would have taken £60,000, plus the £20,000 he said he'd got for the seashore display. Next time he advertised, we would give him a home visit.

Our good contacts with the north Wales police wildlife officer, Sergeant Pete Charleston, made it simple enough to get a search warrant and off we went, with Roger and an expert from the RSPB investigations department, Duncan McNiven. I'd become good friends with Duncan over years of co-operation but especially on a trip to Belgium to recruit an informant. With that done we went to a bar to celebrate and introduced our man from the RSPB to the tipple of the senior service, the RSPCA, which was Belgian Trappist beers. We worked our way up through the strengths to Chimay Blue, which is 9%, swapping stories which got funnier and funnier until Duncan fell off his stool onto the floor. He always blames me for not telling him it wasn't ordinary lager. I tell him that as an RSPB expert he should be able to tell a Chimay Blue from the other parrots.

Redfern's was a simple detached house, off the main road with a bit of land and a wonderful array of sheds and outbuildings which reminded me a little of the shanty towns in Accra, and there was the white Astra van in the driveway. The police blocked it in and fetched Redfern from the house. I stayed in the background. It didn't really matter now if he recognised me but it would be better if he didn't. I needn't have worried. Over the next hour or two, Redfern was far too busy watching his business collapse to notice me.

They unpacked the van, which was loaded seemingly for an imminent delivery. First out was a double breeder cage, routinely used for canaries and budgies, a large oblong construction about 3 feet by 18 inches by 18 inches with a removable dividing partition. This one had about 40 quail in it. Another, smaller cage had 20 or so quail. Two more double breeders, dirty and, like the first two, without water drinkers, had crossbills and hawfinches.

Next they tackled the sheds. The idea is to get the owner to go in and retrieve the birds so, if they are in a bad state, he can't claim mistreatment by the search party. Redfern would do this, say what the species was, Duncan would confirm or question that, and Roger would give his view on whether they were wild-caught.

In the first shed, which had a bare earth floor and puddles of water, all eyes immediately went to two pure white egrets These are wading fish-eaters, something like a small heron but with fancy plumes that once were fashionable in ladies' hats, almost causing the species' downfall. You used rarely to see egrets in Britain but recently they've been breeding in south-western counties and you see them in the estuary shallows there. Even so, you would not expect to find two in rural North Wales. Nor would you expect to see oyster-catchers in a Welsh shed. The best place for them is on the beach by the rock pools, where grow mussels, or in places like Morecambe Bay where the cockle beds are.

Redfern had lapwings in there too, also called peewit because of the call. They're plover family, strictly speaking a wader but a short-beaked, land-based one. You used to see them pretty well anywhere there was pasture or marshes but marshes get drained and pasture is managed for maximum profit, and the lapwing has declined to a third of what it was only 25 years ago. Lapwings were the farmer's friend, feeding on wireworms and leatherjackets. Now the farmer sprays his land instead, and if you want to see this fantastical bird doing its pre-mating aerobatics and flying somersaults with full sound accompaniment, your best places are the high pastures where no plough ever goes.

The lapwings were not ringed and Redfern had no supporting paperwork. Three birds were seized for further examination. His other paperwork was all from a well-established Belgian outfit called Aviornis International, which acts as an official registration office for its members who are genuine breeders of wildfowl, game birds and those species which readily breed in captivity. 'Aviornis closed rings and certificates are proof of captive breeding'. The problem is that it's not compulsory in Belgium to register aviary-bred birds and so the system is lax and full of the kind of loopholes which unscrupulous dealers will always exploit, which is one very good reason why the word 'Belgium' crops up so often on the darker fringes of the bird world.

Also in this damp shed were redshanks, curlews and a few dunlins, one of the smaller waders not much bigger than a blackbird. Roger had a better time with these, finding oversized rings which he could slip off, proving on the spot that they were not captive bred. Redfern had no paperwork for the redshanks either and his trade was looking very shaky, as indeed was the man himself. He had not expected ever to meet someone like Roger, the avian equivalent of Uri Geller who could slip these tiny, tight-seeming rings off birds' legs if they were only slightly iffy. He also looked for other signs, such as damage caused by repeatedly flying against the mesh of a cage, which wild birds will do for a very long time before they become reconciled to imprisonment, and swellings or bruising on the leg where someone has forced a ring on. These are supporting pieces of evidence, helpful if Roger can't get the ring off, but if he can, that's proof in itself.

When he picked up a bar-tailed godwit and slipped the ring off that, Redfern had every appearance of shortly needing an ambulance. These birds breed in Siberia and other Arctic quarters and stop off around the big UK estuaries for the relatively warm winters, or pass through on the way to somewhere even warmer. A reasonable explanation of how a few specimens came to be living in a shed on the Welsh Marches in the British summer would have had the most silver-tongued barrister struggling, and Redfern knew it.

The next shed was furnished with conifers and various bits of tree and shrub, to make the place more homely for the tawny owls which were living in it, next door to another shed with about ten turtle doves, only two of which were ringed. Roger did his trick and soon none of them were ringed. This was the first RSPB red status bird seen here, a migratory small and very pretty dove which comes to southern and eastern England to breed in the summer. It used to be common and its call widely heard from April on, a cross between a cat purring and a British landline dialling tone. The call is usually rendered 'turr-turr' and is how the bird had its name. Nowadays the turtle dove figures in the usual story. Intensified, super-efficient farming means fewer uncut hedges and wild places to nest in, fewer weeds to provide the seeds which are its main food, and four fifths of the turtle doves gone. Perhaps we could try persuading sportsmen not to shoot so many on their spring migration over Greek and Italian airspace.

Our next surprise was in an ordinary, potting-type shed which, instead of the usual clutter of seed trays, garden implements and tobacco tins, had neat stacks of cardboard boxes on a floor covered inches deep with bird muck. Ten of the boxes had a curlew inside, unringed. When asked for his comments, Redfern said it was complicated and he'd rather not go into it just at the moment. Complicated was something of an understatement as we opened another box to find a crossbill, and another with a corn bunting. Here was our second red status bird, a plain and portly creature which has declined rapidly without much notice being taken, possibly because it is so unremarkable to look at. Farmers sow cereals more often in the autumn so don't leave stubble fields over winter as much; they cut grass early for silage rather than leaving it for hay and the safe nesting of corn buntings; the sprays kill the weeds and the insects. Result: another disaster.

If only the blackcap were equally unremarkable it would have a much better time of it, but the determination of some people to kill what is lovely makes life very hazardous for this attractive little warbler. It's one of our first arriving migrants, having flown from Africa through some mass-murderous technology devised by Greeks and Maltese. Powerful public address systems play the male blackcap's call as the flocks go by. The females come down to investigate the possibility of a suitable mate only to be caught in nets stretched between trees. This is an illegal activity but that doesn't stop it, and the birds end up on the pantry shelf in a special Mediterranean delicacy, jars of pickled blackcap. Of course there is a long tradition in this region, going back to classical times, of eating tiny creatures with hardly any meat on them, and the less likely the bird to satisfy your hunger the greater luxury status it attained. Maybe that has something to do with it.

The good news is that there are also European populations of blackcaps which increasingly are wintering in Britain and breeding there. Possibly the pair of birds found in another of Redfern's cardboard boxes had not endured the long and perilous flight, past the guns, nets and amplifiers of those who wished to see them on gourmet menus rather than warbling their cheerful song in the sunshine.

This was a very successful raid. We took away a great many birds which were wild-caught, plus Redfern's computer and a small mountain of paperwork, diaries, address books and so on which, with a lot of hard graft, was bound to lead us to suppliers and wider horizons. We also had the story of the jays, a much persecuted species, which has become extra wary and wild over centuries of enmity from gamekeepers and from fishermen who love those brilliant blue feathers for dry-fly tying.

We hadn't worked very far into the Redfern evidence before it became clear that this case had a big international, cross-borders dimension to it, and once you have that you start getting involved with government departments. There is a traditional reluctance in the RSPCA and other organisations to pass information to these people, partly because it is always one-way traffic. There's a view, founded in truth and experience, that the government department will run off with the charity's investigation and take any credit that accrues, depriving the charity of that kudos so essential for fund-raising. The other thing that can happen is nothing, which might be understandable if you're an under-budgeted, overstretched little department at the end of the corridor, perhaps not so if you happen to be a blackcap or an avocet, and I've always been on their side.

I was keen to follow up some leads we'd discovered in Belgium and Holland and expose the scandal in a big media splash. My bosses shared my enthusiasm and plans were made. Chris Kerr of the British government wildlife department, to whom I'd passed all the information, counselled caution. The thought was that an official investigation, co-ordinated through the various European police forces and wildlife offices, stood a better chance of catching everyone involved and closing the operation down completely.

This was the right approach in an ideal world, but we had our doubts about whether it would get anywhere in among a lot of transborder complexities. Meanwhile, a little intelligence gathering would not go amiss so Ian and I set off for Belgium. Redfern's account books had shown up a major supplier, of avocets, godwits, oystercatchers, crossbills, turtle doves and, would you believe it, red squirrels and snowy owls. These white owls are quite magnificent, one of the biggest of the owl family, living in Arctic and sub-arctic areas although they do nest in the Shetlands sometimes and may come further south in cold winters. They like the big open spaces of the tundra and generally eat lemmings, but they'll take other prey such as birds, fish and hares – a 4-pound snowy owl can carry away a 2-pound hare in its talons. With global warming they're going to be in serious trouble unless they can adapt, but at present they're numerous, particularly in those years when the lemming population explodes.

It's always difficult operating in a rural part of a foreign country. You're never sure what attitude the locals take to strangers and, in the flat region of Belgium we were in, it was fairly easy for us to be spotted while lurking. The premises looked fairly standard for an old farmhouse with outbuildings. It was at the end of a lane, next to a railway embankment which offered the possibility of a slightly elevated view over the farmyard.

Next morning, Ian dropped me off some way away and I crossed the fields to my position before it got light. As dawn broke I could see, over the 6-foot fence, one large aviary with maybe ten different species of wading birds in it. Outside it, loose, were a Rottweiler and two other large dogs. During the next few hours I made sketch maps, listed vehicles and noted all persons coming and going, so that anyone in future executing a warrant would have an information start. With that in my pocket, I slipped away.

Next on our list was another Redfern lead who'd shown up on the computer as supplying egrets and night herons, more precisely black crowned night herons, which are much smaller and shorter in the leg than the grey heron in Britain. Night herons are widespread in the New World and the Old, but not often seen in the UK except in zoos where they can breed well. They seem fairly comfortable with people and might just as well build their shaky, untidy nests in trees on a busy city street as out somewhere in the bush. Where our lead was nesting we never did find and we had to give up on him.

Another Belgian had been offering avocets to Redfern at £200 a pair, black winged stilts £300, black-tailed godwits £300, oyster-catchers £180, little egrets £600, squacco herons £500. He also had nuthatches and skylarks on his list, birds which are impossible to breed in captivity. We found he lived in a modest town house with a couple of garden sheds, not the place to be keeping avocets and herons, and we couldn't get around the back anyway so we told ourselves we had collected negative intelligence. At least we could cross off this address if not the man.

Next was a huge property in the southern Dutch countryside with 20 or more big sheds with runs, not far from the Belgian border. We had a not terribly good vantage point to spy from, but all the bird species we'd seen at Redfern's place we could see here. If we'd thought Redfern was a fairly big fish to catch, here was the great white shark. It would need a military operation to stage a proper bust. All we could do for the moment was map the place, note the access points and so on, ready for when such a raid could be planned.

In a small, ordinary Belgian town called Itegem was a garden centre which we believed had a secondary range of stock: wild-caught small birds. It proved almost too easy to get in there with our hidden camera, posing as tourists on the look-out for finches, even though tourists in Itegem must have been one of the rarest species of all. At the back of the place, beyond the trellises and plastic ponds, were three aviaries packed solid with jackdaws, crossbills, hawfinches, fieldfares, yellowhammers, greenfinches, bullfinches and every other sort of finch, hundreds of them. Jackdaws were €45, siskins €16, all prices in between and all the birds glaringly obviously wild, bashing themselves against the cages, fluttering about in panic. We could also have had a red squirrel if we wanted, €120.

Thanking the main man there for his business card and promising to be back later, we left with our film. The problems now were looming and large. If we were to mount a successful, synchronised, all-out attack on these people, get them prosecuted and seize the birds, we would need resources equivalent to a major police action. We could expect little help from the continental equivalents to the RSPCA and RSPB, not for lack of willingness but because they are mostly small and not geared up for this sort of thing. Here we were with one of the biggest international wildlife crime networks we were ever likely to see, and we were going to be beaten back by the sheer scope of it.

We did go to the Belgian RSPB and heard about yet another big wheel in this machine, an ex policeman who smuggled birds in from Russia and Poland, like king eider ducks and Steller's eider, both species under great pressures. He also specialised in white storks, birds which mate for life and return to the same nest every season for up to 30 years. This copper-turned-criminal had a secondary range of stock too, in drugs and firearms. We offered to try to infiltrate his organisation and to recruit and run informants. The Belgians perked up at this idea but decided to try it for themselves, and they did it very well.

Back in England, the first phase of The Avocet Man project was coming to a happy ending. All the birds we'd seized from Redfern had gone to Colchester Zoo, where they were looked after in the very best possible way, in vast aviaries like aircraft hangars with deep litter on the floor. There was no possibility of releasing them back into the wild. They'd been in captivity too long and we didn't know quite where they all came from. Colchester was the best answer.

Redfern was up before the beak, in the shape of Wrexham magistrates, at three hearings. At the first, he pleaded guilty to advertising wild birds for sale and to transporting two jays in a manner likely to cause suffering: £100 costs. Next, he pleaded guilty to six charges of illegal possession and one of neglect: £100 costs, 120 hours' community service, disqualified from keeping birds for five years.

After such ferocious punishments we naturally expected the third and biggest case to result in hanging, drawing and quartering, or transportation at the least. After pleading not guilty to 33 charges of illegal possession, Redfern was fined £350 and had his traps confiscated.

I got Ian to give him a phone call, suggesting a meeting but not to tell him what it was about specifically. He could imply that it might prove financially beneficial, that was all. Redfern was agreeable and the meet was arranged at an Indian restaurant. Ian and I got there first. We sat waiting with a bottle of Cobra each, and in he came. I stood up and shook his hand. Those who remember having to put an old penny into a large and sturdy brass device on the door to get into a public toilet, or pressing Button A or B in a telephone box, will understand the clunk and clatter which can accompany a penny dropping. As he realised I was the fellow who'd bought two avocets from him at the Oswestry Little Chef all those months ago, the look on Redfern's face changed from confident to puzzled to recognition to fury in a few seconds, and the colour changed with it.

Normally when you used to press Button A, the person on the other end just said hello. Redfern said all sorts of things and I thought for a while that Ian and I would be dining à deux that evening, but he calmed down and had a Cobra. Several Cobras and a few biryanis and pathias later, he described the method his Low Countries associates used to catch avocets, one of the species which breeds in colonies, usually in wetlands. In Belgium especially there were avocet colonies breeding on islands in shallow lagoons. The poacher would spot a colony, wait until the eggs hatched, then wade out to ring the hatchlings with the correct rings. Young avocets can walk about and feed themselves within hours and so the thieves had few problems when, a few days later, they came again and took all the young birds from an entire colony, which could be as many as 500 or even more, with up to 150 pairs hatching three or four young each. Fed on submerged layers pellets these birds soon grew into healthy adults, in a far better ratio, Redfern was quick to point out, than in nature where many young avocets die before reaching maturity if the weather is poor and food is not so plentiful.

Thanking Redfern in lieu of his high-minded colleagues for their efforts on behalf of avocets everywhere, we asked him how other birds were trapped and how easy it was to fiddle the paperwork. By the end of our talk we could see that the wild bird trade in Belgium was pretty well unchecked, that there was also considerable traffic in rare mammals, and that therefore the country had become a prime centre for traders from other countries, like the City of London is for financiers.

He was willing to be our agent, our snout or, as the modern parlance has it, our chis (covert human intelligence source) to be run by Ian, but he wanted £1,000 up front. This seemed to us a small price to pay, considering the information he'd already supplied and the potential of a truly massive operation, but we knew we had two problems. One was the RSPCA bureaucracy. Wheels can turn very slowly in a large charity. Two was Redfern himself. If he didn't get his money soon, his attachment to us would break and we'd lose him.

Since virtually all of the RSPCA's big successes come from informants, you might imagine that there would be an efficient system for dealing with them, and a planned route direct to a senior manager who would be able to say yes or no to a budget proposal and sign off certain amounts of money to pay these extremely valuable people. You might imagine it, but that's as far as it gets. The system is there but it's Byzantine, and in the Redfern case it took months to be given the okay, by which time our man had lost interest, moved house and disappeared from view.

The upside was that, as usual, I had passed everything we had to the government wildlife crime unit, which in turn collaborated with the Dutch and Belgians who staged a number of raids with the help of Belgian RSPB informants, seized thousands of wild-caught birds and successfully brought a great many charges against dozens of operators. This was great but it needs government and public willpower to break the circle for good. Ian and I knew, as we heard about the prosecutions, that it was highly likely that these same lowlifes would be back in business soon.

Chapter Six

THE YORKSHIRE FALCON AND THE MALTESE FINCHES

Name one big difference between these two common UK practices: (a) catching wild birds and keeping them in cages as if they were tame; (b) keeping tame birds in cages and shooting them as if they were wild.

The former practice is illegal; the latter is not.

Perhaps things were different in the old days, when shooting game birds was the exclusive sport of the land-owning aristocracy, a small group of people who had been taught how to use a gun from childhood. Perhaps. In modern Britain, game-bird shooting is an industry. It's still not for everybody but sport can be had by a much larger group of rich people, who often see it as a symbol of their arrival among the elite of society. The aforementioned landed gentry provide the facilities for these wealthy oiks, whether they can shoot for toffee or not, and charge the earth for it so that they can continue to be landed, and gentry.

Key figures in the industry, as ever was, are the gamekeepers. The difference is that instead of having to make sure that his Lord- and Ladyship and house-party guests have an occasional good day at the butts, the gamekeeper now has to guarantee 12-bore fodder in huge and frequent quantities for those who have paid thousands of pounds for it and who demand their money's worth. That the fodder may end up wounded, by the lousy shots whose only qualification is money, and so may die a long, slow death, is not a factor in the equation. That the many birds killed by the better shots may end up as landfill, because there is little demand for them as meat, is also neither here nor there.

The forelock-tugging, straw-chewing, old poacher-turned-gamekeeper, wise in country lore, oo arr, probably never existed except in The Archers. If he did he's long gone, because that is most certainly not the profile of the modern gamekeeper, the archetype of which I came across through a very unusual phenomenon, the gamekeeper-turned-poacher, or should I say informant.

This man was an underkeeper on an estate owned by a wealthy non-aristocrat who had made his millions by building houses which, reputedly, did not always conform to the highest standards of workmanship and materials. The underkeeper was lodged on the estate in the smallest of small cottages with no room to lie straight in his bed and nowhere to make his growing family comfortable. The head keeper was unsympathetic, the owner equally so, which was good coming from a housing squillionaire. Seeking his revenge, the man left his job and came to me.

The story was a grim one. The estate was the focus of the village, the pub was named for the family which used to own the estate and the head keeper was traditionally an important figure. The current incumbent took his social position seriously and, being an especially short-tempered and brutal hard case, had established himself as a kind of local one-man Gestapo. Even the village bobby would not confront him. Woe betide anyone who sat in his chair in the pub. In fact, woe betide anyone who got in his way at all, as could be witnessed by walkers in his woods whose faces had been lacerated by dangling fish-hooks, by ramblers across his moors who had been beaten up, by courting couples in his beauty spots who returned to their cars to find the tyres slashed.

Anyone on his patch was deemed likely to disturb his pheasants and so was the enemy. The same prohibitions applied to those many non-human creatures which he saw in the same way. Populations of foxes, stoats, crows, magpies and birds of prey were kept as near as possible to zero by poisoned baits, with collateral damage to other scavenging species such as hedgehogs. The poison of choice was alpha chloralose, which is a Part II poison under the Poisons Act 1972 and should only be sold as a mouse and rat poison by a qualified retailer to someone known to be a proper person to make such a purchase, or to someone with a signed authority from a police officer. No problems there then. All such sales must be entered in the poisons book and the record kept for two years. In small doses, alpha chloralose acts as an anaesthetic; in larger amounts, it generates symptoms similar to and just as fatal as those of strychnine. Our man had some very large amounts stashed away in a hidey-hole in a stone wall.

My plan to curtail his activities was simple and obvious: plant dead pheasant doctored to look as if killed by goshawk; gamekeeper would expect hawk to return to finish meal; video gamekeeper administering poison to corpse. Bingo.

First I had to check if it was legal to act as an agent provocateur in this way. Apparently it was, because it would be the gamekeeper making the decision to turn a harmless dead body into a potentially fatal bait. Next we had to be sure of the age of the pheasants currently being reared. Again this was no problem, just a simple bit of moonlight espionage with, it has to be said, a discomforting tingle at the thought of happening across the head keeper.

Once this information was acquired I needed a dead bird of that age, which my informant would get for me while I briefed the team: Ian, Barry and Geoff. A few days later we met at the Royal Hotel, Scarborough, which is interestingly situated across the road from the town hall where, some years before, the decision had been taken to use alpha chlorolose to reduce the numbers of seagulls. We went up to our room with the underkeeper who instructed the surgeon, Ian, while I filmed the operation for evidence. This may well have been the only occasion on which the Royal has hosted an RSPCA inspector imitating a goshawk by removing a pheasant's head, plucking feathers from its breast and removing pieces of flesh and breastbone with surgical scissors. I wanted to flush the bits down the loo but was reminded that the feathers wouldn't go, so had to hope that the room cleaner wouldn't look inside the double carrier-bag wrapped parcel of pheasant remnants in the waste bin.

By 3am next morning, Ian and I were creeping across a mile or so of moorland to the woods where the pheasants were kept. A well-worn track leading away from the pens showed where our man would come from. I left the pheasant near the pens, the occupants of which squawked and chuntered at my arrival, and scattered some feathers about. Our target couldn't miss the bait, nor could he miss us if he saw us hiding in a bush near-by. This was a genuine concern. Our underkeeper had told us we were sure to be given both barrels and all our assassin would have to say was he thought it was a fox.

We had taken every precaution and left no trace of our journey, no downtrodden heather, no dew trails, nothing. Our hiding place was good and thick. Barry and Geoff would warn us by radio when the target was approaching. Ian would make some last minute alterations to our hide with his birthday present, a cheap imitation of my Leatherman (an American Swiss-army knife with pliers), and I had to giggle when the pliers broke at his first attempt to cut a thin twig.

The sun rose at half five and we settled in to enjoy a beautiful morning. If there had been a meadow, there would have been a bright golden haze on it. At half nine, Barry reported the expected red pick-up truck and we checked and rechecked our camouflage. Half an inch of white underpant waistband can be enough to get you spotted. Our man arrived and we heard him banging about with feed tins and whistling to his pheasants. This is an old gypsy trick originally used to get dogs to come unfailingly when you call. You whistle to them when you feed them as little puppies, so they forever associate your whistle with rewarding din-dins. This gamekeeper was training his pheasants so that, as grown-ups, he could better organise them into orderly ranks on the day they would be shot.

I trained my camera onto the dead pheasant and soon our man came into view wearing, as they all do, green checked shirt and brown moleskin trousers. He picked up the bird, shook his head, said a few words and threw it down again. Perfect. I'd got the lot. As the evil one drove away, we could relax. It was almost certain that he wouldn't be back until the evening feed, when he would poison our carcase.

At 6.30pm, after a lovely if somewhat cramped day in the countryside, Geoff radioed with our warning. Here he was, rattling his tins and whistling again. I focused the camera on the bait. Hearts thumped beneath the bush. Nerves jangled. And the sod got back in his pick-up and drove away.

We had been in that bush for 18 hours and not a sausage had we. At the debrief I asked the underkeeper if he'd let anything slip in conversation.

'Er, well, no,' he said. After all, I had emphasised the need for secrecy time and time again.

'What does "er, well" mean?' I asked, suddenly all suspicions.

'Well, I didn't tell anybody, except the policeman, and another gamekeeper. I mean, they wouldn't ... oh ****. ******* ****.'

Quite. No wonder our target had come nowhere near the dead bird. The wonder was that he hadn't turned up with a shotgun and a box of cartridges. There's nothing like a near miss to make me more stubborn and determined but I couldn't think of a way to turn this around. The dead bird trick would never work a second time, my boss would never sanction another potentially lethal surveillance as ownership of the cache of poison could easily be denied.

Then I remembered a West Highland White terrier owned by a certain viscount, whose glorious estate was only a few miles away. His Lordship had rather old-fashioned views about many things, a clear perception of his own importance and his ancestors had been important figures in British history, but a man's a man for a' that.

I was an inspector in Bridlington, it was two days before Christmas and I was on my way to York for our annual RSPCA staff dinner. These were brilliant events and I was really looking forward to it. All our calls would be fielded by the neighbouring RSPCA district, as we'd already done for them, and we could have a stress-free evening.

One of our office girls phoned me. There was this problem, it was on my way, it wouldn't take a minute, it's just that the man was very insistent, and he did own half the East Riding. She filled me in on the details. Said viscount had been out two days before watching a shoot and had taken her Ladyship's West Highland White with him for the walk. Wanting to see something particular he'd stuck his walking stick in the ground, fastened the terrier to it and gone off for a few minutes. When he came back the terrier had vanished and my Lord realised he'd parked the animal right next to a badger sett. His staff had conducted a complete search of the estate and two nights' vigil by the sett, with no result. As I arrived, Plan B was about to be implemented.

'Ah, Inspector, thank goodness you're here. You can advise this fellow where to start.'

'This fellow, sir?'

'Yes, he's going to drive the JCB thing.'

'I'm sorry, but I can't let you dig up a badger sett with a JCB. It's against the law.'

'What's that got to do with it? I'm chairman of the bench.'

'I don't care if you're the Archangel Gabriel, you're not digging up a badger sett.'

I don't think he was used to people standing up to him and he was quite nonplussed. He took me on one side to explain the gravity of the situation, man to man.

'Look here, Inspector. It's my wife's dog. It's surely gone down the sett. My wife and daughters have made it plain to me that Christmas will not occur this year if I do not retrieve that which I have lost. The entire festive season and very probably the rest of my life will be spent in cold isolation. You see?'

A parade followed, his Lordship striding in the lead, me following with my bundle of slim iron rods, a rubber mallet and my stethoscope, and about 15 miscellaneous estate workers in line astern. We reached the sett which, by the size of it, was an ancestral home for a family going back even further than his Lordship's. I began my methodical exploration, driving a rod into the soil and placing my stethoscope on it to listen for vibrations. The silence around me was one of awe, as if the spectators were in the presence of the prophet himself.

I left my mallet behind as I progressed and, since it was more or less at his feet, I asked his Lordship if he'd pass it to me. 'Perkins,' said he to a man 20 yards away, 'pass that mallet to the Inspector.'

I could feel my magician's aura beginning to slide away as I drove in rod after rod with no result. Despondency was taking its place as I bent over to listen yet again, and a little wet, grey, bedraggled, frightened bundle of hair on legs rocketed out of a badger's tunnel and straight into the arms of the viscount.

If I said joy was unconfined I'd be understating it. Obviously, if his Lordship was in bother with her Ladyship, that meant everybody who worked on the estate was in bother too, but hallelujah! They were all saved. Although I must have dislodged by accident a stone or something which had been trapping the terrier in there, as far as they were concerned I was Good King Wenceslas on toast. I had never been hugged by a peer of the realm up to that moment, and a moment later when her Ladyship arrived I was given innumerable noble kisses too.

A happy band trooped back to the great house, the butler was instructed to bring champagne and I was told to name my heart's desire. I thought of asking if he had a time machine to take me to the do in York but I just did my 'oh, all in a day's work, don't you know' routine. He promised a substantial donation to the RSPCA and said that if ever he could render me a service, any favour whatsoever, ever, I only had to ask. And so it happened that a few years later I had this telephone conversation.

'Hello. This is Chief Inspector Spamer of the RSPCA. Could I speak to Lord X, please?'

'Chief Inspector who?'

'Spamer. The one who rescued her Ladyship's terrier.'

The secretary put me on hold and the next voice I heard was his Lordship's, still fresh in his gratitude for my having spared him whatever terrors his wife might have had in store.

'Mr Spamer. Chief Inspector now. Good show. How are you? Never forgotten what you did. Saved my life. What can I do for you?'

'It's one your neighbours,' I said, and explained who it was. 'You know him?'

'Know of him, Mr Spamer,' said the noble lord with some distaste. 'What's he done? Invented the 10-stone pheasant?'

'No, it's his head keeper. Poisons anything that moves that isn't a pheasant and I can't catch him. I was wondering if you might have a word.'

And so it came to pass that the local dole queue was lengthened by one, a man who, when filling in his forms, put down 'gamekeeper' as his profession although he knew that he'd be very lucky to get a job in that line ever again.

Poor birds. If they're not being fattened for the gun they're being poisoned, and if they're not being poisoned they're being trapped and sent into bird slavery. Just as poisoning wild birds is illegal in the UK but goes on all the time, so the whole business of wild-bird trapping is illegal but the country remains a big exporter and British aviaries never seem to go short of 'captive bred' birds with false rings. Finches are the main wild birds wanted by the caged-bird trade – goldfinches, greenfinches, siskins and the RSPB red-listed bullfinch – but other species such as tits are taken. It makes a significant difference to UK bird populations although generally people think that's all to do with loss of habitat.

The British trapper who is in business on a modest scale will use sticky birdlime, or he'll have a double cage. This is a small dual-chamber trap, with one half occupied by a decoy bird. Others of its species will alight and walk in out of curiosity, and the trap will spring shut. Somebody in your street might have one of these. It doesn't need watching unless it's necessary to take out the caught bird and set the trap for another. If one finch a session is enough, it'll do its work while the trapper is out at the day job.

The big traders have trapping sites established in remote parts of the countryside with elaborate systems of nets. The birds are enticed with food and the net falls, catching dozens at a time. Another type of trap is the clap net, like a huge pair of open hands which shut when triggered.

That trapping exists is self-evident; the only possible reason for taking the birds is for the caged trade; all birds sold into the trade are captive bred. Something wrong somewhere?

Here is an extract from a British government consultation paper on potential action over caged birds:

Finally, there is the very large, combined bird show and trade show, such as the national cage and aviary bird exhibition staged annually by the management of Cage and Aviary Birds magazine. This is by far the biggest cage bird show of its kind held in Britain and ranks only second in size and importance to the international bird shows held annually at various locations across the continent. It involves both a large competitive bird exhibition with an average of 7,000 to 9,000 birds and a trade section in which large numbers of birds are displayed for sale as well as all kinds of appliances. The national show attracts large numbers of fanciers, being almost a pilgrimage.

The defenders of such shows used to point to long tradition, the potential for exchange of stock, information on breeding, feeding and the latest on animal health, showing new advances in equipment and generally helping to educate the novices into graduation mode. Said defenders also pointed to Crufts and the like, and said nothing can equal the pride and joy of a certificate for your canary, best of breed at the national show.

A lot of this is true and, with many of the fancy, cruelty and abuse are not an issue at all. The difference with Crufts is that no dogs are offered for sale in a market and the Pet Animals Act prohibits the sale of animals in markets and other unlicensed places. The big national show has been shut down, which means that the opportunity has gone in the UK to unload large numbers of wild-caught birds over one weekend, but the more things change, the more they stay the same. If you want a wild-caught bullfinch, shall we say, in the UK you will need to go to the black market, to the trappers and their friends, or a local garden centre with an aviary at the back, or a bird club, and whisper. You will not be able to buy a pair or a hundred at the NEC or any other open regulated market, and there is at least one good reason why this is so.

The national show had been held at the NEC in Birmingham for years, then it was switched to Telford International Centre, then more usually known as Telford Ice Rink, home of the Telford Tigers. There, in among the annual conferences of the Association of British Asphalt and Roadstone Associations and the Dr Who Lookalike Society, our intelligence from the previous year's show suggested there would be a major deal going on. We suspected an invasion from Malta.

Malta has a disproportionately large number of shooting folk and a police force which largely turns a blind eye to unregulated hunting. Consequently, not a lot of birds live there. For example, no birds of prey ever breed because they are shot before they get the chance. A great many birds stop over during their migration but a much decreased number carry on their journey. This means that birds protected in many European and other countries, often the subject of conservation programmes, are shot by the Maltese. They also trap birds to use as decoys for hunting and, in even greater numbers, for the pet trade.

According to the conservation agency Birdlife Malta:

Trapping currently occurs in Malta at such a high level that only a handful of each of the common finch species regularly breed on the islands, despite breeding in abundance in other areas of the Mediterranean. 73.2% of all finch recoveries in Malta come from the Czech Republic, Hungary, Italy, Slovenia, and Croatia.

Lack of finches is very keenly felt in Malta. There, almost every household, by tradition, has a greenfinch hanging in a small cage, often a very small cage with barely enough room for the bird to hop about, in the porch or a window and, perhaps more bizarrely, in some areas it is not uncommon to find men wandering around the villages with greenfinches in cages under their arms. It's nice to give the bird a bit of fresh air.

Possibly the reason it is such a popular cage bird, given that it's not the best singer, is that it is very easy to trap. The vast majority of greenfinches for sale in Malta are wild-caught although trapping wild finches is illegal throughout the European Union. When Malta joined, an agreement was made to phase out this practice by the end of 2008. At the time of writing, autumn trapping is still allowed of seven finch species: greenfinch, linnet, goldfinch, chaffinch, hawfinch, serin and siskin. The problem is the trapping lobby and their electoral and financial clout. Recent aerial photographs showed 5,317 trapping sites, used by 4,600 registered trappers and, presumably, more than one unregistered trapper. The most recent official figure for greenfinches trapped in one year is 37,924, and that's a figure collected from trappers whose interests do not include exaggeration and which does not account at all for the other six species.

Wild-caught finches tend not to live very long, especially in tiny cages, and so here is a market desperate for supplies. Enter the shrewd businessmen of Malta.

Telford bird show rapidly developed into one of the most complex surveillance jobs I ever had anything to do with. Firstly we approached the security people at the ice rink and told them our story. They readily agreed to let us join their company temporarily, as it were, and lent us the uniforms. We had floor plans of the exhibitors and stall holders, hundreds of them, and we decided to place our Welshman Barry on top of the near-by multi-storey as project co-ordinator. We of the ice-rink security guard would keep close watch in the main hall and around the show, looking for our Maltese. When they were spotted, their movements would be tracked and messages passed by covert radio to Barry on the roof with his floor plan and coloured pins. Two of us were members of the public, kitted out with covert cameras to try to catch the Maltese in the act of purchase.

There were four of them and they led us all around the place, obviously making a very thorough reconnaissance before committing themselves. We identified the stallholders who were the likely beneficiaries of the trade, which seemed to be everybody with any greenfinches for sale, and our radio messages confidently predicted an early conclusion. Having inspected all the goods, all the Maltese had to do was hand over some cash and the job was done.

Such a straightforward business technique can't have appealed because three of them swung out of the ice rink and started an equally thorough inspection of the shopping mall, leaving one behind at the show to be watched. We followed the shoppers on foot and, as a precaution, I asked Ian to pop into the mall security office to tell them what we were up to. They not only gave us the okay. They trained their CCTV cameras on us and our quarry and recorded everything.

Bryn, member of the public, followed them to a public telephone box. It was clear to Bryn that they, unfamiliar with local custom and practice, were having no joy in their attempt to order a taxi. If they wanted a taxi they must, he thought, be going back to their hotel, the identity of which would be priceless information for us. Putting on his Prince Charming-cum-Good Samaritan act, he offered to help them out. He was about to take a cab; would they like to share it and he'd drop them off? They were so pleased it was pitiful, so Bryn whistled up a cab from the rank around the corner, much to Maltese amazement, and they piled in.

I was watching all this from the ice-rink doorway with a plain-clothes police officer just as a taxi drew up there. We jumped in and told the driver to follow that car. He was delighted. He said he'd seen it so many times on the films and he'd always wanted to do it. Telford's not a massive place but it was busy and we were having difficulty keeping up. 'Can I jump red lights?' said the driver. I looked at my police travelling companion. 'Whatever it takes,' said he, and the taxi driver was grinning from ear to ear.

We followed the targets into the hotel and up to their rooms, meaning to come back the following day while they were out. Meanwhile, the fourth man was being observed paying for greenfinches, buying officially approved live-freight boxes at the show, and having the duty veterinary certify the birds as free from disease and so conforming to regulations for export which, as the birds were all ringed, meant tacit approval of them as captive bred.

Next morning, with some difficulty the hotel manager was persuaded to let us in to a room with every spare square inch taken up with bird cages. We'd counted as far as 120 greenfinches when the door opened and in walked one of the Maltese dealers. Our police officer quickly persuaded him that we were hotel security doing a routine fire-precautions check of all the rooms on that floor and the guy seemed happy enough with that.

To have kept this number of men under surveillance for two days was unique in my experience at the time and in animal welfare anywhere, I'd have thought. It all went like clockwork with everyone carrying out their role in a truly professional manner. We watched them hire a van and fill it with the freight boxes, and I followed them to Heathrow, where the finches were seized. Their rings were removed, proof in itself that they were wild-caught, and they were taken out into the country and released into the wild. The Maltese businessmen also had to be let go and there was no possibility of getting them back to the UK for a court case.

Afterwards my colleague Cliff, who has done more than anyone to battle the wild-bird trade, established a protocol with the airlines to tip us off should they receive any bookings for shipments of birds to Malta. It worked very well. We were bombing up and down the motorways to Manchester and Heathrow for a year before the trappers and dealers gave up.

While this provided some respite for greenfinches in the UK, it increased the pressure on those in Malta and elsewhere. If the majority of the Maltese population want to keep a greenfinch as they always have, where is the government that will make keeping greenfinches illegal? If there is no law against keeping greenfinches as 'companion animals' in Malta, will they all change to captive-bred canaries? No, because they already keep canaries too. All right, so what good might a trapping ban be?

According to Dr Andre Raine of Birdlife Malta:

Not making finch-keeping illegal will of course leave a large loophole in the law which no doubt will be exploited. Insisting that birds are sold only with closed rings does not solve the problem as it can easily be circumvented, as is seen with wild caught raptors sold in the UK. The main issue at the moment is whether the government is going to make good on its promise to ban finch trapping from December 2008 onwards, as we have seen no progress in the matter to date. They are allegedly carrying out a captive breeding project to provide an alternative source to wild-caught finches, but there is a loophole in this as well: 'small numbers' of finches will 'need' to be caught from the wild to keep the gene pool 'healthy' in captive bred populations.

Also not too worried about all of Heaven being in a rage, are some members of the Flemish parliament, who are attempting to reintroduce chaffinch trapping at the behest of so-called bird lovers who hold bird-song competitions. They say the song of a captive-bred finch is not as good as that of a wild-caught bird. I wonder why that is?

Chapter Seven

THE RHINO HORN MURDERER

My friend and colleague Phil, new at the time, took the call. Puzzled, he passed it over to Alan, who was more experienced. On the other end was a young man who worked on the help desk at the Stock Exchange. He'd just been speaking to a Stephanie Grant who had wanted to know what the current market price was for rhino horn. Instincts on the help desk said that this call was best handled with a 10-foot barge pole, so Ms Grant was asked to leave a number and she'd be phoned back with the information. The young man phoned the RSPCA help desk and was transferred to the SOU.

My boss then, Don, was another wildlife and conservation nut like me and therefore an endangered species among RSPCA senior management. Like me, he was highly enthused about the idea of a case involving rhinos, all five species of which are threatened with extinction, but he had a terrific fight to get permission for us to take the case on. He'd recently come back from secondment to the Hong Kong society, and we knew that China was the main purchaser of rhino horn. Within half an hour he'd established the going rates for various types and qualities of horn, whole and powdered, and Alan rang the stock market man, Darren. He was to phone Ms Grant, tell her the news, and give her Alan's mobile number saying that this was a chap who dealt in such matters, a trustworthy type who would exercise discretion in such a delicate situation.

Our plan was that Alan would pose as the go-between while I would be the expert on rhinos and their horns and the one with all the business contacts in the two big Chinatowns, in London and Manchester. I would also have contacts in the secondary market, the rich Arab aristocracy, where rhino horn, which can polish up beautifully, is considered the correct material for fancy dagger handles. The horn that all the fuss was about is not ivory, or bone like antlers, but compressed hair, keratin, like a horse's hoof. To show how mad the world is, nine out of ten rhinos that die are killed by poachers for their horns which, when powdered, are chemically almost indistinguishable from the poachers' own toenail clippings.

All we could do was wait for Stephanie to call Alan. I did know quite a bit about rhinos but I felt the intervening time would be best used swotting up on them further. The first thing to go was the misconception that the horn is revered for its aphrodisiac properties. Journalists and broadcasters constantly recycle this myth and the Chinese do nothing to deny it because the truth is much more mundane and much, much more depressing. Rhino horn is used in Chinese medicine as a blood cooler/thinner and pain reliever, in much the same way that everybody else uses aspirin, except that aspirin works. Proof that rhino horn has no medicinal qualities of any sort has been obtained experimentally by scientists in laboratories, and empirically by an acquaintance I made at a well-known British broadcasting corporation who, as a student, had been employed in a zoo. One of his jobs was to trim the horns of their rhinos, to stop the beasts hurting each other and to make them less tempting to would-be robber gangs, Chinese or otherwise. After one trimming session, he sequestered a quantity of shavings, took his loot home to his student digs and put it through the coffee grinder.

He invited his girlfriend round, and his flatmates did likewise, and they had a Chinese takeaway and a great many beers. The performance-reducing effects of the excessive alcohol were confidently expected to be more than compensated by the Viagra-like consequences of mustard-spoons of magic rhino powder. When the said consequences did not materialise, more powder was washed down with more beer. When the powder ran out but the beer had not, the girls went home.

Rhinos belong to an ancient order of herbivores with hooves, Perissodactyla (meaning odd toes; they have either three digits or one on the rear foot). The horse family, the tapirs and the rhinos make up the order, of which only the domestic horse, donkey and wild zebra look likely to survive in any numbers. One member of the order already extinct is the indricotherium, which reconstructions from fossil bones suggest was a very large and dopey-looking, slightly horse-like rhino weighing maybe 11,000 kilograms, perhaps 15,000 for a really big one, making it at least equal to the mammoth and possibly the biggest mammal ever. Currently the elephant is our biggest, at 6,000 kilograms top weight, with the white rhino second at 3,500 kilograms.

All but one of the rhino species are CITES I. Except for females with young they are solitary, which works against them for breeding when there are so few. They are not the brightest of animals and have poor sight but acute hearing and sense of smell. These characteristics, added to a tendency to grumpiness, can make them very dangerous in a charge-first, ask-questions-later sort of way.

Our smallest rhinos, the Sumatran, are a mere 9 feet long and 4 feet high at the shoulder and weigh but 1,000 kilograms. They have two horns and, uniquely, a hairy coat on their tough, leathery old skin. The female can have young from about four years onwards, one at a time, which are gestated for 400 days and weaned at 18 months. They eat shoots and leaves, 50 kg a day, and are fond of the water, even going in the sea occasionally. Their natural enemies are tigers and Man. Seeing as we've pretty well got rid of the tigers in those parts, it must be Man who is accountable for this animal's decline to almost zero.

Badly off as the Sumatran rhino is, it's not so perilously close to extinction as its single-horned, slightly larger Javan cousin. One colony of about 50 animals lives in the wild in a remote part of Java, a few exist in a Vietnamese national park, and that's it. The Indian version, single horned and larger still with males up to 2,200 kg, also preyed upon only by tigers and Man, was headed for extinction, seemingly irretrievably, until the Indian and Nepalese governments put in a huge effort. The population is back into the low thousands, all in protected reserves, and the number of armed guards doing the protecting is in the high hundreds and needs to be, with a kilogram of horn furnishing the price of a new car. Unavoidably, the more the trade is driven underground, the more difficult and dangerous it becomes to get the horn, the higher the price rises and the more desirable the prize.

There are two species of African rhino, the black and the white, neither of which are those colours, each having subspecies resulting from local evolution, all with two horns. The black is grey and is having mixed fortunes. The populations under heavy protection, mainly in southern Africa, are relatively thriving and up to the low–mid thousands. The western subspecies has gone.

The white rhino, grey like the black rhino but bigger and with a widje (Afrikaans for wide) mouth, is the least bad tempered of the lot and the only one without a prehensile top lip to help it graze. Almost certainly about to become extinct is the northern white, which is down to its last dozen or even fewer in its only remaining habitat, the Congo. The southern variety has been successful enough under close protection to be downgraded to CITES II. O joy, this means that international trade in them can take place with the right permits.

The call from Stephanie came while Alan and I were in the car going to a job. He put it on speakerphone and set the recorder. She was very, very cautious, saying only that she had access to a large quantity of rhino horn which was for sale. Alan told her he knew a man who would be interested and who had bought large amounts before. There should be a meeting between the three of us. Stephanie, perhaps doubting that we were big enough dealers for her project, told us how many horns she had: 127 horns weighing approximately 530 pounds or 240 kilograms.

'Are you sure, 240 kilos?' Alan asked her. She was absolutely, which confirmed in our own minds what she had possibly thought, that this case was too big for us. My history of squeezing money out of the RSPCA had been confined to a few hundred pounds here and there. I didn't think it likely that they'd come up with several million for the rhino horns. In fact, like Stephanie, I was absolutely sure.

Stephanie wanted to refer to her partner in business about the meeting and so would come back to us the next day, which gave me time to develop a further plan. I knew if I went to the management with what we had so far, they would pass it straight to Customs and Excise, the official body for dealing with CITES matters. We would then be cut out of the job entirely and maybe it would go right, maybe not. I phoned the police, the national crime squad with whom we'd done surveillance training over the years and where I had some good pals. Soon I had a call back, from a DC with the regional squad which covered our area. They were keen to co-operate and mount a joint operation, which news was enough to prevent the case being shipped out to Customs.

Stephanie rang again, saying she wanted £12,000 a kilogram, or £2,880,000 altogether, or an average of around £28,000 a horn. She would meet us in the bar of the Garden House hotel in Cambridge with her partner, David.

The following day Phil, Alan and I met our DC and a DS in Cambridge to take a look at the hotel. The police would conduct general surveillance; we would go into the meeting. We were finalising details when Stephanie rang and changed the venue to the Holiday Inn. Bright lady, we thought.

Our equipment, RSPCA issue from the charity shop and not really of the latest design, was not going to be up to the task in hand whichever hotel we were in. The police, not yet fully committed to the investigation without proof that it was worthwhile, had not brought any useful gear, so we stopped off at an electrical goods place and bought some. We needed two small, light, easily hidden microphones with radio transmitters, a receiving set and a recorder. Alan and I would be miked up with devices very like the ones used for interviewees on television. Phil would book into a room on the first floor and set up with his receiving and recording kit.

We taped the mikes and transmitters to our persons as if we had broken ribs. There was a chance we would be frisked and so we lashed on a good layer of adhesive bandages, not thinking about how we were going to get them off again. Excitement was high. You don't get many multimillion investigations in the RSPCA.

We met Stephanie in the foyer - tall, early 40s, slim, long hair, elegantly and expensively dressed, a woman who meant business and was used to having things her way. We had expected to go into the bar for a drink and a chat. No, Stephanie had hired a proper meeting room, on the fourth floor. This was bad news from several points. We would be in private and vulnerable to whatever tricks she pulled, which could include a few of her bodyguards giving us a thorough shake-down. Also our transmitters might not be powerful enough. And, it would be her room and her meeting, and she seemed a powerful enough personality to dominate. Certainly she dealt with us in a most assured way.

Up we went, making sure we said out loud that we were going to the fourth floor. In the room sat a shortish, plumpish, older man. This was David, the partner, and he was another who gave a misleading first impression. Any amateur psychologist, drawing derogatory conclusions from an obvious wig and a bottled suntan, would have been wrong. It was a smart meeting room with large table and chairs, water cooler, soft drinks cabinet, tea and coffee in the machine, and David sat there with some papers in front of him which he soon dished out after the hand shaking and pleasantries were complete. Each of us was given a copy of a short report setting forth the way things were going to be done.

1. Initial meeting to establish credibility on both sides. Buyer to establish availability of commodity and seller to establish evidence of availability of finance.
2. Date to be determined for banker's draft and inspection and weighing of commodity.

3. Method of payment: banker's draft drawn on a UK clearing bank, to be available on the morning of inspection/weighing, with seller's attorney in attendance to authenticate said draft.
4. Inspection to take place at a secure warehouse with two separately calibrated weighing machines so that buyer and seller can arrive at an agreed dry weight for each part of the goods.
5. Exchange of banker's draft and goods between buyer and seller to be witnessed by the attorney who will be thus satisfied that the ownership of the goods has been transferred.
5. The commodity is warranted free of rot and beetle infestation, also free of any metal screws or nails, and to have been kept in a dry environment.
6. Transport of the commodity having been purchased will be the responsibility of the purchaser.

The appendix to this succinct document was four A4 pages headed respectively Box 61, Box 62, Box 63, Box 64, and each page was a list. Box 61 was 35 items numbered and weighed and totalling 69.48 kilograms, 32 items in Box 62 and so on. David, sitting in for Magnus Magnusson, then gave me ten minutes of questions on my chosen specialist subject, rhinoceroses and their horns from prehistoric times to the present day. He seemed satisfied that we were the genuine article and we believed that he and Stephanie, who hadn't said a word to the matter in the meeting, were in possession of this very large quantity of contraband. We said we also accepted the price, which would give us plenty of room for manoeuvre in London, Glasgow, Manchester and Hong Kong and, for a few of the very finest horns, our man in Damascus, through whom we reached the Arab princes.

We adjourned to the bar where I was given a less formal but just as penetrating inquisition on my record as a horn dealer, what amounts I'd sold in the past, to whom and for what, while Stephanie flitted about buying drinks. She had had the same role in the meeting room, that of coffee slave and general minion to his majesty king David, and he treated her like a used doormat throughout. Seemingly content, they went. We would be in touch soon about a date for the exchange.

We dashed up to Phil's room to find him despondent. He had not been able to receive a word of our conversations in the meeting. After the initial chatter in the foyer, all he had on his tape was the repeated interference caused by the lift doors opening and closing on every floor of the hotel. This was not quite the disaster it might have been because we had the business document and those lists of the numbered items, although nowhere were the words rhino and horn mentioned. Nor was it quite the disaster that taking our mikes off proved to be. Alan and I both have a reasonable covering of body hair, at least we did until we started ripping those adhesive bandages off. I understand that some men in certain professions have their hair removed voluntarily by means of sticky tape, in order to further their careers. They're welcome to it, and I have to admire their dedication.

The police came in with their notes on general movements, vehicles, times. When they'd finished laughing at our pathetic and cowardly attempts to remove adhesive bandages, they decided they had better interview us while the day's events were fresh in our minds.

From here, the regional crime squad took the lead in the investigation. Their equipment was much better than ours, their experience with crooks on this scale much greater, but Alan and I were to continue as the little pigs in the middle. Several phone calls came in from Stephanie, all of them edging around the crux. Show us the colour of your money, no, you show us the colour of your rhino horns. A second meeting was arranged at the Holiday Inn, to which David would bring a specimen horn.

The police found out that, as before, she had booked the Tennyson conference room so they set about bugging it with audio and video, and installing their receiving and listening post in the room next door. This time, much to everyone's relief, Alan and I would not have to carry hidden microphones. Another difference was an extra man, an experienced undercover policeman who had worked a lot among crooked art dealers and antique fakers. He was smooth, laid back, just that little bit flash by the right amount, and he would be the chief investor in our deal. Potentially the police would have to stump up a banker's draft for almost £3,000,000. We understood perfectly why they might want their own man in on the job.

At the appointed hour we waited in reception for Stephanie, who took us into the bar, bought us all a drink, chatted to our new man, and led us up to the Tennyson.

David was there, sitting at the table, with a socking great rhino horn in front of him, about 3 feet long which is as long as they get. Ignoring it completely he launched on a quiz to Pat, the undercover copper, but was soon happy and accepted our new team member completely.

For a while he talked about anything but rhino horn, which was a psychological ploy of course with a lump of keratin on display worth £100,000 or more, but we went along with it politely. Eventually he was surprised to discover an enormous horn in front of him and passed it to me to verify. It was an unusually dark specimen but I was pretty sure it was right and, in my capacity as world expert, I would have to give my verdict on sight. Which I did, while quietly scraping a bit off the base of it with a penknife, intending to take my sample to the Natural History Museum to have it definitely authenticated.

To establish availability of commodity, Pat produced the latest copy of the Antiques Trade Gazette and asked David to have a photograph taken as soon as possible, showing the horns as a complete collection with the magazine there in the picture. This was agreed, no problem, so now all that remained was for us to come up with the spondulicks at £12,000 a kilogram. This we said we would have organised within two weeks.

While I went off next day to the Natural History Museum to get expert certainty on my little piece of horn, the police reviewed their recordings. After we had left the meeting, David had launched into a self appraisal for Stephanie's benefit in which he told her how he was without doubt the world's greatest businessman and prime negotiator. Look how he'd got the price he wanted. Look how he'd reduced those mighty millionaire criminal horn dealers to feeble putty, kneeling before him and touching the hem of his gown. What a terrific fellow he was, and if Stephanie looked, learned and inwardly digested, she might pick up a few hints which might help her progress from her current lowly status in the commercial milieu. By now we knew that Stephanie and David were a live-in couple. We wondered how she put up with him.

He also made some comments which Stephanie understood but which an outsider would find puzzling without knowing the background. He had to visit someone, and wondered when this person would be out. When paying a visit, we thought, one normally wonders if the person would be in. The puzzlement disappeared when the police followed him and Stephanie all the way to an open prison where they visited a convicted murderer called Wilfred Bull, currently serving a life sentence. David was not the owner of the horns after all but was acting as an agent. Bull, a London antiques dealer, had been having a six-year affair with a widow, one Carol Scotchford-Hughes and had decided that she was a preferable permanent consort to his wife Patsy. After a few domestics on this subject, rather than go through all the unpleasantness and acrimony of a divorce, Bull decided to kill Patsy. He would stage a mock robbery on his antiques showroom in Coggeshall, the Essex village previously famous for witch executions. On one of Patsy's days on duty at the showroom, the robber blasted her with a 12-bore.

At home later, wondering idly where his wife might be and why she was not yet home from the showroom, he suggested his teenage son might pop along and see what was the matter. The son discovered the body of his mother and called the police, who at first made their enquiries along the robbery line. Bull had already been implicated in two other killings, one involving his brother-in-law, but nothing had been proved and no charges brought. Third time unlucky for Bull, though, and down he went. He was a wealthy man and, before he went to prison, he had bought the rhino horns which was not illegal at that time. Now that it was illegal and the horn was consequently more scarce, the value had increased substantially. With only two or three more years to serve, Bull was organising his rhino horn coup from his cell via Carol Scotchford-Hughes and two of her friends, the loving couple David Eley and Elaine Arscott, aka Stephanie.

Knowledge is power, and we thought we had it all. Alan went on leave hoping that we wouldn't close in for the kill until he got back, and left me his phone. Bryn was driving me home one night when it rang. It was David, in a stew. He'd seen in the papers that the police had staged an operation against wildlife criminals and seized some rhino horn. He wanted to know what the legal position was. Under no circumstances would he be involved in illegal deals. He was a businessman, not a criminal and they didn't come any straighter than him. Then he suddenly asked me two completely unrelated questions. Was it possible to make rhino horn look older than it was, and did I know anybody in the RSPCA?

The answer to both was no, and what had the RSPCA got to do with anything? We were keen to buy the horn whether it was, strictly speaking, illegal or not. I was aching to say that I knew it had been bought legally and so the new law might be irrelevant anyway. I could only say that it would depend on when it was bought. When had David bought it?

He wanted the legal position explained to him properly, by an expert, which was why he'd mentioned the RSPCA. I didn't quite go for this and thought there was something else. In fact, the legal position was a bit of a sore point. There had been no cases brought under the new law and so there were no precedents and no rulings. A judge might go one way or the other. Regardless of how it had been obtained originally from the rhinos, could it be illegal to sell something which had been bought legally?

David rang off after agreeing to meet me to discuss all matters connected, then rang again and once more rabbited on about how honest and upright he was and how he'd rather die a thousand deaths than sell a stolen paper bag. My own view was that he was protesting rather too much, as if he was trying to wriggle out of a trap before anyone accused him of being in it. Furthermore David, the planet's most capable businessman, had not come down with the last shower and so had set his favourite private investigators onto us and, as well as that, he had contacts throughout the security business. He had checked us out and, he wanted to know, why would Alan's phone number be owned by the RSPCA? Rubbish, I said, it isn't. Oh yes it is, said David. Alan is RSPCA. How long had I known him? He could be under cover.

I said this was a lot of nonsense. I'd known Alan for ten years. In any case, the RSPCA would never get involved in a sting like this, to do with rhino horns for God's sake. They were cats and dogs, the RSPCA, and cruelty to gerbils. What did they want with rhino horns?

It was true there had been enquiries at RSPCA HQ, from an alleged corporate security firm asking about some mobile telephone numbers, mine and Alan's, and some fool had faxed out the information without bothering to tell us. It was clear that David had lost faith in Alan and, by extension, me. Although he'd only managed to trace my number to our fictitious import/export company in Salford, the case was rocking badly.

We had to do something, and quickly, or we were lost. The suggestion I now made was that we should stage a double-cross. Alan and I should be cut out of the deal and Pat, who was the moneybags anyway, would propose a direct arrangement between himself and David, meaning he would have no irritating commissions to pay the middlemen. Such treachery was right up David's street and he was soon on the phone to us saying the deal was off, it was illegal, he could not touch it, goodbye.

Over the following days, Alan and I had to sneak into work. We were in the silly position of being undercover agents operating out of RSPCA HQ, and any surveillance team could have spotted us and put the deal in even more jeopardy. It was the sad truth that our great schemes for exposing multimillion pound crimes against endangered species were only illusions. The RSPCA was not up to it, the resources and facilities were not up to it and, as a consequence, we were not up to it. Maybe the big boss was right. Maybe we had better forget the wildlife killers and stick to what most people believed the collecting tin was for.

Pat had another meeting with David who passed over two horns as a gesture of good faith. I was called in to identify and verify at the police station. The larger of the horns was worth about the same as my house. And so the operation moved into its final phase. Pat would meet David in Norwich and hand over the banker's draft. A phone call from Pat would set his transport going to an address in London that David would give him, where a mystery woman would be in attendance to show where and what.

David Eley was arrested as he accepted the banker's draft. He could do little to help himself except give Pat the London address. On mobile surveillance in the police van, we heard the call come through that Eley was nicked and the horns were to be gathered in. Playing the part of White Van Man was another undercover police officer, and we followed him as he drove to the address and picked up Carol Scotchford-Hughes. She directed him to two lock-up garages in Kensington.

Inside the lock-ups it was like Sotheby's with paintings, sculptures, furniture, gilded mirrors, clocks, all kinds of antique valuables, plus four anonymous grey plastic boxes with hardboard lids. Carol showed us what was inside: hundreds of rhino horns, mostly the larger African ones but with some Asian. While the cops were arresting Carol, I photographed the boxes, loaded them into the police Transit and drove off across London with £3 million. The police would be taking charge of the prosecution but they would need our evidence, including our verification and valuation of the horns, the most valuable items ever to sit on my desk at the RSPCA. They weren't there long because they had to be put into official police custody at Cambridge where, contrary to the warranty previously issued, the wood-boring insects infesting them must have taken flight, mated and laid their eggs. That police station was plagued with exotic woodworm for years afterwards.

In the months before the trial at King's Lynn Crown Court, I did some serious thinking about rhinos, the RSPCA, and what we and other similar organisations could do to help this magnificent animal. To be involved and partly responsible for bringing about the biggest rhino horn case in the world, and the first in the UK, was all very well but what did it do for the rhinos now alive and not yet born? As ever, money was the problem. What could we do with £3 million …

To attract attention, get media coverage, set up a fund, get government help, all those things, we needed a stunt, and the plan was to burn Mr Bull's horns on the South Downs where beacons used to be lit to warn of invasion or celebrate coronations, royal births and suchlike. Maybe this could be the birth of something even more important. I got quite excited about it.

The lawyer involved in the deal, mentioned in the original business plan but not a visible player, had already been acquitted at a different trial, before the main case began. Bull, Eley, Arscott and Scotchford-Hughes all pleaded guilty. Judge Peter Langan QC gave Eley nine months in prison, Arscott got 120 hours community service and Scotchford-Hughes' sentence was deferred. Bull got off very lightly. Although he was given 15 months imprisonment it was to be served concurrently with his life sentence, so it made no difference to him, plus £700 costs which was no more than a flea bite to him. The big hurt, the confiscation of his horns, he was going to contest on the grounds that it was legal when he bought them. Our lawyers thought he had a good chance of winning if the case wasn't handled properly.

All the nationals carried the story. The Daily Telegraph, the BBC and others once more stated as a fact that rhino horn is used as an aphrodisiac.

More fiasco followed. The police and in particular DEFRA put out press releases and other publicity, taking all the credit for the investigation and successful prosecution, not bothering to mention the RSPCA, while Bull appealed against the confiscation of his horns. He had no proof that he had bought them legally, but neither had the Director of Public Prosecutions any proof that he hadn't. It was decided that the horns could be handed back if Bull accepted a DEFRA proviso that he wasn't allowed to sell them. So he agreed. Well, he would, wouldn't he?

The prosecution lawyers in the case had failed to turn up at the hearing, which is an indicator of the regard in which wildlife actions are held. I am quite certain that had the RSPCA's specialist legal team been allowed into the appeal, they would have won it, kept the horn, and we could have burned it on the Downs in glorious pyres, to raise funds for a noble cause, to help save those bad-tempered, half-blind, stupid, splendid, magnificent animals from extinction at our own hand.

Chapter Eight

COMPULSORY RETIREMENT, MAFIA STYLE

Zebrzydowice is a small town of about four-and-a-half thousand people in southern Poland, Silesia, on the Czech border and not very far from Auschwitz. It is a popular resort for train spotters, being a place where railways meet, and it has special advantages for some of those whose main interest is road transport.

For years now it has been the focus for a trade that illustrates perfectly two of the great truths of animal welfare. One, if there's money involved, the animals lose. Two, if there's a law which increases the difficulty of maximising the money, the law will be got around.

The money in question here is that to be made from the production and sale of salami sausage and butcher's meat in France and, more particularly, Italy. The meat is horse. The going rate at the many horse sales in Poland could be up to a Euro a kilogram for the best animals but you might get lucky and buy a live horse for almost nothing. Fresh horse meat might go in the butcher's shop for

€10 a kilogram, salami three or four times that in the deli. If a horse weighs 600 kilograms, say, and you get perhaps 250 kilograms of meat from it, and from that you make 175 kilograms of salami, you can see that the sums look good, even if the meat has done quite a few road miles to get to the butcher's.

Some of the meat does many, many road miles, alive. The horses mostly used to come from Poland and Lithuania but supplies are getting thin there and so the dealers have to go further afield, to Romania for example, and the old Soviet republics like Belarus. In such countries, much poorer than Italy and France, working horses on farms cannot look forward to a peaceful retirement. Their owners get as much work out of them as they can but cannot afford their keep if it's not being earned. As these countries modernise and become wealthier, the farmers buy tractors so you have a raft of redundant horses as well as retired ones.

Given that the appetite for fresh horse meat and horse salami is hearty in all the richer EU countries except Greece, Portugal and the UK, and given that redundant or otherwise useless central European horses are not going to be sent by the thousand to old horses' homes, the answer might be to build slaughterhouses and salami factories in Poland.

There are several arguments against this. Italians believe that some other countries don't bother sufficiently about hygiene in their abattoirs. In any case, people like their horse meat fresh. They don't want it frozen and they don't want it a long time dead because it goes a funny colour, so it has to be killed locally. People like their meat to be local and so they should. Curiously, while they can easily see cattle, sheep and pigs in the fields being reared for meat, they never see horses. And nobody ever wonders where the horse meat comes from.

As for salami factories, there can be no advantage building in Poland when there are already so many excellent factories in southern Italy, France and so on. Ah but, you might say, what about the problems of transporting thousands of horses alive over distances of a thousand or more miles? There are EC regulations about the vehicles, the numbers of animals per cubic metre of space, tethering, how they can't be driven for more than 24 hours without being given another 24 hours' rest, how they can't be driven for more than eight hours unless the vehicles conform with the regs, how they must be fed and watered every eight hours, kept at certain temperatures, given plenty of fresh air and all that good stuff. In fact, regular feeding and watering is especially important for horses because they are what is termed 'continuous eaters'. They don't have any internal storage facilities.

Of course, if they were monitored and all the proper paperwork was filled in and inspected, the regulations – inadequate though they are – would have to be observed. As they are not monitored, and most of the vets and police and border guards and government officials who are supposed to do the monitoring do not give a tuppenny damn, then there remains no case for building facilities near the source of supply. It is much cheaper to transport the horses right across Europe, avoiding Austria because the police there can be rather fussy. Problems? What problems? Time and money can't be wasted on doomed animals on route to Italian slaughter houses under the management of the Mafia, whose accountants are very cost conscious.

Here is the objective stated in European Union Council Regulation (EC) No 1/2005 on the protection of animals during transport and related operations. It applies only when animals are being moved for a commercial purpose:

No animal shall be transported unless it is fit for the intended journey, and all animals shall be transported in conditions guaranteed not to cause them injury or unnecessary suffering.

Quite how we might define suffering as being unnecessary is not clarified. The implication is that where suffering is necessary, that's all right. We might also ask how a 20-year-old horse which has spent its whole life on a farm, serving the same family, pulling the plough and the hay wain, being given the good fellowship of kindly country people and never having been inside a motor wagon, could ever be fit for the intended journey.

Here is the same objective, as amplified by DEFRA:

No animal shall be transported unless:

The journey is properly planned and time is kept to a minimum and the animals are checked and their needs met during the journey.

The animals are fit to travel.

The vehicle and loading and unloading facilities are designed, constructed and maintained to avoid injury and suffering.

Those handling animals are trained or competent in the task and do not use violence or any methods likely to cause unnecessary fear, injury or suffering.

Water, feed and rest are given to the animals as needed, and sufficient floor space and height is allowed.

You and I might say that if we were to use the principles of common sense and common humanity, we might well come up with exactly the same things, again with a caveat on the nature of the fear, injury and suffering deemed necessary or unnecessary. The difficulty is, with all this fine statement of intent, who is making sure that the evil bastards in the world are doing what they should?

SOU had been receiving intelligence for some time about the traffic through Zebrzydowice, mostly from Animals' Angels, the German all-women outfit that I so much admire and respect, and we were very interested in trying to do something about it. Colleagues Bryn and Martin made some enquiries and received information from a sympathetic vet about departure dates from Poland. This was what we needed to begin planning a most complicated and difficult exercise. We had to establish the workings of an entire trade and gather sufficient hard evidence to go to the European Commission with an unanswerable case. We would need everybody in SOU and all the resources we could muster, to track the horses across several countries from Poland to a place near Bari, where there was a huge slaughterhouse for horses.

Continuity of surveillance was essential. We knew what was going to happen but we had to prove it: that horses would not be fed and watered properly, that they would not be rested or even unloaded at the stopping places, called lairages, and that they would travel all the miles and all the hours with no decent care. We would have to stay with them every inch of the way without arousing any suspicion, eat with the drivers in the same roadside cafes, maybe stand next to them in the gents. We couldn't know what they might do if they clicked, bearing in mind a strong suspicion of Mafia involvement.

We decided that a recce was necessary. Bryn, Martin, Phil, Alan, me, we'd all been to different bits of the route at one time or another and we were all used to following vehicles, but Poland was new ground and, from what we could gather, this was a piece of Poland dedicated to the assembly and transport of livestock. At Zebrzydowice they used to send horses by rail. Now we found a modern collection centre and a motorway leaving the town with a special lane for livestock hauliers, signposted with a graphic of a horse's head. Note that it is a collection and forwarding operation. All the horses have already travelled to get there, sometimes hundreds of miles, before they are loaded for their final journey of a thousand miles to the warm south.

We split up into three pairs and checked all the border crossings, from Poland into Czech Republic, Slovakia, Hungary, Slovenia and Italy. At each, we mapped out observation points for the lairages, hiding places for our vehicles, checked radio signals, staff numbers and whereabouts, every little detail. After a few weeks back at home, we had the message from our Polish vet. All systems go.

The plan was for Andy and me to do the whole journey, with other teams covering it in relays. We began with one vehicle in Poland, another just into the Czech Republic. Bryn was watching the Zebrzydowice lairage as we settled in for the delay which seems inevitable with every job like this. We grumble about our trains not running on time. Try sitting around through the night in Poland waiting for some villains to load up their horses.

In the early hours of a Tuesday morning in high summer, the wagon rolled. It had two drivers and 40 horses on board, which would not have been too bad a number if they had only been going ten minutes down the road. As it was, 30 hours later, mid morning on the Wednesday, we were in Bari. It sounds so easy when it's put like that but pursuit of an unpredictable quarry for that time and distance requires enormous concentration. The Polish wagon drivers were geared up. They had a bunk in the cab and knew their route, so they just took turns and kept going more or less continuously except for diesel, food and toilet stops. Our teams had no bunks and had to be awake all the time, one map reading, one driving. Without sleep or decent rest stops, following about a kilometre behind, having to inspect every pull-in to see if they'd gone into it, having to get up close at turn-offs, and all without being spotted in their rear view mirror or anywhere else – it certainly takes toll of a chap. No matter how much coffee and cola you drink and how many caffeine tablets you take, it's only will power that keeps you awake. By journey's end we had been on the job for 44 hours. We were exhausted, smelly, uncertain if we were coming or going, and almost bereft of any ability to complete the task. Even so, we were very, very well compared to the horses.

No horses had been unloaded at any border crossings and no rest had been given. Why the drivers even bothered to have a quick glance at their cargo wasn't clear. They would never have done anything, whatever they saw. Dehydration was inevitable in most if not all the animals. They were not given enough water and the stress of the travelling made them less likely to drink anyway. An average horse in comfortable conditions will drink 40 litres of water a day. I'd be surprised if this lorry load of 40 animals were given that quantity between them over the whole journey.

Some horses will not urinate when travelling. In a group like this, there were bound to be some which, in a horrible irony, would suffer from fluid retention. As for food, they were given hay, a paltry amount, doubtless of poor quality with little nutritional value. Horses need two or three meals a day; most of the horses on this journey got nothing.

Horses that do not know each other are more liable to fight. Horses in confined and crowded circumstances are even more liable to fight. If that were not enough, with too many animals in the wagon they can't stand properly with their legs braced, so they fall around as the wagon accelerates, brakes and takes corners, causing more disagreement and kicking. More fights would occur when the pathetically small rations were doled out.

Add to all this the intense summer heat, the manure which was never cleared out and so made the wagon floor slippery and filthy, and the well-established fact that dehydration, stress and poor ventilation all increase the chances of shipping fever (pleuropneumonia), which can be fatal, and other dangerous diseases, and you begin to marvel that any of the poor beasts survive at all on this frequent and regular passenger service.

When they get to the slaughterhouse they still have not finished with their unnecessary fear, injury and suffering. Many will come off the lorry with laminitis to a greater or lesser degree, greater if they had contracted it before the journey and it was left untreated. This is a really painful condition caused by inflammation inside the hoof, usually one of the front hooves. In normal horse life it is often triggered by overeating; in Polish horses transported in barbaric conditions, stress brings it on, or a blood malfunction. A horse with laminitis tries not to put its foot on the ground because it hurts so much. Perhaps you can imagine the torture it goes through if it has the pain in two feet, or even all four.

We humans, tired out and feeling in dire need of beer, bath, sleep, shave and breakfast in that order but not feeling any pain, were in no condition to present ourselves at reception and ask for a visitor tour. That would have to wait for another day but there was an imperative to get film of our horses being unloaded, to show their condition and prove continuity. To try to work out what to do, Bryn and I hid in a small olive grove near the premises, which were in a built-up area with four- and five-storey blocks of flats all around. The good citizens were out on their balconies taking their morning coffees and late breakfasts, and hanging out their washing. Any shenanigans we got up to would be seen and would probably result in a call to the carabinieri or, worse, to the local equivalent of Tony Soprano.

One of our men, the team humorist Cliff, is a lightly built guy and so he was elected unanimously to clamber up the surrounding wall of the slaughterhouse and take what video shots he could. As I was in charge of operations, I was elected to bend over and let Cliff climb on my back and shoulders.

When the horses came out of the lorry they were in the most pitiful state. One had an eye hanging out and bleeding. Another had a massive gash on its leg. Another had laminitis and was compulsively scraping its front hooves on the ground. Several had loose shoes, there were more laminitis cases, another with an eye missing, yet more showing with laminitis by having their front legs sticking out straight before them, sometimes crossed over. Every one of them was dehydrated. They went directly for the water, drinking and drinking in desperation, even overcoming their obvious pain to get to the troughs. Some could hardly walk at all but they had to get to that water. One skewbald was doing a weird kind of dance on its back legs, waving one front leg around in the air while it tried its hardest not to stand on the other front leg, both front hooves being terribly swollen. Nobody with eyes to see could have failed to register the agony this horse was going through but nobody did a thing about it. Obviously, this suffering came under the heading of 'necessary'.

There were men walking about in the yard, tethering the horses in rows in what looked something like bicycle sheds, so as well as the balcony breakfasters we had the more immediate likelihood of being spotted with a camera and Cliff's head poking over the wall. Very soon, enough had to be what we'd got, so we made for our cars and our hotel in the hills.

Back home, we set up a bogus agricultural college in Shropshire on whose headed notepaper we wrote to ask if we could amplify our comparative studies of meat production methods by seeing around the slaughterhouse, with a view to including a horse meat module in the new course we were devising. All calls and mail to the college were redirected to RSPCA SOU and we soon had the reply we wanted. The management would be delighted etc, and so off we went.

We got there early and set up observations from 5.30am, so we could knock on the door when we knew there'd be a Polish lorry unloading. In one came at 6.40. It's a super-modern abattoir, everything stainless steel, EU-approved and designed for efficiency but with no consideration of what a horse might feel while watching its fellows being killed and skinned.

Our guides were a glamorous lady vet and the director of the establishment, Alfredo il Cavallo, Alf the Horse. We had made some checks with Interpol before setting out. Information from them about the abattoir's business connections made thoughts of horses' heads in beds irresistible.

As we walked in there were 250 or so horses tethered and waiting, and three more lorries arrived in short order.

The vet told us that they killed 6,000 horses a month, their stock coming from Poland, Hungary, Slovakia, Serbia and Romania. It takes three days, you know, for them to come from Poland, she confided.

They sold the meat to local shops and salami processors, the blood for fertiliser and the skin to furniture makers. The heads went, not to be used as letters of intent but to a supplier specialising in horse's head as a delicacy for the local gourmets. Quite how they managed as many as 6,000 a month became a puzzle when we viewed the place of execution and the chief executioner, who appeared never to have seen a humane killer before. Maybe he was having a bad day or the gun was faulty, or maybe he used a different method when there were no guests around, but he was needing three or four shots a horse before they dropped. Such crass incompetence was truly frightening the horses, which were already disturbed by the smell of blood. The poor victim in the crush cage at the front of the queue, waiting to be dispatched by Mister Bungle the Butcher, could see the previous corpse being strung up and skinned and its head being chopped off, no more than 3 feet away. The one waiting behind was beaten with heavy sticks as its eyes rolled in terror, having seen the horse in front fall dead out of the crush cage it was now being forced into.

Our covert camera had packed up the minute it was turned on so I went for it and took a camcorder out of my bag and started recording the scene for posterity. The Italians didn't seem to mind and Alan and Barry kept them nattering away and distracted from what I was doing. An invitation to lunch was politely declined, on the grounds that we had to drive north to see more abattoirs specialising in pigs and cattle. Instead we scuttled out, took the road towards Rome, and soon found ourselves a nice little trattoria with fish on the menu, cold beer, and a good view of all the girls going by.

We had done what we set out to do. We had evidence which could not be gainsaid, showing the whole disgusting trade from A to Z, and we could write a report which the RSPCA could take straight to the European Commission and the Italian government. What actually happened was that we did the whole thing all over again with a Daily Express reporter in tow, so that he could write a story about how the fearless Express, in the person of himself, had investigated, uncovered and exposed this disgraceful and shameful trade, by the way with a little help from his friends in the RSPCA.

Our report disappeared upwards. I don't know how far it got. The European Commission made some noises and some amendments to the rules, but if you want to know if anything has changed, ask Animals' Angels. They'll tell you. They follow these horse wagons all the time. Go to www.animals-angels.de and you'll see what a burgeoning, vital operation they have. Ask the European Commission why it is, if their rules and regulations are so great, that we desperately need more and more people like Animals' Angels?

Chapter Nine

GET ME A LEOPARD. DON'T DAMAGE THE SKIN.

There have always been two threads to the reasoning behind the preservation of dead animals to look as if they were alive: education and trophy display. The same reasoning applied even before taxidermy, literally 'skin arrangement', was thought of. In the 5th century BC, the Carthaginian admiral Hanno set sail from modern Tunisia, around the African coast beyond modern Sierra Leone, and brought back gorilla skins to show everyone what marvels lay beyond the horizon.

Early methods of taxidermy were fairly primitive. They cured the animal skin with salt and oak bark so it didn't go off, stuffed it with straw, hay or wood shavings, and sewed it up. Early customers were mainly the wealthy aristocracy whose collections, from the 16th century AD onwards, proved that education itself can be a trophy. Wood-shavings stuffing was insufficiently flexible as a technique to show the animal involved in its natural behaviour, but strenuous efforts were made in early

Victorian times to provide painted backgrounds, theatre sets as it were, to give the whole thing a better gloss, and the museums took over from the aristocracy as the education providers.

Moths and other insects preyed on stuffed animals but poisons were developed to deal with this problem, and new techniques were designed to revolutionise the art, as they would have it, of taxidermy. Sometimes using the skeleton, a mannequin of the body would be made from plaster or other imperishable, workable material, accurate in every respect, so that when the cured skin was applied it truly looked like the real thing. A taxidermist had to be a naturalist too to pull this off, and the great pioneer of the new taxidermy was a Frenchman, Jules Verreaux, who stunned the visitors to the Paris International Exposition, 1867, with his tableau of an Arab on a camel being attacked by two lions. Presumably the chap on the camel was a model.

Commercial taxidermists were always in the trophy business. At one time every pub had a fish in a glass case and a deer's head on the wall, and every hunter had trophies in his study. As cinema and television have largely removed the need for educational taxidermy so the practitioners of the trade have become fewer and, often, more secretive. So, nowadays, you can see a tiger in the zoo, see tigers on the wildlife programmes, or stand next to a life-like dead one in the museum. Or, as we shall see, if you have enough money you can stand next to your very own dead tiger in your sitting room and stroke it.

An honourable taxidermist, such as my friend Dave Astley and his fellow members of the Guild, will go to any lengths to ensure that his specimens came by a natural death, even threatening to inform the authorities when people turn up with a dead creature but no provenance. Others don't care where their animals and birds come from and, in my early days in the SOU, they seemed like legitimate targets. It was not difficult to set up. We had animals dying on us almost daily, especially injured birds that concerned folk brought in, so my source of specimens was ready made.

My plan was thus. Any really handsome tawny owl, kestrel or similar which died, I would take home and put in the freezer. I'd ring up a taxidermist from Yellow Pages and say I'd found this bird by the roadside in perfect condition, and I'd like it mounted to give to my girlfriend for her birthday in three months' time. The taxidermist would agree and I'd go round there with my specimen. The three months would be plenty of time to get to know the person and maybe be invited around to the house, where I might be able to spot things which looked dodgy. The only flaw I could see was that if my timing went wrong, I would end up going to my boss asking for the money to pay the taxidermist for the stuffed owl on my office window sill.

The first case went so smoothly I could hardly believe it. Denise had been making increasingly frequent remarks about the boring existences of those poor people who only have peas and ice cream in their freezers and threatening me with buzzard risotto for supper, but I knew her complaints fell on deaf ears. Anyway, I was now on with the job, taking birds out of the freezer rather than putting them in, and with my first taxidermist I laid it on thick, saying I'd been really interested in the subject as a boy but never had been able to do anything good with it. The man began showing me the secrets of his craft and took me to him as a kind of disciple. He trusted me and was quite happy to leave me alone around the place, so I could find badgers with bullet holes, rare species with shotgun-pellet marks and exotic venomous snakes, clearly very recent work, which are difficult to find as roadkill in Britain.

I caught him taking a commission for a hen harrier. This is a very rare bird with probably not many more than 500 breeding pairs left in Britain. The few that do remain are heavily and disproportionately persecuted by game-keepers because they sometimes will take a grouse chick. The taxidermist didn't seem to have a hen harrier about the place but that was of no concern. He was intending to pay to have one shot – at least, in my ignorance I assumed it would be shot. I found out later that these people have quite different methods. Confronted with this evidence, he confessed to several other charges, was found guilty, fined, had all his collection confiscated, and I was highly pleased with myself.

After this first case, we had a surprise visit in the SOU, or should I say a truly astonishing visit, from the director general of the RSPCA. He walked into our office; we'd seen his photograph so we knew who he was. Our boss wasn't there so, instead of a meeting, he made a simple announcement. There would be no more of these taxidermy cases. These were dead animals and of no concern to the RSPCA, an animal welfare organisation.

It took quite a long time to get this decision reversed but, thanks to some very hard work by my managers Don and Tony, who pointed out that not all taxidermy subjects died from natural causes nor did they come from plentiful species, we did get going again. Over the next couple of years, this simple idea of investigating a clearly visible trade would lead to dozens of prosecutions and the repossession of more than 1,000 illegally taken specimens from badger cubs to wolves and tigers.

After reinstalling my patent taxidermist catching system, my next call proved to be to one of the honourable members of the profession, in Middlesbrough, who was pretty hacked off about some of his so-called colleagues who were getting the trade a bad name. I thought there might be a good source of information here so, while going along with my barn-owl-for-my-girlfriend story I was quite happy to encourage him to drop some of his fellow taxidermists right in it. Sidney Hoyle of Blackburn was one, and an Italian baker called Franco di Canto another. Their chief supplier was a gamekeeper, Dennis Frazer who, like the Italian, lived in the Edinburgh area.

My Middlesbrough man had no addresses, just a general picture in his mind of the authentic little Italian bakery and pizzeria where he said he'd seen many specimens of birds of prey in this fellow's freezer beside the pizza dough. How did we manage before we had freezers? Anyway, thinking there couldn't be all that many such places in Edinburgh we decided to go up there and, with the help of an old friend, a SSPCA inspector called Mike, find ourselves a Quattro Stagioni with extra peregrine.

Bryn and I, with Mike, drove around Edinburgh for hours. It's a really good city for Italian bakers. There are scores of them, Franco's, Ruffino's, Tony's, Alberto's, and we took photographs of all the shop fronts. We also went inside hoping to see Signor di Canto, a man believed to be in his early 50s, 5 feet 6 inches, good belly on him, thinning hair, prominent aquiline nose. Without wishing in any way to slight as fine a body of men as the brotherhood of Italian chefs, bakers and pastry cooks, we did not find that this description narrowed the field very much.

Back in Middlesbrough, my man didn't recognise any of the shop photos but had had a thought that the one we wanted might be in the Mount Pleasant district. Off we went again taking him with us and, within a mere two hours' scouting, found the spot. It was yet another Franco's but this time the bakery of the aforesaid di Canto. With Mike, we quickly organised a search warrant at the Sheriff's Office. Mike also had found out that the gamekeeper, whose address we'd traced easily, had convictions for assault and GBH and was somewhat notorious in certain circles.

Two simultaneous dawn raids were organised with the local police. Mike, some more SSPCA and several large constables went to the gamekeeper's place, a semi on a council estate. There was nothing in the house which was out of the ordinary but the freezer in the garden shed made them gasp and stretch their eyes. It contained five tawny owls, a little owl, seven sparrow hawks, a dunlin, a goshawk, five buzzards, a golden plover, a badger cub about 12 weeks old, and a hen harrier in a woman's nylon stocking. This is how they kill the prize birds, not with a gun but with a stocking. They lure the harrier or whatever into a trap baited with a pigeon, wrap it up tightly inside the stocking so it can't move, then put it alive in the freezer, thus preserving the body without blemish.

When Bryn opened di Canto's freezer he was equally stunned. There were two otters, two roebuck heads and a wildcat in among the frozen panettoni and whatnot, and in the living room already mounted were a long-eared owl, a waxwing, two tawny owls, two kestrels, three sparrowhawks, a barn owl, a corncrake and two buzzards. Still they weren't finished. In the shop were a waxwing, two little owls, two sparrowhawks, a wildcat and an otter.

Everything went back to the SSPCA HQ and they began procedures against di Canto and Frazer. All the specimens had been shot or poisoned apart from a few which unharmed and so presumably had had the stocking treatment.

My job then was to go to Blackburn and see what I could do about Hoyle. With a sparrowhawk in a carrier bag I went to his house, a two-up, two-down terrace in central Blackburn. Sidney Hoyle answered the door, a short man, about 5 feet 3 inches, bald, in his mid fifties, a very quiet-looking kind of guy you'd expect to find in a routine job, pushing paper around a desk or driving the community bus, whose idea of excitement would be two halves of mild in the pub before coming home to watch Question Time. First impressions can be so misleading, can't they, and doubly so in Mr Hoyle's case.

I explained about the sparrowhawk and my girlfriend, and he let me in to the house. Well. The expression 'gobsmacked' hardly covers it. I stood amazed. In that hallway I swear that, above dado-rail height, there was not one square inch of wallpaper visible. It was lined on both sides with a 3D jigsaw of animal heads like some sort of weird and scary piece of installation art. Otters, foxes, badgers, squirrels, deer, stoats, polecats, Soay sheep, mountain hares, so many I couldn't count them nor remember them all. I had no hidden camera with me and it wouldn't have worked in that dim light anyway. I tried to take mental notes but the sight was overwhelming. Alfred Hitchcock could not have dreamed up a better set for a horror movie. Everywhere you looked were teeth, horns, eyes and more teeth, in heads which were so, so realistic and lifelike. I knew how Mole must have felt when he was lost in the Wild Wood.

Hoyle could see I was impressed and took it as a compliment. We went on to the rest of the show, starting with the sitting room. There may have been chairs and a sofa in there but I didn't notice because every wall, every surface, mantlepiece, sideboard, window sill, coffee table, everywhere was packed with stuffed animals and parts of animals. Foxes' brushes, otters' paws, baby badgers, albino badgers, every bird of prey you could think of, every British mammal and many of the reptiles, more than you would see in the museum. It was another mind-blowing sight. He took me to the main bedroom and it was the same there. On top of the wardrobe was a glass case with an albino hen harrier and two badger cubs. Next to them was a really small badger cub that can't have been taken at more than three weeks old. Mrs Hoyle had kept her dressing table free of taxidermy but that was all. I thought, how she must have longed for a picture of some flowers in a vase, or even some real flowers in a vase, but there was nowhere to put such a thing.

I left the sparrowhawk with him, said I'd return in a few weeks, raced back to the office and set about getting a search warrant. We expected this to be the final act of the investigation into this particular gang so I would go along on the raid with Bryn and PC Maria Thompson, the Lancashire Constabulary wildlife officer and one of the very best I've ever worked with. I tried to prepare them for the shock which awaited them in Hoyle's hallway but no amount of description could numb the senses enough. Like me when I first saw it, they stood, open-mouthed, unable to believe their own eyes or, more accurately, unable to believe that there existed a man on earth who could or would do this to the hallway of a terraced house in Blackburn, Lancashire.

Sidney Hoyle was open-mouthed too, having been summoned from his bed at dawn to be cautioned by the police on his own doorstep in his pyjamas. He must have assumed that it was all to do with his previous form as a drug dealer disposed to violence. When he realised it was his beloved taxidermy, he went red with fury, and spouted. All his specimens had been legally taken. We had no right to be there nor to impugn his good name and reputation in the profession. How dare we be banging on his door at this hour. All these years producing work of the highest quality, and what does he get but a slip of a girl policeman telling him what's what. And then he saw me.

I thought he was going to do a Tom and Jerry on us and inflate into a barrage balloon, float up to the ceiling, crack up all over and explode into a thousand pieces. Maria had just about got him cooled down when Mrs appeared, spitting, frothing, cursing and setting the fireworks off again. Professional that she is, Maria managed to turn the storm into calm but rather a fragile calm as we saw when the business of removing the specimens began. The pair of them went berserk again. They showed exactly the same kind of behaviour as those wild-caught monkeys in cages at Accra Zoo. They were beside themselves with anger, fear, frustration and what they saw as the most outrageous injustice which they could do absolutely nothing about.

Almost 200 specimens were taken from that house. We could make a well-informed guess that most if not all, apart from one night heron, had been taken locally – Forest of Bowland, Westmorland fells, Lake District, southern Scotland – and when we X-rayed them we found what we wanted. With a dead specimen straight from the freezer, finding shot in the body is easy enough with a metal detector or X-ray machine. Taxidermy removes the lead shot itself, of course, but fragments often stick in the skin, in the layers beneath the fur, and this was what we were looking for.

The great majority of Hoyle's animals had been killed by shooting, even including the badger cubs. Some utter bastard had waited outside a badger set all night, and maybe the next night and the next night, until the sow badger brought her offspring out for their first smell and sight of the big wide world, and bang. The single very small cub on top of the wardrobe, three or four weeks old, was too young for that scenario. It must have been dug out.

In court, Hoyle pleaded guilty to illegal possession, for instance of the badgers which had been shot, but our pleasure at that soon turned to anxiety as we saw the way the stipendiary magistrate was dealing with the case. He seemed very interested in all the mitigation being put forward by Hoyle's lawyer, but indifferent to the prosecution's evidence. Was he a huntin', shootin', fishin' kind of magistrate? Was he Master of the local hounds? Or an amateur taxidermist? Or a member of Hoyle's golf club? Several times he cut off our solicitor in full flow, finally giving Hoyle a conditional discharge with £500 costs.

Things were not so much better in Scotland, where Frazer and di Canto were fined £1,500 each with £700 costs. Bryn and I were in the pub afterwards, not knowing whether to laugh or cry, when Frazer came in. He was quite forbidding looking physically and we did wonder what was going to happen next, but he shook our hands saying he bore us no grudge. He wasn't letting us all off, though, and by golly gosh he was going to get that cad of an SSPCA bounder, or something like that, if it took him the rest of his days. We tried to explain that the initiative had come from us, from England and the RSPCA but he wouldn't have it, no, that SSPCA expletive deleted was behind it all. For years afterwards, whenever he'd had a whisky too many, Frazer would ring Mike up and tell him in excruciating detail how the process of taxidermy need not be confined to those animals with wings or four legs.

It's not confined to Blackburn and Edinburgh either, and my system was taking me all over the UK to case after case. One seemed to lead to another to another with bits of information, like gypsy code in the woods, always telling me to turn right or left and there would be another illegal taxidermist, sitting, waiting for me, in a trap he'd built himself. I almost began to wish the Director General would descend from on high again and ban me from it. And then I came across Mr Jarvis.

He was a taxidermist living way up on the Northumberland moors near Hexham, and a few little stories I heard about him seemed to put him beyond my girlfriend-and-sparrowhawk ploy. This chap was, it was said, only interested in the exotic and the very rare, and he was hard to get to know. By this stage I had many contacts in the taxidermy world but nobody seemed able to get me an introduction to the great man.

Without a dead member of an exotic or endangered species, my normal approach had no chance. I had dreams about people bringing dead dodos into the office but no such luck until, on a holiday in France, I came across the body of a snake which I didn't recognise. At home it was identified as a western whip snake, Coluber viridiflavus, also called a grass snake although it's very much bigger than the British grass snake. It can grow to 6 feet; this one was about half that, striped, with yellow and green markings. They're not venomous but will bite if they have to and will hiss alarmingly if threatened. They're not all that rare either but would be unfamiliar to your average naturalist studying British wildlife.

Despite what people say, flattery can get you into all manner of places and flattery was my only weapon. I would knock on Jarvis' door, tell him that I'd heard marvellous things about his wildlife expertise, so I'd come all the way from Carlisle to ask him what this snake was and could he mount it for me. Good plan? Probably not the best but it would have to do. His place was a farm, really isolated, miles from any village, with what at first I thought was one of those conversions of stables into holiday cottages. They were not cottages but they weren't active stables either, all refurbished around a paved courtyard and looking very trim indeed. The whole set-up had a moneyed air about it. This guy does not draw his wages from the sheep sales, I thought, as I rang the bell. He was a big chap too, well over 6 feet, mid 30s, black curly hair, athletic, muscular build, the type you'd want playing at number eight in your rugby team.

By his accent, that would have been a team from Rotherham or Barnsley, or maybe Doncaster, my old stamping ground. He spotted I'm from Hull and, two Yorkshiremen together in a foreign land, we were soon getting along famously. He knew what my snake was, for which I was duly thankful, and it can't have been more than 10 or 15 minutes before he offered to show me round, starting with one of the converted stables which had enough locks and bolts on it to protect the Crown jewels. I've seen the Crown jewels and very nice they are, but what I saw in that stable was a hundred times more exciting. Any dividing walls had been removed so you looked down a very long single room, and the stalls on either side had each been turned into galleries. Here, in the first gallery, was a fully grown tigress with six cubs, two of them play-fighting while the others idly and curiously watched a small animal creeping towards them. It's not surprising they looked curious. The animal was a duck-billed platypus. In another gallery there was a mixed display, as if waiting proper arrangement, with a grizzly bear up on its hind legs, a leopard, a flamingo, several species of the pine marten family, one swan a-swimming, the front half of a seal and various unusual species that Noah might have recognised but I didn't.

The next gallery was given over to birds of prey, perching on a mock tree or flying on wires. Another had a big boss male lion, a lioness, some half grown cubs and some very young cubs including an albino. Next a full-sized leopard attacked a (very) startled gazelle, and another leopard crept beneath another tree stacked with falcons, vultures and harriers in an assortment you would never see in nature.

Monkeys, hyenas, golden eagles, zebras, a display of elephant tusks but no whole elephant, black bears – surely there cannot have been another collection like this outside the major museums. It was mind-boggling. And then there was the British corner, with ospreys, hobbies, hen harriers, and a wryneck of all things. The wryneck used to be common, a type of woodpecker that looks something like a sparrow and rarely pecks wood, feeding on ants on the ground instead, but loss of ant-favourable habitat has made it extinct, or virtually so, as a British breeding bird. If you're lucky you might see a migrant or two, autumn to spring, around the south-east coasts.

Some of the things the man said made me realise this wasn't a static collection. Specimens could be for sale or, if I didn't see what I wanted here, it could be got for me. He didn't come right out and say so but the clear implication was that if I fancied a stuffed leopard or lion, he could oblige. Where, I wondered to myself, was he getting his animals from? The number dying in zoos could hardly account for his apparent ability to provide whatever the market wanted. I doubted if he was directly connected to big game poachers. The obvious answer was dealers, probably in Belgium and Holland, possibly Germany, who in turn would have their own local dealers in Africa, India and so on. The costs of such an exercise had to be high. Some people were clearly willing to pay huge amounts of money for a stuffed lion.

I said my goodbyes, promised to return, hoped he wouldn't find my whip snake too boring a project, and set off to get my search warrant. I had to have a chortle to myself as I drove away, thinking about the size and scope of the job my colleagues would have to do, seizing and cataloguing all those specimens.

The marathon proved worth running although we did not have an outright win. There were lots of very rare animals in there, severely threatened species, and many of them had been shot, poisoned or snared, but the sheer numbers and variety defeated us. It would have taken time to gather and formalise the evidence on all the exotics, which would have come under CITES and therefore have been Crown court-indictable offences. It was RSPCA policy not to pursue such cases, with all the legal palaver that entails. We had to concentrate on the indigenous species which were Wildlife and Countryside Act and so summary offences for the magistrates to deal with. Jarvis, therefore, was up on only a fraction of the rightful charges. Even with these limits, he was convicted on 193 counts of illegal possession and was sent down for five months. Three furniture vans full of specimens were distributed to museums.

Chapter Ten

ANYBODY WANT A MAMBA?

One of my favourite notices is on the edge of a wood in east Devon. It says 'Beware of Adders. Sidmouth Hospital 1½ miles'. So much more effective than 'Private, keep out' don't you think?

Every pastime has its hierarchies. Just as the most ambitious rock climbers want to open up new and more difficult routes and conquer the most remote peaks never trodden before so, in the world of reptile keepers, poisonous snakes are the very zenith of achievement. The more venomous and dangerous they are, the more satisfaction there is in keeping them.

They're ideal in some ways. Snakes generally lead fairly lazy lives, eating occasionally, snoozing a lot, taking a drink now and then, so if conditions are right they're nothing like as demanding as a red setter. When they do eat in the wild, unless they are of the specialist egg-eating types, they capture their prey alive and don't always kill it or paralyse it before swallowing. If the prey is large, they don't so much swallow as pull themselves over it, and if they lose a tooth or two in the struggle it doesn't matter because they have junior sets of teeth lined up and ready to move into place. Some snakes live in the water but most live on land. Most lay eggs but some have live young. Some eat other snakes, or insects, and of the 2,300 known species of snake about a quarter use venom, modified saliva, when hunting. Of these, relatively few can kill a human or want to, but some do, and a very nasty death it can be.

Everyone would like to know which is the most venomous snake of all. For pure strength of poison that is probably a water dweller, the faint-banded or hook-nosed sea snake, Hydrophis belcheri, but they hardly ever bite anybody. They just can't be bothered. Fishermen pick them up and throw them back in the water. Ten of the most venomous species occur in Australia but again hardly ever bite a human because they don't live where people live. The African black mamba is probably one to fear the most as it is both deadly and aggressive, but you would also get votes for rattlesnakes, moccasins, cobras, kraits, coral snakes, copperheads, rhino vipers and so on. If you define the most venomous as the one causing the most deaths, that is Russell's viper, Daboia russelli, also known as the chain viper, which ranges right across South-East Asia although associated mainly with India. Adults are 3 to 4 feet long, in camouflage patterns of earth colours, usually a brown or orangey brown background with darker patches outlined in black. They have big eyes with gold flecks. They do not like being disturbed but otherwise are slow to anger, although the young ones will rise easily to provocation. They are responsible for thousands of deaths a year, largely because what they like best to eat – rats, mice, that sort of rodent – are plentiful where Man is active. The person most likely to be killed by a Russell's viper is a man out working in the fields or the farmyard in the evening, in the Punjab or somewhere along the south-west coast of India, when he treads on one. Sidmouth would not be the only hospital too far away to save him.

Snake venom is the most complex of all poisons. It is a mixture of dozens of ingredients, the formula varying from species to species and within species according to environment, age and time of year, but having several things in common. There will be toxins which paralyse muscles and/or paralyse the nervous system and/or destroy the proper functions of the blood. There will be enzymes, over 20 different types, which accelerate and spread the toxins in the prey's body by, for example, breaking down tissue barriers such as cell walls.

Thus if you are bitten by an unseen venomous snake, you don't quite know what to expect. You might have internal bleeding sufficient to give you disastrous loss of pressure and severe shock. Your blood may lose its ability to coagulate, leading to kidney failure. Your nervous system might shut down, so your breathing or your heart stops, or both. Your muscular structure might go into paralysis, also leading to cardiac arrest. If you get through this phase, you might later get gangrene where you were bitten, or septicaemia. Oh, and in almost every case there's the pain. Quite, quite agonising, apparently.

If everything points to putting the greatest possible distance between yourself and the poisonous serpent, why does anyone want to have one as a pet? Well, they are absolutely fascinating creatures, horrifyingly handsome, mostly quite undemanding to keep, and … no, I'm not that keen on it either.

Evidence that many people are keen on it is amply provided from my own life in animal welfare, a career which seems to have featured venomous snakes at every turn. Luke Yeoman, a man who lived in D H Lawrence territory at New Eastwood, near Nottingham, was the subject of my first undercover case. He'd applied for a licence under the Dangerous Wild Animals Act to keep such snakes but the licence had been refused. The suspicion was that he was keeping them anyway so I went round there to his smallholding, listened, noted the positions of several very large tethered dogs, heard someone busy doing something and knocked on a Portakabin door. I asked the young man who answered if he might have a garter snake. My son's birthday was coming up and the lad was very interested in reptiles. I thought garter snakes, which are a family of North American species known to be relatively easy to keep, feed and even breed, would be a good place to start.

The Portakabin was fitted with shelves and there were plastic tanks everywhere. I picked out a nice looking garter snake, gave the man my £10 and asked what else he might have. In another shed were tanks with covers over them so I couldn't see what was inside, but I did catch a glimpse of the chubby striped body of a puff adder, that's the highly venomous African snake of that name, Bitis arietans, not the harmless North American hog-nosed version. This was enough to justify a proper search and, after giving my garter snake to a man I knew would take good care of it, I arranged a raid with the local authority, the police and one of the UK's leading herpetologists, Tom Langton.

The police took the case very seriously, not surprisingly when there was someone on their manor, no older than 23, keeping animals which can kill people. There was a superintendent and a chief inspector at the briefing that January morning, Hucknall police station, and off we drove in convoy through a countryside thickly covered in frost.

At Yeoman's door, the environmental health officers told him that he was being inspected under the Act on suspicion of keeping dangerous animals, to wit, venomous reptiles. He'd had this before and had managed to bluff his way through because those inspecting, along with a general practice vet, had not been confident enough in their knowledge to identify a snake as one species when Yeoman said it was another. We were better armed than that.

After he'd stopped ranting and raving at me for getting him into this mess, he took us first to a breeze-block shed which was heated and humidified to tropical standards. In here were one or more of anaconda, boa constrictor, Burmese python, red blood python, white lipped python, Pacific island boa, Madagascar tree boa, Argentine boa and a sailfin lizard which is a spectacular Philippine lizard 3 feet long, also known as the sailfin water dragon, Hydrosaurus pustulatus. He had water monitors in there (Asian lizards growing up to 9 feet – only the komodo dragon gets any bigger), also a Bengal monitor and an emerald monitor. None of these are classified in the terms of the Act as dangerous but they are endangered. All the boas, pythons and monitors are CITES II at least.

The next building, another breeze-block effort, stopped us all in our tracks. The walls were fitted with shelves and tight-fitting plastic tanks which slid in and out like drawers. This is what's known as the American system for keeping snakes. Any fool could see there were exotic species in great variety and numbers, and once Tom Langton started reeling off the names with a few brief descriptions we realised we were in the presence of something very special indeed. Here is Tom's list, and not once did he look anything up: mangrove snake, puff adder, Indian cobra, Egyptian cobra (Cleopatra's asp), Gaboon viper, rhino viper, king cobra, Honduran milk snake (a type of king snake supposedly able to suckle from a cow but cannot), Sahara horned viper (very like the American sidewinder but without a tail rattle), green mamba, Wagler's pit viper (South American, also called whitetail lancehead), western diamondback rattlesnake, African tiger snake, Mexican cantil (Mexican moccasin), Ottoman viper (Greek islands, parts of Turkey, one of the few really poisonous European snakes), Innes cobra (Egyptian rarity found only in southern parts of Sinai), forest cobra, canebrake rattlesnake (very rare, found only in some districts of Virginia), white lipped viper, blacktailed rattlesnake. This was a collection of which most zoos would have been envious.

Pit vipers, Crotalinae, form a big family of nocturnal predators found all around the world, including the rattlesnakes, moccasins, fer-de–lance, the mind-boggling bushmaster (up to 12 feet long) and the tiny eyelash viper at 18 inches. Members of the family live in deserts, rainforests, water, all kinds of habitat but none of them live, as I once thought, in pits. The pits are a pair of small organs on the head which act like eyes except they 'see' heat rather than light, sensing infrared rays with quite remarkable sensitivity, so that a prey animal only a fraction warmer than the night air can be 'seen' and struck as if by daylight. Their modus operandi is the ambush. They sit and wait, if they're feeling hungry. One, the Chinese island pit viper, goes back to the same branch on the same tree every year to wait for the migratory birds flying through.

Wagler's viper is another tree dweller, up to 3 feet long and a stunner to look at in green with black scales and yellow markings. In the vivarium containing Yeoman's specimen I noticed two bedraggled and dispirited little zebra finches, which are colourful and chirpy Australians hugely popular with cage and aviary enthusiasts. Those finches would never have seen a Wagler's viper but they seemed to know what fate awaited them. I took a photograph, hoping to bring a cruelty case against Yeoman, and asked him to take the birds out of the box, which he did.

There were also nine iguanas and a red-eared terrapin, so called because of its two lateral red stripes and rapidly becoming a seriously endangered species. The young are taken in large numbers from the wild – southern USA, Mexico, central America – and sold into the pet trade. Naïve folk buy the few little darlings that survive transporting, put them in the childrens' fish tanks and watch in horror as they grow as big as the tank, up to 10 inches long. Usually, their owners then release them into the nearest pond where they decimate the local fish and insect populations before dying of cold.

While the official list of snake species was being compiled, I took a walk around the place to see what I might find. Mostly I found dog food. This was Yeoman's business, making dog food for local pet shops, and his outbuildings were largely made over to this process. In the corner of the largest barn I saw an area screened off with solid partitions. I opened the door expecting to see perhaps an office or a small laboratory for testing dog food samples, rather than five Nile crocodiles, one of them 7 feet long, relaxing in a concrete paddling pool. At least, they were relaxing until I came in, when the big one slid off its ledge, jaws open, hissing loudly, and came towards me faster than I had believed a croc could go. I reversed out through the door faster than I'd believed I could go and slammed it firmly shut.

There was no choice but to leave all the specimens with Yeoman for the moment except the crocodiles, which we rehoused to a safari park, and when the court case came up he was found guilty of illegal possession and told not to be such a naughty boy ever again. We fared better with the zebra finches. This was the first charge ever to be brought against someone for feeding live birds to snakes, under a law enacted in 1911 against cruelly terrifying an animal. A specialist vet called Martin Lawton gave a brilliant testimony on the finches' behalf while Yeoman pleaded not guilty and was defended by the famous TV snake-man, Mark O'Shea. The court was impressed by Martin

Lawton and Yeoman was found guilty on two counts of cruelly terrifying a zebra finch and one of causing unnecessary suffering. He was fined £1,100 and ordered to pay £2,500 costs, which was a good result for those days and, of course, without precedent.

Later cases featured a chap who was keeping cobras, mambas and vipers in his garage, and another who sold me a beaded lizard while being secretly filmed by ITV. Beaded lizards are CITES II and the only venomous lizard apart from the Gila monster (also CITES II). From Mexico mainly, they bite, hang on and chew in defence, rather than strike for food as a snake does, but with its rattlesnake-type venom a fully grown beaded lizard could kill a man.

Regardless of CITES or other classifications, international laws, treaties, accords or any kind of formality on which authorities might agree, there will always be somebody who will sell you a beaded lizard or a green mamba in a plastic box for cash. It's the way of the world. There are arguments, too, about how worthwhile it is for people like me to stop them. There are probably rather more beaded lizards being bred in captivity, occasionally biting their keepers, than there are in the wild. We might argue that it's not natural, keeping an animal like that well fed, in the ideal climate, secure from predators, but we have to ask what the beaded lizard might think about it.

Anyway, whatever the rights and wrongs, I was gradually becoming a malcontent at the RSPCA, unhappy with the big-company politics and management protocols that always seemed to work against we front-line operators. I felt that there was not enough support for me or the unit and, alone and palely loitering as I so often seemed to be, I felt I was battling but losing. What could I do? Was I firing at the right targets? Was I making any lasting difference to anything?

That was when I had the idea of going freelance. I would set up a training company. I would give others the benefits of all my experience. Instead of just me and the RSPCA SOU, I could equip the Europeans who were just as motivated but with much less know-how on how to get in among the evil-doers. Yes, that was the answer, Europe, and we could go and live there. So Denise and I began looking for a place where we could do training, and offer hospitality, in an area strong on wildlife. We got very excited about it.

We found the place all right, in the French Pyrenees, and set up in business offering walking holidays, bird-watching and so on, while I finalised my plans for the Spamer School of Skulduggery. Then I was ordered to a medical.

I had been working undercover at Appleby New Fair in Westmorland, the most important UK gypsy gathering of the year. It always used to begin on the Thursday a week after Epsom Derby Wednesday, which gave the horse-drawn caravans time to trot up the A1 and across the A66. They've moved the Derby to a Saturday but the Fair has stayed where it was. Not that the Fair itself is much like it was. Yes, there's some horse trading, and they wash the animals in the river, and there's the occasional wedding. The ancient fairs up and down the country always used to attract gypsy dealers, showmen and fortune tellers. Now they're mostly just funfairs like Nottingham Goose, if they're there at all. The biggest remaining annual week's gypsy conference and piss-up is Appleby and it has degenerated and attracted a new set of dealers and traders. It's reached the point where you hear the old Romanies say they're not going to come any more, because it's been spoiled by the crooks and the hooligans.

These were the very boys I was after when I went to the Fair of 2004, not my first by any means but the first one I'd seen with armed police. There were rumours of scores being settled, guns being acquired on city streets by warring factions, and the whole thing was going to kick off. I was looking for wild-caught finches, not a gun battle, and on the first day I bought some. The next day I was out for more, and hoping to gatecrash a cockfight, when I went down with a bad allergic reaction. I should have given in and gone home but I stayed, it got worse, and I finished up taking a week off work with a chest infection. When I returned to the office, my boss Barry sent me to the doctor.

The doctor pointed out that I had a long record of suffering from very extensive hay fever symptoms. I replied that I'd never taken anything like the time off that the symptoms justified, but that wasn't what he meant. He wasn't attacking my attendance record.

'This is an allergic reaction, Chief Inspector Spamer.'

'Yes, doctor, I know.'

'And you are allergic to … ?'

'Animals. Well, not all animals. Only the ones with fur, feathers, hair, er, you know. And I take cartloads of antihistamines. Just that the horses charging about at Appleby, with all that dander and dust, and the hot weather, it, well …'

The doctor looked at me as if I was as mad as my medical record suggested. He didn't bother to ask why a man who was allergic to animals should pursue a career in the prevention of cruelty thereto. He just said he was signing me off work and further steps would have to be considered. I couldn't argue, nor could I understand. When I was clearing my desk, I said to one of my colleagues that I was being sent on gardening leave because of my allergy. Oh, he said, they're frightened you'll sue them.

So, after 27 years of not suing them, I was compulsorily retired on medical grounds. I wasn't ready to jump but I was pushed. My plans for my academy were not ready and the wonderful World Wide Web was producing absolute zero in terms of Pyrenean holiday bookings, so wasn't I glad when the BBC turned up with a programme idea. I was to be filmed showing what I knew to be true, that there is always a way around the animal laws. I was to buy venomous snakes illegally in the UK, and show how you can go abroad, to Germany and Holland in particular, and buy whatever you want and bring it home to UK-on-Sea.

The loophole in the law is that, while it is illegal to be in unlicensed possession of a dangerous animal under the terms of the Act, it is not illegal to transport it. Also, if you have a licence to own a pet shop, you can keep pretty well any animal temporarily, if it is in transit to a zoo for instance, or an authorised collection. Needless to say, this slackness in the law is an open invitation to some dealers in venomous snakes. Snakes are easy to transport, easy to hide, easy to keep alive, and there is an inexhaustible market. Hundreds and hundreds of snakes and juvenile dangerous reptiles come into the UK every year. If the customs stop the courier at a port of entry and find a Gaboon viper in the luggage, it's part of an errand being run for a certain pet shop. Or, it goes through the green channel anyway.

The two big reptile fairs in Europe are at Nijmegen and Hamm, and Nijmegen was coming up soon. I put out a few feelers around my contacts in the snake fraternity and called also on my old friend and colleague, Jim of the SSPCA, my Scottish equivalent as was, running their version of the SOU. Jim, an investigator of the highest class and supremely professional, was rather stretched to say the least at that time but his department was about to be given a 100% increase, from one man to two, and he was interested in a group of Scots dealers who would, he thought, be going to Nijmegen.

I picked Jim up in Rotterdam and we drove off to recce the Nijmegen fair, opening the next day. It was to be held in a sports centre, not a very big one, and I'd been there before anyway so it wasn't much of an exercise. More to the point, it was the Dutch Queen's birthday, much celebrated with street parties and a great excuse for a wingding, so we joined in the fun not realising that everything started late the day after, including the car park where our transport was locked in. We were anxious to get to the fair early. My experience of it was similar to being in a football crowd, having to go the way everyone else went, so to do any dealing and filming we needed the space we hoped earliness would give us.

After running around like the fly with the blue posterior, we found a taxi driver who had not taken Her Majesty's birthday as seriously as the rest of Holland and we got to the sports centre just as it was opening. We made straight for the snake hall, a room about 30 feet square with, I was surprised to see, a security man on the door. Someone must have clicked on the pandemonium that could be caused by an escaped rattlesnake on the floor of a small room with 80 people in it, plus many more snakes in boxes on the tables onto which people might be trying to jump. Now the security guard would only allow customers in a few at a time.

There were seven or eight stall holders with trestle tables, for all the world looking like the village produce show or the farmers' market in the church hall. Instead of cakes and jars of marmalade and a couple of ladies from the Women's Institute, here were spitting cobras, Gaboon vipers and puff adders, ranging in size from babies a few inches long to the full-grown adults. While the Scots dealers Jim was watching put in an order for five puff adders to be delivered, we expressed a lot of interest in one particular Egyptian cobra because the vendor said it was wild-caught, which rather set the thought processes going. Here was a snake which, a few weeks before, had been making its living by an oasis in the Sahara, or maybe on some scrubland or savannah in any one of 20 or more African countries, or maybe it was used to hanging around a village in Saudi where there were chickens and rodents. All of a sudden it had been snatched up, put in a box and sent to Holland in April. No wonder it was off its food. It was far too thin for a healthy specimen, a very slim and scrawny 5 feet of cobra reputed to inflict a quick and painless death. Probably this one, in such poor condition, wouldn't have been quite up to a fatal dose although they do keep a hold in the bite, giving extra time for the venom to flow.

Jim managed to get some video pictures of me buying this cobra for €100, including the vivarium that I planned to lock into a metal container bolted to the floor of my car. We could have bought 20 or 30 more venomous snakes if we'd wanted, and every time the same number of questions would have been asked about our experience in keeping them, our knowledge of feeding and watering, our facilities for their comfort and well-being, where we were taking them and whether we planned to serve them that night roasted with barbecue sauce.

The BBC team wanted an interview with me, which was simple enough, and to film the cobra displaying its hood, which was slightly more difficult in an hotel. Egyptian cobras are ever quick to display, which is one reason why they are popular with snake charmers but Jim and I had no qualifications as charmers on a hotel room carpet so the BBC had to make do with filming the cobra through the clear Perspex sides of its tank.

That night we went back to England on the ferry and drove straight through Customs at Hull, which was just as well. We had a perfectly good story in case we were stopped – we were taking the snake to my pal George, licensed pet-shop owner – but a combination of sea sickness and Jim's bottle of single malt had made both of us reluctant to converse. We got to George's place in West Yorkshire and put forward our serpent for the great man's verdict. He took it from its tank with his ultra-sophisticated professional deadly-snake-handling equipment, a bent bit of coat-hanger wire. Having secured its head by pinning it down with a wooden ruler he must have nicked from school, he examined it and pronounced it half starved, then passed it to me to hold. While the BBC filmed me I could feel its ribs and backbone. Later, George began a force-feeding programme with a dead mouse.

George is another Bryn; not even in the slightest detail does he look the part. You might not look at him anyway, because your first impression would have told you that he was likely to come across and dot you one. If you did look, you would see someone who perhaps might have played scrum half for Leeds Rhinos since he was a baby, not tall but with muscles on his muscles. I bet he used to be in the special forces, you might say, or a circus strongman, or one of those blokes who drives cars over cliffs in the films.

I don't think George ever played rugby professionally but he claims to have done all those other things, and it was his circus connections which led him into the animals trade. In those days, before the Dangerous Animals Act, the only requirements for a successful importer of exotics were the know-how and the contacts. Regulation hardly existed but George, for all his forbidding exterior, has a heart as hard as Turkish delight when it comes to anything with four feet or wings or, more accurately, any non-human animal held captive. He feels the same whether it's CITES 1 or next door's stick insect, and this was always a great help to me when I urgently needed board and lodging for a rescued animal. The zoos, by and large, are not interested if it's a common species or if they already have some. With George, no matter what, there is always room at the inn.

George's signature dish is the one he uses to wash his reptiles. Whether it's a frog, a lizard, a snake or whatever, if it will fit in his dish he will fill same with warm water and then gently scrub and rub until his subject is as clean as could be. He'll dry it with the nearest tea towel and hold it up, like an expert on The Antiques Roadshow admiring a piece of Fabergé, and speak the immortal words: 'What a belter. What a belting animal'.

A chap living in a flat had a puff adder and a full grown gaboon viper. Well, they were both full grown, as big as I've seen, five or six feet long with girth in ample proportion like a man's thigh, which in snake terms made them obese and unhealthy. Rolf Harris and his Animal Hospital team were at RSPCA Manchester at the time and they heard about these snakes and wanted to film them. George had built a very secure place for them, like a small roofless room inside an ordinary room, but the TV people wouldn't go in. Their risk assessment had come out as too risky. This apparently didn't apply to George and me, so while the camera operators poked their noses over the wall, we went in to move these giant snakes into transport cases for their journey to a permanent home.

They were too big for George's normal piece of bent coathanger padded with masking tape. He wouldn't use proprietary snake tongs because he said they might damage the snake, so he made a longer, stronger version of his coathanger out of a bit of flat metal rod. In we went, me second, and the first thing George did was light up a massive cigar. I thought this must be a new snake charming trick. He and his ex business partner Pat were legends in the snake world for their handling. Pat would put his hand inside a sack of cobras and pull them out one by one. George wasn't quite that legendary but he certainly had the knack. The cigar wasn't part of it, though. He said it was simply that if he was hit by one of these snakes, considering he'd recently had a triple heart bypass, he wanted to die smoking a big cigar. I looked up at the cameraman and the sound engineer as I cradled most of a fat gaboon viper in my arms. They looked like I felt. If only I'd had a camera too.

Back with the BBC again, that was half the appointed task complete. I now had to show that I could do much the same thing here in the UK. I'd been taking various phone calls from contacts and I was soon led to a man in Leeds who rang to tell me he had several different venomous snakes for sale, or would have shortly. He would ring me when he was ready, probably with a puff adder and a Gaboon viper. I didn't have his number so had to wait, and suddenly it was all happening. I got the message: next Thursday, M62, Hartshead Moor Services, eastbound, phone boxes, 9pm. We were there, the BBC and I, in the afternoon, with cameras, Emma the presenter, Andy the producer, security man, sound man, the lot. They were going to operate largely from inside a van which had a good view of the phone boxes but as the time drew near it was another van which caught everyone's eye. It was parked away from every other vehicle, with the door open, and the driver kept getting out and heading for the bushes behind the phone boxes, where he crashed about doing we knew not what, then went back to his van, then came out and did it again. This was not conducive to a smoothly running sting.

My man turned up on time, a tall fellow in dark clothing, hood up, scarf over lower face. We had a chat about the difficulties of a snake-keeper's life. He was scornful of the Dangerous Wild Animals Act, a tissue-paper sham as far as he was concerned, and would I be interested in any more snakes because he would be able to get me anything I wanted. I said I would be, but meanwhile here was the £150 he wanted for the puff adder. I counted it out slowly in front of him for the benefit of the camera, thinking all the while that it was extortion. I was being ripped off. The price was about three times what I should have been paying on the black market for a puff adder.

This man had been jittery throughout our dealings and I could feel him getting more so as our unexpected guest wrestled with his demons in the bushes near by. With nervous glances in the direction of the noise, my dealer passed me the vivarium, picked up the sports holdall he'd brought it in, said he'd like to introduce me to his girlfriend and disappeared. I switched my hidden recorder to transmit and told the BBC team that I thought we'd lost him. Searches around the service station confirmed it, which was disappointing for me as I still had no idea where to find him, but the TV people were happy. They'd got their programme, it could be transmitted to a shocked public, and Nijmegen Fair would be on next year just the same, and my man from Leeds would still be in business along with dozens of others.

Probably the only real beneficiary was the puff adder. It would be domiciled in peace and fine comfort with George, for months if necessary until he found a home for it, a zoo probably, and like the Egyptian cobra it would never go hungry again.

Chapter Eleven

A MEAT AND LIVESTOCK COMMISSION IN GREECE

In a pig breeding and slaughtering set-up in Ioannis, north of Athens, the electric stunner wasn't working. Like a pair of tongs touching each temple, this type of stunner is supposed to render the animal unconscious, painlessly, before its throat is cut. If the tongs are out of order, the pig knows all about the knife. It can see it and feel it, and this pig did. It had already been beaten with sticks to force it into the crush cage. The slaughtermen seemed to think it was a matter of pride, to show who was the master, the he-man or the pig, and so much was this the purpose of the exercise that the death of a single pig could take ten minutes. This was a show which would run and run.

In Thivas, north-west of Athens, in the municipal abattoir there, after the slaughtering had finished, sheep and goat carcases lay about the place, none of them with the wound in the skull which shows a humane killer has been used. The veterinarian on duty, a podgy man in his fifties, insisted that the animals had been shot with a captive-bolt gun. If he was right, this must have been a special Greek type of self-healing gun which left no mark on the animal. In fact, the only equipment in this filthy, stinking hole, swimming in blood, were the electrical hoists for raising the carcases into a position convenient for butchering. Surrounding the Thivas municipal abattoir was the Thivas municipal rubbish tip on which a few of the local ragamuffins were scavenging. Occasionally, one of these poor folk would walk off the tip into the slaughterhouse, begging, and be given a plastic bag of offal.

Next day, at 5.30am, about 20 goats and 15 sheep waited outside the place. Very little attempt had been made to clean up from the day before, or the week before come to that. Cobwebs, dirt, dried blood, excrement, bits of rubbish blown in from the tip, it was all there. Three slaughtermen, ignoring such everyday matters as dung on the floor and blood caked on the walls, had long knives in their belts and strode about, while sheep and goats peered around the corner looking to see what was next. What they saw was a sheep dragged over to the blood drainage channel. One man knelt on the sheep, another sliced its throat open. Blood spurted out in a fountain. While this animal kicked its last nerves away, the next was brought over and laid next to it, or on top of it. Slice, spurt, kick, next, just the way it used to be done years ago. Soon there were two dozen dead animals laid in a line, and all except the first had watched its fate enacted before its own eyes, in advance.

In Soufli, northern Greece, there were the usual macho men strolling about with their knives when an old pick-up arrived with a bull and two cows in the back. These were killed with a humane bolt gun; the bull in the pick-up, the cows in the abattoir. A little green van turned up with a nanny goat and her two kids, hog-tied. A man carried the kids in, one in each hand, left them lying near the blood drain, and went back for the mother. With the nanny watching, he slit the throats of her two kids and then dealt with her.

Another open-topped farm truck came, with ten pigs. They were making a row, as pigs will do when moved, and carried on making it as they were herded inside the abattoir. One of the slaughtermen had a humane killer but instead of shooting the pigs between the eyes, which drops them stone dead, he did it behind an ear, which does not. He shot them with as much care and attention to accuracy as a Hollywood cowboy might, firing his Colt 45 while sheltering behind a wall and hoping to hit whoever's coming down the street at him.

Soon there was a scene of blood and mayhem which could not be equalled by the most imaginative artist after a fortnight's researching in Hell. Half-conscious pigs, having taken one or more terrific whacks behind the ear, were wandering about, squealing, slipping and sliding, trying to find a way out of this damnation, wading in the blood of their brethren which had been caught and throated and left to die where they fell. One pig, gullet slit wide open, refused to die and went into a spin, literally, getting tangled in a hosepipe, whirling around on the ground bathed in its own and others' blood, winding the hose around itself like some horrific parody of a forkful of spaghetti in tomato sauce except the sauce was going everywhere. This was a big pig, too big to go near in its death throes, so until the spinning stopped all waited and watched, including the two men who were tiling a wall about 10 feet away.

Bryn and I got into all these places posing as mature English students attached to Athens University, with our credentials written in Greek on official-looking paper and with a false ID provided by the Hellenic Animal Welfare Society. We didn't understand any Greek and without exception this was a good thing. Any interrogator soon gave up and let us do what we liked, filming, taking still shots, they didn't care, and sometimes they acted up for us, waving their knives and shouting. We didn't know what they were saying but we knew what they meant.

Our film was shown on Greek and UK television and the report went to the Greek Embassy in the UK as well as to our own government and the European authorities. We had several letters from the Greeks, thanking us for our efforts and promising action, and eventually one came which said that special financial aid had been granted to abattoirs which did not meet legal requirements, to upgrade facilities and educate staff. Furthermore, over 50 abattoirs which could not be updated had been closed permanently. The situation would be monitored continuously from then on.

Some years later, British sheep were going to a Dutch dealer called Van Veen, in a small town called Zuilichem not far from The Hague. From there the sheep were going to Greece. The British government's attitude was that once the sheep had spent a few days at Van Veen's place, they were no longer British sheep but Dutch and so could not be of any more concern. I thought they were a concern whatever nationality they happened to be and, with my SOU colleague Ian, set out to follow a Greek transporter lorry with some of these international animals on board. We'd seen British ear tags. We checked them on the ferry out from Italy, while the drivers were asleep. We knew what they were and we followed them to a farm where, presumably, they were given Greek citizenship and which, we were interested to note, was just a couple of stone's throws from Thivas.

We thought we might as well take a look and set up surveillance at the Thivas abattoir early the next morning. When they were well on with their business we sauntered up, saying or rather miming that we'd broken down, trusting that nobody there would recognise me from ten years before. We began making dummy phone calls to breakdown recovery services. When the moment seemed right, I went to the loo, fixed up my covert camera and walked into the slaughtering area. Within a few seconds a man was pointing at me and shouting 'Camera! Camera!', so I shrugged my shoulders, waved my hands about in a less than meaningful way, and left as rapidly as I could.

My filming that day might have been useless but Ian and I had both seen that the animal carcases had no injuries from a bolt gun and we couldn't see any electrical stunner gear anywhere. We dashed excitedly back to Horsham with the news that the Greeks had not changed their ways. All their promises had been empty. What we'd seen at Thivas could not have been an isolated incident. Thousands of animals were still being slaughtered in the old, unenlightened, cruel and painful way.

Previously, my work in Greece had been part of an RSPCA campaign mounted with full resources, all bells ringing and whistles blowing, but the campaign had run its course. No matter how much Ian and I jumped up and down, Greek slaughterhouse practices were no longer of interest. It was about this time that I too became of no further interest to the RSPCA, and soon after that a staffer in Compassion In World Farming (CIWF), Liam, called me to ask if I might be able to have another go at the Greek slaughterhouses. He explained that several different attempts had been made to infiltrate by various groups but they had failed. In view of the reception I had just had in Thivas, this hardly surprised me, and I told Liam that such a project might prove too difficult. Liam was quite sure I'd think of something and showed his confidence by arranging, through the highly professional and admirable Iris of Animals' Angels, for an interpreter, colleague and helper called Angela.

It's always hard anyway to mount a repeat undercover operation over the same ground. The high barrier here was to come up with a method of getting in to the abattoirs which we knew would still be leery, after all these years, of anyone from the UK with a far-fetched story. Vets, owners and politicians would fear exposure again and everyone would be on their guard. After a lot of thinking at my home in the Pyrenees, where I had been collecting bones from the local slaughterhouse to feed vultures and eagles, I had a brilliant idea. I would go to the Greek slaughterhouses asking about the relationship between contemporary farming practices, bones, and vultures.

The bird I had in mind was the lämmergeyer, aka bearded vulture, a very large bird with a wingspan 8 feet or more, which I'd seen on walks from my home. There are about 80 pairs in the French and Spanish mountains and there used to be many more, and there are small populations on Crete and mainland Greece. In fact, Greek ornithologists had recently mounted a project to see what could be done to increase numbers of a bird which would surely otherwise disappear, the few remaining often killed by poisoned bait left out for foxes and crows.

That its numbers fell to such a perilous level in the first place was at least partly due to a folk myth that it would take live lambs, drop them from a great height, then feast on the shattered remains. Some of the more gullible country folk believed stories handed down about these huge birds doing the same thing with human babies. They do drop things from a great height but these are always large pieces of dead animal. The intention is to break the bones, and in most languages that is how they get their name, bonebreaker. This is what they eat, bones, and they swallow the manageable ones whole. They are also fond of tortoises, broken open on the vulture's favourite rock.

If I was going to pose as an academic researcher into the life and times of the lämmergeyer I thought I had better find out more than I could sitting on a Pyrenee. Two of the most ancient references are in Greek history and the

Bible. Deuteronomy, chapter 14, verses 11 and 12: 'Of all clean birds ye shall eat. But these are they of which ye shall not eat: the eagle, and the ossifrage, and the osprey.'

The ossifrage, the bonebreaker, comes second in a very, very old list which also includes cuckoo, owl, pelican, cormorant, raven, kite and another well-known unclean bird, the bat. In Greek olden days, the ossifrage was said to be unintentionally responsible for the death of the poet and dramatist Aeschylus, around 456 BC. Clutching a tortoise in its talons the mighty bird, seeking a rock or a hard place on which to drop it, saw the bald head of the noted tragedian. Mistaking it for a stone, with an aim which would do credit to any dam-busting bomb aimer, the great vulture felled the poet with the tortoise and thus prevented the writing of a further quantity of Greek tragedies.

More reliably, the bird is known to rub its chest and underside on iron-rich rocks and mud to turn its otherwise dull white feathers ruddy brown. Why it does this, however, is not known. It also has a 'beard' or tufty group of white feathers under its beak, hence its other name of bearded vulture. It is indeed a vulture but looks more like an eagle or large falcon. Madame lays two eggs in mid winter and, like many of her kind, only ends up with one young. The parents try to feed the smaller of the two but unless it's faulty the larger will always push its way forward to eat most if not all that's on offer. Should the little one survive for any length of time, its bigger sibling kills it.

I began creating my new identity, as an academic conservation scientist from a fictitious organisation in Scotland, with the usual headed notepaper, fax numbers and so on, but with some serious looking questionnaires for the Greeks to fill in. Our story would be that we were investigating the causes of the decline of the lämmergeyer, one of which might be the reduction in numbers of fallen sheep and goats up on the mountain pastures. The farmers who brought their animals to the slaughterhouses would be asked about this, and we'd quiz the slaughtermen to see if they'd noticed differences in the numbers of injured animals coming in.

It all looked pretty thin. We had to rely heavily on the working man's belief that all academics are a waste of time and possibly insane, and the Greeks' belief that British academics would naturally be more so. The more peculiar the cause seems, the more willing people appear to be to credit it, so to reinforce our eccentricity I had some T-shirts and car stickers made.

With a fictitious government grant to conserve the species against changes in farming methods, wearing our 'Save the Lämmergeyer' T-shirts and driving a hire car with 'Help our bearded vultures' stickers, my Greek helper Angela and I set off for the Kassandra peninsula and a modern abattoir with a very decent chap as the veterinarian. We were not really expecting to find much animal abuse here but were road-testing our cover story and our equipment, which had been supplied by CIWF and Animals' Angels. Everything went beautifully. Our story was swallowed with all the positive certainty of a lämmergeyer with a leg bone. The slaughtering procedures we recorded were exemplars of best practice and the covert equipment functioned without hitch. With no expectations of cruelty or evidence to gather, everything worked.

Next we went to Larissa, capital of Thessalia (Thessaly), the central periphery (governmental district) of Greece, home to the ancient gods and the centaurs, where rises Mount Olympus and through whose mountain passes came Xerxes and Julius Caesar. Most of the country is a flat plain but there are mountain ranges all about. Larissa is an important agricultural hub where we should have expected an up-to-date abattoir and I watched in admiration as Angela charmed our way in to it. Being pragmatic rather than politically correct, there is no doubt that a pretty girl works wonders in this kind of situation. Almost always the target in my work is male and fairly macho with it, which is to say easily distracted by an attractive female. I had asked for my helper to be such a person and Angela was that all right, plus she was a natural actor and the holder of forthright views on animal welfare. She was perfection but, alas for our project, here was another abattoir which was well up to the mark and two whole days had gone.

They only slaughter in the early morning so we could never do more than one place a day, and our intelligence from Iris, about which abattoirs might be the bad ones, was about probabilities, not certainties. Our routine immediately established itself: up at 4am, finish researching and filming by 8, drive all day to the next place, eat, sleep, up at 4. CIWF had hired me for a five-day exercise. This was Day Three and a town called Trikkala, also in Thessalia. There was pressure from CIWF to come up with some results and this was getting to Angela. She was having doubts about our story. Trikkala wasn't lämmergeyer country, she said, and it wasn't going to work. She had a point. Trikkala was not actually in the mountains but it was, according to my studies, within range of the birds, which have enormous territories and will fly vast distances to find their bones. In any case, it was the only story we had and it was doing us well so far.

Once more the lovely Angela charmed and flirted our way in, and this time there was a clear prospect of success. We could see no signs of stunning gear anywhere and the carcases from the first round of slaughtering had no captive-bolt wounds. Beside the drainage point on the floor was a long, low bloodstained table, not unlike the benches traditionally used for pig sticking, and around the corner was a holding pen full of sheep and goats. I had a quick word with Angela. As soon as they looked like starting up again, in we would march to the slaughter room waving our questionnaires.

Sure enough, number one big guy with very long knife finished his coffee and cigarette and was ready for business. A sheep was dragged towards him. Simultaneously, at the moment my finger pressed the record button, in walked a man who was clearly office, not shop floor, saying something in Greek which stayed the hand with the knife. We were ushered away, no option. This was the manager, late for work today, and we were on his premises without his permission or foreknowledge. He was annoyed, very annoyed, and we were kicked out in a flurry of loud, emphatic, hand-waving Greek, which I took to mean something like 'Hit the road, Jack, and don't you come back no more', which linguistic intuition Angela confirmed as we drove away.

Kalambaka is a historic heart of Greek Christianity, world famous for its 24 monasteries built on top of the rock pinnacles of Meteora, and other fabulous churches by the source of the River Pinios and below the Pindus mountains. We reached there mid afternoon, having been cut rather short in Trikkala, so had some time to wander around this spectacular spot. Later, Angela chatted up the hotel manager, telling him about our research and our hopes of finding suppliers for feeding sites. He was most forthcoming, telling us when the local abattoir began work and that we should be very careful not to take cameras with us.

Why not? Well, two Englishmen from an animal welfare group had been to Greece years before and publicised the abattoirs' lack of proper equipment, how they didn't use electric stunners and all that. There had been ructions locally and nationally but they wouldn't give up their traditional methods just because some interfering English wanted them to, and though the government closed 50 and more slaughterhouses they opened again soon afterwards. That was the trouble with Europe. Too many petty regulations. Next thing, they'd be telling him his retsina was 2% too cloudy, or 2% not cloudy enough. Anyway, no cameras if we were going to the slaughterhouse, or we might end up being slaughtered ourselves and hung up with the sheep, ha, ha.

We were there at 5.30 next morning and had to hang around until the manager came. Half an hour went by and he still hadn't turned up so I had a bit of a wander. Inside, the place looked exactly like yesterday's, and the similarity continued when an angry manager, with a fruitlessly fast-talking Angela in tow, came charging in demanding to know what we were doing there. Within a minute or two we were off site and wondering when our luck was going to break. Tomorrow was Day Five, our going-home day. I rang Liam and asked for an extension. Like the senior police officer giving the maverick detective just 24 more hours to solve the crime, he agreed.

South of Lamia, at Atalándi there was an abattoir that represented our last chance of gathering any evidence and I was not happy. Angela said she had a long-standing evening engagement to keep near Athens but would certainly be back in time. As the time would be 4.30am, I had my doubts. Our camera had been playing up all week, chewing tapes. The auguries were not auspicious.

The morning came and no Angela. By the time she did arrive, and we'd had a frantic drive to the slaughterhouse, they'd nearly finished. Disaster loomed. They had had a shipment of sheep from Romania and there were only half a dozen left. On our side of the balance, the men had taken a break so we had a few moments to compose ourselves. This was fortunate as I now noticed that the camera was dangling from a couple of thin wires. Terrific. Our last hope, the last few minutes of the last day and the blasted equipment was falling to pieces. I ran to the car and tried to effect repairs while Angela gave me useful encouragement through the window. Thanks to my trusty Leatherman I soon ran back with a non-dangling camera, cursing all designers and manufacturers of cheap and shoddy equipment everywhere.

What followed was, as the sports commentator put it, déjà vu all over again. I'd seen it at Thivas and other Greek abattoirs years before; I'd seen it in Spain before that. The sheep were led in one by one and held over the drain in the floor while their throats were cut, and all but the first watched its companions die in this cruel way. Nothing had changed, not since I was last there, not for thousands of years since a man realised he could make a knife out of metal and sharpen it.

Plus points were that we'd got the film we wanted, and our elaborate but flimsy story had stood its tests. One lesson learned was to keep working hard on my cover stories, always remembering that, when you're fooling some of the people all of the time, or all of the people some of the time, it's a good idea to be crazy because it's more believable that way. Another lesson was to buy my own kit and become a complete, reliable package for hire. A third was to work wherever possible with colleagues who have had undercover experience or, if not, to make sure that they fully understand the implications and mutual accountabilities which rule out long-distance evening liaisons mid-project.

These worthy resolutions were soon eclipsed by a fourth: never get in a car with someone who drives Greek-style. Charged up with the adrenaline of the successful completion of a difficult task, Angela decided to leave the abattoir yard with a flourish. Had her flourish been a few miles an hour faster, our car would not have grounded as she reversed over a 25-foot cliff but would have hurtled right over the edge. As it was, we hung there like the closing scene of The Italian Job. Our gently rocking, critically balanced car had just enough forward weight to allow us to climb out and, while Angela stood in mortified silence, I went into the slaughterhouse and beckoned the men out.

The tavernas of Atalándi would ring with laughter for a month. The mad English professor of vultures and his glamorous assistant, having been poised for the drop, had to be rescued by the abattoir workers with a rope and a 4 x 4. I didn't mind the embarrassment and nor did Angela really, as it soon became clear to her that the car reversing was my fault. What I did mind was having to betray our rescuers when all they were doing was earning a living as their fathers and grandfathers before them. The lack of regulation and refusal to invest in proper equipment was not their responsibility.

Perhaps I shouldn't have worried. Our pictures and a report appeared in a CIWF magazine but I don't suppose for one minute that any action was taken as a result. So, our friends in Atalándi will still be cutting throats and, over a glass of wine in the evening, they'll be saying 'Do you remember, when the English came, and we had to pull that car … ?' and laughing until the tears fall.

Chapter Twelve

MAD REINDEER DISEASE

Why would hundreds of reindeer be thundering around and around inside a wooden corral, charging flat out for ever in a continuous circuit, seeking a freedom which was not there? Had they been domestic farm animals like sheep or cattle, they would have accepted their lot. Fenced in, they would have looked for something to eat or somewhere to lie down. But these were reindeer. Reindeer are not farm animals. They are wild. They roam the wilderness according to their instincts, and their instincts now were telling them to run, run, run away, run anywhere, just run.

How I came to be there, in Norwegian Lapland, with a herd of reindeer careering around at full pelt, is a story of pressure. The reindeer has always had pressures, naturally. It has predators like the wolverine, Gulo gulo, aka glutton, the largest of Europe's pine marten/weasel family, which in the summer is a voracious devourer of carrion and small mammals. In the Arctic winter, when many of its customary prey disappear from view, the wolverine feeds itself and its family almost entirely on reindeer and will sometimes kill more than it needs at the time, to fill the pantry for later. When spring comes, so the brown bear's fancy too turns to reindeer meat. There aren't very many bears in Norway but they are on the increase. Luckily for the reindeer, there are no wolves any more.

The European reindeer, Rangifer tarandus, mostly eats one thing: so-called reindeer moss, which is actually a lichen. It looks like a low tangle of branches of miniature grey-green seaweed and grows successfully where light is short and there is little warmth. Hardly anything else eats it. Although people use it for flower arranging and make a thickening powder from it for cooking, it would seem that the reindeer evolved simply to eat the lichen and feed the wolverine.

In ancient times the Lapps, nomads from Mongolia, gradually driven into less and less hospitable places, eventually ended up where, at the time, nobody else wanted to be. Some of the Lapp tribes went hunting and fishing. Some, like the Sámi, looked at the clumsy, galumphing, docile reindeer and saw in it a constant source of food, clothing and tenting, and so grew that primitive kind of beneficial relationship between Man and Nature which used to be everywhere and now is hardly anywhere.

Lapland was never a country, only an area. Other folk, concerned with politics, religion and economics, drew national boundaries, disputed them, redrew them but always respected, or took no notice of, the Lapps who continued to roam and follow the migrating reindeer across their own tribal bits of northern Norway, Sweden, Finland and Russia as far as the White Sea. In September, each extended family would kill the first reindeer and make a stew out of select cuts from the back. The tongue, the offal and joints of reindeer sirloin would likely be sold at the local market and the rest of the beast would be butchered and salted down for the winter. When the weather was favourable, some of the salted meat would be hung out to dry, making an almost imperishable source of nourishment. As and when the family needed more meat, another reindeer would supply.

Then came modern civilisation. Cities wanted more hydroelectric power. The people of Norway, Sweden and of other countries farther away began to take holidays in the Arctic, in reindeer country or, as the Norwegian government puts it, 'During the past 20 – 30 years, deer populations have become important commercial and recreational resources and an important part of the wilderness experience.'

Pressure from wild predators can be borne. There is a balance in Nature which allows for it, but pressure from the greatest predator of all, Man, cannot be withstood without help. Once you're an important part of the wilderness experience, boy, you've had it unless you get some protection, and these Norwegian reindeer are the last viable herds in Europe.

Everywhere Man builds a road, a railway, a dam, a reservoir, a line of pylons or even a log cabin, the reindeer will retreat. They will not go within miles of such structures and so, as Man extends his kingdom into the last wildernesses, the amount of grazing land wild and remote enough for reindeer reduces. Migration routes are cut. The herds must share what little is left, so we have overgrazing.

Nature compensates by reducing the birth rate but can't keep up with Man's careless greed, and the inevitable follows: culling. There is insufficient food for the reindeer, so we must reduce their numbers. Why is there insufficient food? Because there are too many reindeer in too small a space. Er, just a minute …

So far, so normal. Norwegian reindeer numbers came down from around 60,000 in 1960 to 30,000 in 2000; the forecast is 15,000 in 2020. The same story of habitat pressure has been repeated in all sorts of wildlife species all over the world; nothing out of the ordinary in that. Then, suddenly, came something entirely unlooked for. The people of the West, overweight on too much of everything and worried about their heart attacks, discovered that reindeer meat is low in fat and cholesterol and high in vitamin E. This essential vitamin, only discovered relatively recently and not yet fully understood, is widely available in vegetable oils, seeds, nuts, beans, whole grains, milk, eggs and oily fish, but Mr and Mrs Heart-Attack don't eat nuts and seeds. They get most of their E from its use as an antioxidant in processed foods. So, let's take the healthy option. Let's hear it for The Reindeer Diet.

The demand for reindeer meat in restaurants shot up, far outstripping any traditional method of supply. Tourist hotels and restaurants in Scandinavia put on reindeer feasts and barbecues. Elsewhere in Europe, but especially in Germany and France, reindeer became the meat of choice wherever the fat and/or fashionable gathered together. The street markets of Lapland were no match, but never mind. Reindeer are easy to kill. The wolverine finds them so, and the bear.

Besides the health kick there is also the rich countries' desire for exotica. An advertisement for reindeer pâté illustrates what I mean perfectly. 'Antlers not included,' it says, with sparkling wit. 'Arctic delicacy. Farm raised relative of Rudolph. An indulgent Christmas treat! You'll be jingling all the way to gastronomic Valhalla once you've sampled the delectable delights of Reindeer Paté! It's incredibly meaty, low in fat and deliciously different.'

At £10 or €15 for 190 grams, I'm sure it is all those things, but it's not what it says on the ring-pull tin. Reindeer are not farmed. They are herded, managed in a loose kind of way, but they are wild animals. The advert for pâté goes on to compare it favourably with beef, saying you've never heard of Mad Reindeer Disease.

While I may feel that this particular messenger does need shooting, he is not alone by any means. Reindeer was listed at Number 37 in the BBC's survey resulting in '50 things to eat before you die'. Shark was number 33. And guess what? They used the same witty joke about Rudolph – or is it with an F? 'When Rudolf and friends are not at the helm of Santa's sleigh they can also be found on a Scandinavian plate.' I can't imagine a group of reindeer, fictional or real, at the helm of anything, and sleighs don't have helms, but no matter. 'Reindeer is a regular all-rounder in the northerly reaches of Europe, such as Norway, Sweden and Finland (otherwise known as Lapland). Reindeer stew is seldom off the menu and, if you're feeling brave, reindeer tongue and hearts are also said to be delicacies. In other parts of the world, smoked reindeer is becoming increasingly available. Its strong, gamey, distinctive flavour is very rich in nutrients and doesn't require any fancy seasoning beyond pepper, all-spice, bay leaves and salt.' If that whets your appetite, supplies can be obtained via various websites.

A national UK news service suggested reindeer sandwiches. 'Exports of reindeer meat are becomingly increasingly popular across Europe, with reindeer meat sandwiches even popping up in the UK's favourite Swedish furniture shop,' the story ran. 'Don't opt for traditional meatballs but instead choose a reindeer meat sandwich and enjoy the many benefits of this low fat meat.' The young meat is preferred. Like veal, it's without the fat that comes with overwintering and age.

So, how far up the food chain would the real villains be? The people causing the demand, the reindeer eaters, probably don't realise that there is a problem. The Laplanders, the Sámi, could argue that they're only doing what they've always done, except more of it. Their way of life is very likely doomed anyway, so why not take what they can while it's there? Somewhere in the middle are the people who turn reindeer into pâté and Wiener schnitzel and take the money, but what's wrong with that?

Dyrevernalliansen, the Norwegian Animal Welfare Alliance, was only formed in 2001. It takes on specific issues, unencumbered by the politics and procedures which long-established organisations tend to build up for themselves, like the RSPCA or possibly Norway's equivalent founded in 1859. The staff at Dyrevernalliansen wanted to tackle the reindeer question and got in touch with their more experienced German colleagues of Animals' Angels, who contacted me.

Soon I was sitting in an office in Oslo talking to a very personable and single-minded young woman called Live (pronounced 'liv') Kleveland. She was a lawyer who'd given up the law, and the money, to follow her passion for animal welfare. Totally committed and a vegan by diet, I could sense that her zeal might collide with the usual need in my kind of work, for calm, disinterested professionalism in the face of animal horror. Live had collected information on times and places where Sámi could be expected to be holding their reindeer gathers, traditionally a twice-yearly event with all sorts of tribal significance.

This information had come from various different quarters and was of unknown quality. I wasn't too happy either with Live's plan, which had the virtue of simplicity but not a lot else going for it. She and I would turn up at a Sámi gathering, where we would announce ourselves. 'We are representatives of Dyrevernalliansen and our business as monitoring the Sámi treatment of reindeer, thank you, and here are our video cameras.' The success of such a venture would depend entirely on the amicable co-operation of those about to sell reindeer into the meat-processing industry with, in the background, the meat-trade dealers and slaughterhouse owners. I knew Norway to be a highly civilised country but, I wondered, was that civilisation universal?

I suggested an alternative stratagem, a covert deception, but Live would not have it. She was quite certain that her approach was the right one, and that was that. A young English volunteer called Richard turned up with two hats, something like bee-keepers' hats with full veils around. These, he explained, were essential on the tundra at this time of year, when the flies following the reindeer were like midges on the west coast of Scotland but 50 times worse.

Live was also quite sure that I needed a splendid array of vegetarian curries in the local Indian restaurant, in the company of herself and the other senior people there – Ingrid, Christine, Lill Ann and Adeleid – and in this she was perfectly correct. I didn't know quite what we'd be living on for the next week, 250 miles north of the Arctic Circle, but it wasn't going to be like this.

We were on the aeroplane early next morning, destination Alta, the main town of Finnmark, which is the county of Norway with the smallest population and the largest area. Live told me about the cave paintings, the hotel made of ice and the Cuban bar which seemed to comprise entirely the fleshpots of Alta, but I was hardly listening. Below us was the most fantastic vista of fjords and forests, with the autumn producing a thousand different shades of red and gold among the trees. This too was Scottish, a Scottish scene but grander, on a totally different scale, beyond anything I'd ever seen in any other wild country. We left the plane in bright sunshine, hot it was too, and I thought that somebody had got it wrong about the far frozen north. I was in baking sun, with the deep blue sea over here and endless forest over there, when I had been expecting dull, featureless, chilly tundra. My first hint that sunshine paradise might be temporary came when I noticed that the tyres of the little hatchback hire car had metal studs in them.

Live was never off her phone, trying to pin down a Sámi meeting place, and at last she thought she had it. We were to head for a region called Masi on Route 93, a perfectly decent road in the style of a UK A-road single carriageway with nice smooth tarmac. Live nevertheless treated it with great suspicion, slowing down and speeding up every few seconds as if she might encounter reindeer crossing at 50-yard intervals, which of course she wouldn't because reindeer avoid roads.

We stopped for a bite of lunch. Live had brought a week's supply of her mother's vegan pâté, which suited us a great deal better than the tinned one mentioned earlier, and home-made cookies. It's pretty hard being a vegan anywhere – if you're not going to resort to pills and supplements all the time, your food takes a lot of thinking about – but Live said it's especially hard in Norway, a country of hunters and fishermen who are big on the kinds of protein that run and swim and fly, and a country where anything out of the ordinary is very expensive.

I didn't want hurt Live's feelings so, rather than go into lengthy explanations I just said 'I'll drive', which is how I came to do 99% of the driving that week. Live did the first 1% and I did the rest. After asking the way from several farmers and consulting maps which really didn't have our sort of detail on them, we decided that this rough and narrow track, hardly wide enough for our eurobox hatchback, was it. Live said something about 'only 18 kilometres to go' and off we set. We would never have made it in anything other than the best conditions, which is what we had, but we still had huge potholes to avoid and ruts which could have left us grounded and helpless. At first we were overshadowed by the forest, then we broke into the kind of country I had imagined - the tundra moorland, treeless and lonely, like the high Cheviots or White Moss in Derbyshire only not so welcoming, with the greens and browns of the early autumn foliage reminding me of winter heather and bracken back home on the Yorkshire moors.

As we approached the site I could see a few of the traditional nomad's tents, which are white and called Laavu and which look something like a North American teepee except wider at the base and lower to the ground so they can tolerate the Arctic winds. A typical one can sleep eight people, Live said. Nobody can remember when a Laavu was made of reindeer hide; certainly the Sámi have had canvas since early Victorian times.

Not so traditional was the scattering of 4 x 4 jeeps and quad bikes of the latest type, but only half a dozen or so. I had been expecting a bigger meeting. There was hardly anyone about, just a few folk moving occasionally between the tents. They were not in Sámi costume but I had no doubt that was who they were, with their weather-darkened skin and distinctive facial features. Confirmation was in the massive hunting knives hanging from the men's belts in ornate sheaths. These were knives meant for business, and the men who carried them looked as if they would be highly proficient in their use.

Across from the camp was a curious wood structure in the shape of a magnifying glass – a corridor of fencing about 40 yards long leading to a circular compound about 100 yards across, and all about 6 feet high. I couldn't yet see what was happening inside the compound but I could hear it: a low, grumbling, rolling noise, like a thunderstorm on the other side of distant hills.

Live and I checked our stories. I had to defer to her; she was the local, she would know what she was doing. We would tell the Sámi exactly what we were up to and hope for a good reception. I was fairly pessimistic about the possibilities and had my own plan, which was to film as much as I could of whatever we might see while Live was talking to the Sámi leaders. Then, when we were thrown out, we'd at least have something for our trouble.

There was nobody to stop us so far, so we walked down the corridor to a small makeshift door. The whole structure had a temporary feel to it, as if it had been put up recently for a one-off purpose, and when we opened the door we realised what that purpose was. We stopped dead. I was stunned, astounded at what I saw, which was a herd of reindeer, about 250 altogether with a leading animal who was obviously the boss, charging around and around the pen. The thunder was their hooves and there was no other sound. You can watch migrating herds of wildebeest or whatever on the television, but nothing prepares you for standing next to it. There was no danger. They avoided us and stayed in their tight circle, three abreast, never colliding, willing to run until they could run no more.

They also avoided the little group of people about 90 degrees around the fence from us. These were not reindeer herders, I was further astonished to see, but a television crew: cameraman, sound engineer and a woman who must have been the producer. Perhaps this meant the Sámi were not averse to being filmed. Perhaps we had competition. Either way, I felt that Live should approach the Sámi leader straight away while I got on with my secret filming of the ever-charging herd.

It turned out that the head man was on the other side of the circle from us, which meant Live walking around while I watched and videoed some new activities in the circus ring. Some of the younger Sámi had been given a job. They would pick out an individual animal and lasso its antlers (reindeer and their close relatives the caribou are the only deer species in which the females have antlers, although the males have bigger). Depending on the size of the beast, one or two young Sámi would wrestle it to the ground when they either thrust a tube down its throat and poured some liquid in, which was presumably a worming medicine, or they used their hunting knives to put a nick in the animal's ear. These boys could tell whose deer was whose – the nicks showed ownership - and it was all done without discussion or argument. Clearly the animals were distressed. You could see it in their eyes, but it was all over in moments when the individual was released back into its circling family. Then there was one which wasn't released.

A young man and woman, in their early twenties I would say, dragged this beast from the main corral to a wire-fence compound and I followed. There were already a couple of reindeer tethered in this small pen, and they were continually charging, head down, against the wire netting, much distressed at being away from the herd and imprisoned in this way. They were shouting and bellowing in their anguish, their antlers were dripping blood and there was much blood and tissue on the fence and on the ground.

Antlers are shed and grown each year, and while they're growing they are covered in a skin called velvet which has a well-developed nervous system. Part of the function of the skin is to protect the immature antler by making the deer aware of that immaturity, which is a formal way of saying that if you bash your tender young antlers you go 'ouch!', so don't break them, in the same way we soon learn not to put our fingers in the fire. In deer farming, there is often an annual 'velvet harvest'. Antlers are cut from deer while they are still covered with the skin which, as well as nerves, holds the blood vessels for the growing bone beneath. This procedure, the harvest, during which the antlers are cut off with a bone saw, is acknowledged to cause bleeding and pain and there are regulations governing what must be done to make sure the animal doesn't suffer.

The reindeer I was watching, bashing their velvet antlers against wire mesh, were so maddened by tethering and separation from the herd that the pain no longer mattered. They were so desperate to get back to their own that they were willing to pick hot coals from the fire, whatever it took, while the Sámi ignored them, presumably because that was what always happened.

The couple now had their deer dragged into the pen and the young man took his hunting knife from his sheath while the woman held the animal down. With one firm movement he thrust his knife into the reindeer's ribs, aiming for the heart. I knew this was the way they did it. It's illegal in Norway but it's traditional and, when an experienced man does it, it's a quick death.

This was the old-fashioned reindeer harvest, the killing of the winter's meat. Some would be salted and dried, some frozen. A herdsman out in the woods later in the year with a frozen joint of reindeer would cut slices off it and fry it in reindeer fat. Cornflakes and skimmed milk is no breakfast for a working man in the Arctic Circle.

The young man I was watching had quite a lot to learn about anatomy; it was some minutes before the reindeer stopped kicking and struggling. I managed to get this on tape, and I filmed the poor beasts charging the fence. It was just as well I had some evidence safely collected because the Sámi head man was ready to kick us out. No matter what assurances Live gave him about fairness and reasonableness, he was having nothing to do with any animal welfare organisation, and if we cared at all about our own welfare then we had better be on our way.

I thought we shouldn't go before finding out what the TV crew was doing, so we stretched our departure slightly with a chat to them. Maybe we could benefit each other. It turned out that they were performing an anthropological study of the Sámi way of life for a television documentary programme, a reason for filming that had obviously gone down well with the head man. I thought it sounded like an excellent cover story, since I was quite sure that any more gatherings we went to would be the same as this, with the same reception to the words 'animal welfare'.

As we drove back up the track I asked Live about the legality of killing reindeer with a knife. She told me that an exception had been made for the Sámi people, provided they used a preliminary knife strike into the back of the neck, to sever the spinal cord and stun the victim. Apart from the fact that our Sámi weren't doing it, I had to tell Live that I didn't think much of her government's exemption. If the young man couldn't hit the heart first time, how would he fare with the far more difficult job of finding where the head bone's connected to the neck bone?

I'd seen something very similar in Spain some years before, where they used a knife called puntilla to do the same spinal-cord operation on cattle and, in my experience of it, they very rarely achieved success first time. Most of the animals had several wounds inflicted, and when I asked veterinary surgeons about it afterwards, they said that even if the puntilla did sever the cord, it would only paralyse the animal physically. The brain would still be working, so all sensations of terror and panic would still be there in full force.

Live had not had a good day and I didn't seem to be helping much. She's a really lovely person, highly intelligent, in complete command of her subject, but I felt she hadn't considered the potential value of lies, deceit and trickery in attaining our objective. These tools of my trade had served me well in many different countries and I was sure they would be equally effective here. Live felt compelled to tell me she was a bit of a star in Norway, often on the television as the spokesperson for Dyrevernalliansen debating animal-welfare issues with top scientific researchers, representatives of the meat trade, the transport lobby and so on. Well, we both knew that while the Sámi might live according to thousand-year-old traditions, they also had satellite dishes. I could see it was against her better nature but we agreed that from now on we would be researching for National Geographic magazine into the ancient, honourable and mysterious ways of the Sámi people, and Live would have to try to look as little like her television self as possible.

This was going to be something of a double life because Live, as herself, had already arranged an appointment for us at a slaughterhouse. She had spoken to the owner of an abattoir chain, who had said he had nothing to hide and was proud of his humane practices and modern equipment in the killing of reindeer. Our destination was in the centre of Sámi country.

The slaughterhouse manager we met was no Sámi. He was a professional slimeball, a greasy, Uriah Heep-style individual to whom even his mother must have taken an instant dislike. He certainly didn't like us being in his slaughterhouse. If it had been left to him he'd have called in the heavies and had us inverted on butcher's hooks, but it wasn't up to him. His boss had awarded VIP status to Live and we were to be shown around properly.

First sight to see was the most advanced animal transport ever, a wagon with entirely steel interior and computer-controlled air circulation, air cooling and heating, deep litter in every compartment and a computer-operated watering system. Mr Heep was justly proud of this really excellent vehicle and we were duly impressed, but things went downhill pretty sharply from then on. The reindeer had been due to arrive soon but it was postponed. Better go off somewhere, get a coffee, and come back later. After the third time this happened Live phoned her man, the owner, who spoke to Uriah, who became even more unfriendly in his special greasy way but who admitted that the reindeer were arriving at 6pm. This was bad news for us because the light would be poor for filming.

To make things worse, for our tour of the slaughterhouse we were going to have to wear standard issue disposable overalls. The hidden camera would be useless. I knew from experience that pictures taken through the overall material, thin though it is, are no good at all. As I was putting my set on I 'accidentally' broke the zip, hoping to become a secret flasher, exposing my lens at opportune moments.

At long last the wagons arrived. They were the standard two-tier livestock carriers like you notice everywhere on the roads full of sheep, not the computerised superlorry type we'd seen earlier. Maybe that was for showroom use only. The wagons were backed up to big sheds and the reindeer needed no encouragement to disembark. Beside the sheds was another wooden magnifying glass, a passageway leading to a circular pen about 6 yards across. We were allowed a peep into the passageway and there was Uriah's first set-back, a dead or dying reindeer which had obviously been there since yesterday. Orders were barked out as we were ushered away, ready to watch the perfect system working perfectly.

As the reindeer entered the 6-yard pen from the first passageway, they immediately went into their circling routine, slowed and constricted by the size of the pen, which made it much easier for the Reindeer Selection Operative to grab one and push it down the second passageway, which was a kind of travelator, a one-way conveyor with powered rollers at the sides, which forced the animal forward into a convenient position for the slaughtermen, who fitted restraints to the animals' heads.

Since some of the animals had huge antlers and some very small, this was no automatic job. It was fiddly, and a backlog soon built up. Live and I watched in total disgust as one poor reindeer had to stand for some minutes, its head fixed, watching its fellows from the herd being dispatched, bled, hoisted, skinned and jointed. Uriah Slimeball wanted to usher us away again but Live kept him talking while I tried to get some video pictures. The place was steamy, the overalls were in the way, there were deer carcases hung up and swinging around on their conveyor rails, their antlers quite capable of putting me in hospital but I did get some pictures. When we reviewed the tape later, Live was impressed. These were, she said, the first such pictures ever taken in Norway.

Uriah Heepslime took us back to his office and gave us a short lecture, the gist of which was that we had seen the finest abattoir in Scandinavia, the meat produced was of the highest quality and there were no animal welfare issues at all in the system. We had to agree that the building, the equipment and the humane-killing procedures could hardly be any better. The system would work very well if the animals were not wild and did not have antlers to get in the way. This latter thought would come to haunt me the next day.

As if to finish us off with a parting shot, Uriah described how he had seen one of the most spectacular sights of the far north: hundreds of reindeer swimming across the Altaelva, the river which runs into Altafjord, on their annual migration. He got quite poetical about this dazzling drama which he said he'd seen on a number of occasions, and rubbed it in hard about the wonders of nature and the magic of the reindeer. I guess he knew he was making Live and me feel utterly sick. It was his revenge and he enjoyed it.

Next day we drove to Skaidi, north-east of Alta, and on to Hatter, where we found a smaller version of our first gathering, with a structure made of wire rather than wood and Sámi people who were totally different. They were nice, friendly folk who, to make me feel guilty and Live more so, swallowed our cover story whole and allowed us to film openly. It was much more of a family affair, with young children and grandparents all together for their twice yearly reunion. Still, no matter how pleasant were our hosts, the reindeer went around and around.

The villains we really wanted to expose were the directors and money men behind this business but, as with most such matters, the evidence was being gathered at the sharp end, where the ordinary people were. Much the same procedures were followed as yesterday, starting with lassoing the antlers of chosen animals. This worked fine when it was the older Sámi doing it but the younger ones had to learn too, and they seemed adept at missing the antlers and catching the target by the rear legs. There followed quite a dangerous little exercise of letting the reindeer go again, because nobody would want to wrestle with a reindeer that had its antlers free.

Likewise, when it came to killing animals for their own use, when one of the elders of the tribe plunged the knife into the heart, he did it properly. The young men were not so good and the animal suffered greatly in its death throes, especially when they tried it the legal way, with a knife thrust first into the neck at the back of the animal's head. I couldn't believe that this was the officially preferred method. It was horrific. It would have been kinder to slit their throats. Had the authorities approving this law ever seen it in practice? Obviously not. Well, they would see it now, because I'd got it on tape and Live would make sure the right people came to the film show.

I realised that we were dealing here with a long tradition, the knife in the heart, and I was glad when the old man took over from the lad and showed him – for the nth time, I assumed – how to do it, but I could not see why a humane killer could not be used. In the right hands it works without fail and there is no suffering. Even the young Sámi would be effective with it. It's as near foolproof as it could be, and to hell with tradition. I did feel some affinity with these Sámi families, having spent such a large part of my own life out in the wilds, living in discomfort, getting wet and cold, often with nothing to eat, and I just hoped that all the blame for this dreadful trade would not be heaped on them while the Uriah Slimeballs got away with it, but they had to use the humane killer.

Actually, Live and I had nothing much to eat that day too, because when the Sámi invited us to lunch and we sat down with them, the dish of the day was reindeer tartare, raw fillet steak. The mixture of embarrassment and sheer horror on Live's face would have been amusing in other circumstances but not at that moment. I could see she was about to try to explain how it was possible to enjoy a full life on a diet of beans and courgettes, which I didn't think our hosts would find credible so I butted in, in English, saying we could not eat their doubtless magnificent meat because of our religion, which was Buddhism. They looked blank, not understanding a word I said, so Live spoke to them in Norwegian and, presumably, translated, still looking embarrassed because the clear implication to the Sámi was that the lovely young Norwegian lady was the disciple in faith of the rather older Englishman, and so we must be an item in every other way.

That night in the warm and dry of our hotel, we reviewed what we had and how we might get what we needed for the complete story, a loading of reindeer onto the livestock wagons. Live took two phone calls. One was from the head man who had ejected us from the first gathering, inviting us to come and watch his group doing their loading. Another was from an informant, telling her about a scheduled loading 25 kilometres away. And then we had our third option, the site we'd been at that day.

Live was keen to go to meet our first man again. I was rather less keen, anticipating what might happen if something went horribly wrong while we were filming. Uriah Slimeball had tried to usher us away from unfortunate sights. I couldn't see this guy going in for something so polite as ushering. In the end, Live and I decided to split. I'd hang around the place we'd been to today; she would go to the new place.

Settled on that, we began to consider our supper which, the barman told us, might cause difficulty. Tonight was the annual dinner of the local hunters' club, the restaurant was fully booked, gargantuan joints of meat were being roasted, and would a salad sandwich do us? Things got a bit hectic later as the bar filled with types the Americans would call rednecks, loud, macho, half cut and very interested in a pretty girl like Live. Still, we coped.

Overnight the weather turned. Outside in the darkness, snow was being whipped about by a bitter wind. Live paused to rearrange the postcards in the hotel reception so that the ones showing seal pups being clubbed were not visible, and off we set for my loading site. It was still dark when we got there at seven; we'd come early because we had no idea when the event might be. We didn't want to miss it but there were no lights, no sign of life in the camp at all. I shivered in the cold and turned back to the car to get my warm clothes, my kit of all-weather gear, only to see Live driving off with it.

Well, at least I had my bag with the camera and I had a DPM poncho (Disruptive Pattern Marking – army camouflage) but, dressed otherwise only in cotton trousers, shirt and thin pullover, I had to hope I could get my pictures before I froze solid. On my way over to check the reindeer I could hear thumping and banging, which proved to be a few escapers from the pen desperately trying to get back in. How sad and noble, I thought, when a wild animal has a chance of freedom and life, it must obey its instincts and choose a cruel death instead.

The cold was really getting to me by this time, and I had to hide. I didn't want the Sámi to find me on their campsite yet. I had no reason to be there in the dark, and certainly it wouldn't fit very well with my being a National Geographic journalist, wandering around so early in the Arctic morning wearing such unsuitable clothes. I searched for some cover. There was none. This was the desolate tundra, barren of things like comfortable bushes. I did find a little bit of scrub I could crawl under so I wrapped my poncho around me and settled down for what I hoped would be a very short wait.

Dawn broke and a grey day began. Flurries of snow flew past my hiding place. The Sámi must have decided to stay indoors in this weather until they absolutely had to come out, which would be when the transport arrived. When would that be? Not yet, obviously, not while the rest of Norway was having its mid-morning coffee. My shivering became uncontrollable, which I recognised in myself as one of the first signs of serious hypothermia. I tried to think back to my early days when I used to study and worry about such things. The shivering was a vital way to keep the body temperature up, a natural defence mechanism, but once you can't control it you only have a few hours of shivering before you run out of the muscular energy to do it.

My feet were the coldest part, then hands. If they got very much colder I'd lose the use of them. I tried testing my speech. That's a sure sign, mumbling and making mistakes in talking. And singing. I'm singin' in the rain, just singin' in the rain, what a glorious feeling, I'm happy again. Rudolph the red-nosed reindeer, had a very shiny nose. The boy stood on the burning deck, whence all but him had fled. What was I doing in bloody Lapland anyway? If I had a towel, I thought, I wouldn't throw it in. I'd wrap it around my feet. Ha ha.

At some point in this I fell asleep, or went unconscious, and the next thing I knew was waking up to the sound of gunshots. Looking back, I can see that those shots might have saved my life. At the time I was more concerned that they would shortly end it and, with the new sources of energy the body seems able to produce under such imperatives, I leaped from my hiding place, saw three hunters with guns, one of whom was aiming his rifle straight at me, whipped off my poncho and did a 'Look, everybody, I'm here' kind of crazy dance.

The hunter lowered his gun. We walked towards each other, or rather they walked and I stumbled as if pie-eyed. Like most Norwegians they had good English but unfortunately nothing I said could adequately explain what on earth I was doing, shivering under a bush in the middle of Lapland nowhere, dressed for a light luncheon at a pavement cafe in Cyprus. They decided I was as mad as the English are reputed to be, told me curtly that I was extremely lucky not to have been shot, and went on their way.

I went back to my little bush and made serious efforts not to relapse into hypothermia again. It was past mid-day so the theoretical sun was up somewhere behind the thick clouds and I suppose the air temperature must have been a degree or two warmer although still cold enough to keep the Sámi by their firesides. I saw two sea eagles fly past, and I watched a hawk owl, a bird I'd never seen before or knew much about, consume a small mammal, a vole perhaps, on top of a fence post. I did know that hawk owls like to eat lemmings and I passed a useful and wakeful half an hour trawling my memory for every scrap of information I could have written down in my answer to the question 'Describe the habitat and habits of the northern hawk owl', gave myself two out of ten and vowed to look up its Latin name when I got home (Surnia ulula ulula, named for its purring melodious trill, it says here).

Suddenly, there was activity. Sámi men hurried from their tents and got busy with the reindeer, which had been milling about in only a mild state of agitation but now, with the men in there, began their circular charge again. I began filming, openly. The Sámi believed I was with National Geographic, but they never asked themselves why a magazine would be using a movie camera, nor why the cameraman should be dressed so unsuitably. The men worked hard, shooing the reindeer from their large compound to a smaller pen, a wooden construction like the one at the slaughterhouse. A 32-ton double-deck animal transporter arrived and backed up to the pen. Older men and young women paired up in teams and each team picked a reindeer and wrestled it to the floor so that one of the younger lads, armed with a bow saw, could do the imprecise but hard work of removing the antlers.

I was stunned – again, and enough to forget, almost, that I was chilled to the marrow. This assignment was proving to be full of even more surprises than I was used to. I could see the sense in what they were doing. Reindeer without antlers would fit more numerously into the wagon, and in their panic in transit they wouldn't gore each other. Also, this was the tribesmen's last chance to harvest antlers for the tourist trade, for carving into ethnic souvenirs by their winter hearths.

The reindeer is above all a gentle creature. It asks for nothing from this world but the right to roam and some lichen to eat. You might compare it to a camel in being rather carelessly put together by Mother Nature but it has none of the camel's propensity for fighting back. These poor beasts couldn't really run in such a small space, so they tried to climb the fence to get out. It's a desperate sight, a big male reindeer trying to climb a 6-foot wooden fence. Their agitation was at a peak, I thought. Those animals which had been sawn, and those yet to be, could not have been more stressed and frightened, I thought. Then one of the Sámi men walked in with a chainsaw.

Most of the antlers were still in their velvet. There was blood everywhere, and skin, and the level of disruption increased beyond measure as the noise of the chainsaw drove these animals right out of their senses. It was a maelstrom of terror and alarm, blended with what you might call the calm professionalism of the tribesmen, who went about their business of wrestling and chainsawing as if nothing else was happening at all.

With the antlers thrown in a pile, ready to make knife handles and suchlike, the funnel was set up to force the reindeer into the wagon. By Heaven they didn't want to go but, once one of the big males went, the rest followed. Still the peak of stress had not been reached. Now they were in the most confined space they had ever seen. Such a place is completely alien to a reindeer; it's hell on earth, and they freaked out, thrashing their legs and heads about, bellowing their agony while they were driven away to slaughter.

This mixture of ancient methods and primitive attitudes to animals, with modern means such as chainsaws and cattle wagons, seemed to produce something far more horrible than the straightforward sum of its parts. Even so, I felt guilt about exposing these people, who were doing what they had always done, in a much amplified version admittedly, but they would see nothing wrong in it. I knew what they would see as wrong: some foreigner telling them lies and exposing them to a censorious and distant general public on national television, which was where my film was sure to go.

Live turned up in the car and apologised profusely for driving off with my all-weather clothing while I climbed into it as fast as I could. The next task was to drive flat out for Alta so she could catch a plane for a conference next day in Oslo. On the way she told she she'd got some good pictures of loading but they'd done it in quite a civilised way, without chain saws.

A hot bath and several coffees restored me to normality and I looked forward to a quiet evening, which was only slightly disturbed by the strange looks I was given when my three gun-toting hunters from the morning came in to the bar and saw the mad frozen English sitting in the corner. My last day was to have been spent walking in this marvellous countryside but the weather closed in and there was fog and snow, so I had to make do with a short trip to Hammerfest, fishing port, tourist resort and the most northerly town of the world.

The film I'd taken was indeed shown on television twice in the following weeks, on the main evening news and late news. An MP who saw the film asked a question in Parliament of the Ministry of Agriculture: 'What does the Minister think should be done to end the mistreatment of reindeer in the Sámi parts of Finnmark?' The Minister said he had received reports from Dyrevernalliansen and the German organisation Animals' Angels, based on the same investigation, and was 'aware of highly critical aspects of the reindeer industry that should receive attention'.

This could be interpreted as the Norwegian government promising a complete review of the reindeer industry leading to proper controls and regulations, or possibly not. Some weeks after the parliamentary question, the jury in a Court of Appeal went against the judges' recommendation and ruled that killing reindeer by stabbing in the heart was legal due to Sámi tradition, despite it being illegal according to Norwegian statute. This verdict attracted severe criticism from the Norwegian Food Safety Authority and led to another parliamentary question, this time to the Ministry of Justice: 'Does the Minister think that mistreatment of animals should be accepted simply because of tradition?'

Postscript

Dear Terry,

All sorts of good news. I have been told that our footage really shocked the Director of the Food Safety Authority and that he personally has intervened to improve conditions. The Sámi delegate at meetings between the FSA and the Ministry of Agriculture has stated officially that our film horrified him too, and that such killings are far from Sámi tradition. Also the state prosecution service is going to the Supreme Court to get that Court of Appeal verdict overturned.

This was direct action with immediate effect, which is good because before it was not even thought to be a problem. Meanwhile, Terry, a new Reindeer Act is going through our Parliament to give local authorities powers to control the exploitation of reindeer. At first it had no provision for animal welfare but we managed to get this included, with sanctions against anyone mistreating the reindeer.

However, practical results are all that matter to the animals, so our political work continues until we have evidence that the conditions are improved and the new laws are working. Also, they are considering to establish a national scientific centre for reindeer welfare.

Take care, best wishes, and keep going.

Live

Chapter Thirteen

THE SPORT OF KINGS, LORDS, GENTLEMEN AND OTHERS

Setting one animal against another has been a spectacle for pleasure and gambling ever since people found out it could be done. Bear versus dog, bull versus dog, bull and human, human and human – a fight with blood and wounds and the possibility of death carries a kind of excitement which the onlooker can find nowhere else. Now that bear-baiting is no longer the regular Sunday morning after-church entertainment it once was, opportunities for betting on an animal fight are confined in Britain to dog against dog, cock against cock and, in some Asian communities, quail against quail.

The Athenians were the ones to formalise and give status to cockfighting around 480 BC after the commander Themistocles, on his way to confront Xerxes and the Persians at Salamis, halted his forces so they could be enthused by the bravery and dedication of two cocks fighting by the wayside. After a great victory, the city state of

Athens evermore held annual cockfights, at first in praise of gods and country and later because they liked it.

The practice spread far and wide. The Romans initially thought it a bit girlie and contemptuously called it 'the Greek diversion', but came around to it and soon wives were complaining that all the family budget was being wagered at the cockpit. It may have died out in England after the Romans went, possibly was reintroduced by the Normans, but certainly was fully re-established by the reign of Henry II when it was organised by schoolmasters as a recommended sport for their pupils on holidays. Whether the masters were the bookmakers is not known for sure but they did have the benefit of the defeated and dead birds for their cooking pots. Shrove Tuesday was the special holiday and is still considered the start of the cockfighting season.

Henry VIII added the royal cockpit to his palace at Whitehall, the Stuart kings were great devotees of what had now become known as 'the royal diversion' (Queen Elizabeth I preferred bear-baiting) and Cromwell suppressed it for a while, but it blossomed into a golden era when every town of any size had its official cockpit and backstreet matches were everyday common.

An organised series of matches was called a main, and the grandest main of all happened in Lincoln in 1830. The two rivals were Joseph Gilliver, the most famous breeder of the time, and Edward Stanley, 12th Earl of Derby, great cockfighting patron and originator of the eponymous horse race. There were to be seven cocks a side, with 1,000 guineas (about £75,000 in today's money) a match and

5,000 guineas on top for the main. Gilliver won by five to two and so relieved my Lord of Derby of the modern equivalent of £600,000.

Our language still carries cockfighting terms. The battle royal was a particular type of fight in which half a dozen or more birds were set against each other at once, fighting until only one was left standing. Occasionally, in any kind of fight, a bird would give in, instinctively signifying its cowardly intentions by raising its hackle and showing the white feathers beneath.

Such sport has always attracted a curious social mix. The highest and the lowest could generally be found gathered together, although in the 1830s you needed five shillings (£17.50) to get into the public cockpit on Birdcage Walk in London, which might have put off some of the lowest. These were the last days of legal cockfighting because agitation by the newly formed RSPCA (1824) helped to bring about the Protection of Animals Act of 1835 which outlawed 'running baiting or fighting any bull, bear, badger, dog or other animal (whether domestic or wild) or for cock-fighting'. Prosecutions brought by the RSPCA under this Act eventually resulted in an unambiguous and complete cockfighting ban, which could be policed with powers of arrest, in 1849.

Cockfighting is illegal throughout the EU except in parts of France if it can be shown that they've always done it there, according to age-old tradition. There, the gallodrome is a popular place of resort. Cockfighting is legal in Pakistan, parts of India where they claim the idea originated, Thailand, Vietnam, Indonesia and various other regions of the world. It's the national sport of the Philippines, with TV coverage and on-line betting regulated by local government even though there is a law against betting on cockfights, and they run a kind of world championship.

At the time of writing, cockfighting is still legal in Louisiana, the last of the United States to keep it so. Recently, New Mexico and Oklahoma have legislated against, despite protests from the fans, protests which may seem familiar to those who have observed other aspects of the blood-sports argument.

'A lot of people will go out of business,' said James Tally, president of the Oklahoma game-bird breeders. 'Takings at a motel near here have been down $10,000 a month. At least four game-bird breeders have moved to Louisiana.'

'It's an urban versus suburban issue,' said Larry Matthews of the United Game Fowl Breeders' Association. 'Many city people have probably never seen a game bird. But they vote.'

I can't speak for the USA but in Britain cockfighting can attract some very unsavoury spectators. The main organisers are certain sections of the gypsy and gamekeeping communities who do it for the tradition and the sport. Inexcusable as that is, it never used to be a gateway to dealing in drugs and firearms and other criminal methods of paying off gambling debts, as it is now.

My adventures with the cockfighting fraternity began at the other end of the social spectrum, with a member of an old, exclusive and secretive organisation called The Oxford Club. To join – membership is strictly limited to

100 – you have to be a reputable sort of a chap, a barrister or a doctor perhaps, or a farmer or a successful tradesman, and a known breeder of the traditional types of game fowl. If there happens to be a vacancy, your name must be put forward by at least two current members.

Gambling in The Oxford Club is rare. They are purists, following the old rules, fighting for prestige and using standard steel spurs (heels) of one-and-a-half inches. Birds are trained with all the care and know-how otherwise lavished on those men and women who get their livings in the boxing ring. Game cocks do not need encouragement to fight; that comes naturally to them. To augment their instinctive aggression, their muscles are built up with exercise and special diets, their physique – feathers and comb – is streamlined to offer the minimum target for an opponent, and as juvenile trainees they are battle-hardened with leather gloves over their spurs. Non-traditional aids to victory include anabolic steroids; drug testing is so far unknown in The Oxford.

Members of The Oxford speak in code on the telephone to arrange matches. Injured birds that survive are looked after by the match host until fit to travel home. Cockpits and other gear are hidden behind false walls. Opportunities to find a chink in the circle, to find out anything which might lead to times and places and therefore to a raid on a live fight, are virtually out of the question as long as everyone keeps to club discipline.

Then along came a family butcher called William Ross, from Kelloe, County Durham. He'd been a member of The Oxford Club for 20 years but he couldn't get enough excitement in this restricted and refined fellowship and so began mixing it with the travelling people and the gamekeepers, the blood sports mob. A tip-off said that mains were being held in a barn he had, on his smallholding behind his shop. A month's surveillance produced nothing but a second tip-off suggested that there would be a main tomorrow.

Hastily, arrangements were made and a team of police and RSPCA officers was put together. The police would deal with the gamesters, our lads would deal with the birds. We watched and saw a dozen men turning up with hessian sacks. Anyone who has dealt with poultry will know that fowls go quiet and still in the darkness of a sack, and possibly these fellows were not up to the monogrammed carrying cases favoured by the gentry.

We waited half an hour and called the strike. Most of the men tried to run but only a couple got away. Mr Ross and the rest of his colleagues were arrested while we looked at a scene almost beyond belief. We'd had to wait until we were sure the game was on, but in that time some 20 birds had died. They were laid out in a row, a crumpled mass of blood and feathers, stabbed and raked to death by sharpened steel which, to their small bodies, would be the equivalent of a man being stabbed several times with a gladiator's short sword.

Prison sentences were handed down for Ross and most of the others. Too many of those fine game-cocks had perished while we waited outside, but we could take some comfort in the knowledge that no more would be dying behind Ross' family butcher's shop. Meanwhile, the search continues for a way in to The Oxford Club.

If game-cocks are almost literally the bantamweights of the fight game, American pit bull terriers are the heavy-weight maulers. Whatever any pit-bull owner might tell you about their lovely nature, these dogs were bred exclusively for fighting and have been so for 150 years and more. Various bulldogs and terriers are in the ancestry but the breed was sufficiently refined and distinct to be officially recognised in the formation in the USA of the United Kennel Club, the objectives of which were (a) registration of pedigree American pit bull terriers and (b) the resolution of dog-fighting guidelines.

All along the history of the fighting pit bull and other similar types, breeders were keen to foster good behaviour towards humans. Obviously, you don't want to produce a fearsomely brave and strong fighting machine which then bites the hand that feeds it, or more likely tears the arm off. So, pit bulls became noted for their eagerness to please people, but they are also supreme athletes and are equally noted for their exaggerated and accented prey drive. The prey drive is a trait present in all dogs and is something inherited from their ancestor, the wild wolf. Wolves search for their prey mostly using sense of smell, stalk their prey mostly using eyesight, chase it, secure it with the 'grab bite' and then kill it. Of these five ingredients – search, stalk, chase, grab, kill – in the prey drive, the grab bite is the one intensified in the pit bull, a dog whose forebears baited a very much larger animal, a dog bred to sink its teeth into the flesh of a bull and to hang on.

Hanging on, fighting spirit, gameness in the face of adversity, stubbornness – having these British-bulldog characteristics in large quantity finally turns the selectively bred athlete into the ultimate canine combatant. It reminds me of a prayer I learned at Sunday school: 'to give and not to count the cost; to fight and not to heed the wounds; to toil and not to seek for rest; to labour and not to ask for any reward'. The only bit missing there is the first line: 'Teach us, good Lord, to serve you as you deserve'. I wouldn't like to say what these dogs' lords and masters deserve.

A wolf needs a pack. To a certain extent it's a social animal and for its descendants, the many domestic breeds of dog, Man is the best friend and the substitute for the pack. In most breeds and individuals, the instinct to socialise with other dogs remains; in the pit bull, that packing instinct has been bred out, which makes the dog unpredictable and unreliable among other dogs and, often, among people.

Since the Dangerous Dogs Act of 1991, it has been illegal to breed pit bull terriers in the UK and to own one without a special exemption from a court of law. Although variations in the breed vis-à-vis the legal definition have made the Act difficult to enforce, it has still much infuriated pit bull lovers, who argue that there are no dangerous dogs, only dangerous owners. One has to ask, therefore, are there no faster greyhounds, only better trainers? Have thousands of years of skill and effort been devoted to breeding mastiffs, bulldogs and terriers, in order simply to make them irresistibly cuddly for peaceful owners who want a nice, laid-back kind of a dog to take for walks or a sweet and tolerant animal to play with the children?

In any case, whatever laws are passed, dog fighters are up with the technology and globalisation like all the other criminals. As we shall see, one very successful breeding operation is run by a group of neo-Nazis in Finland. They export on demand to the UK, Scandinavia, Croatia, Holland, Russia, anywhere. It's not difficult.

Dangerous owner is certainly right when you come to look at those enthusiasts for organised dog fighting; dangerous, and dedicated. Six weeks or more before a match, the build-up or 'keep' will begin with a rigorous schedule of exercise and diet. Vitamins, royal jelly and beefsteak are basics; it's the secret ingredients that are as carefully protected as the formula for Coca-Cola. For exercise, there are four aiming points in stamina, agility, strength and skill. Every day of the keep, the dog will run for hours on a treadmill. He'll swim, and gallop along beside his trainer's bicycle. He'll be taught to jump to grab-bite a car tyre hanging from a tree, and to swing from it until he's allowed down. His trainer will bring out the flirt pole, a long stick with a rag tied to the end, and have the dog twisting and turning, flexing and striking as he tries to bite the ever-moving rag. Every owner/trainer has his own special variations, his own wrinkles handed down or invented, and come the day the combatants will be in the very peak of condition, athletes of magnificence if it were not for their trainers' purpose.

My first dog-fight bust resulted in the discovery of firearms, piles of cash, and a punch-up involving blokes somewhat overexcited by the fight they'd been watching and the amphetamines they'd been swallowing. The guest list at that show read like a who's who of the Glasgow underworld, too dangerous a crowd to allow we sassenach cat rescuers anywhere near on our own. SOU had organised the job and set up the methodology but the Scottish police were doing the surveillance and calling the shots.

The whole of the SOU was there, plus as many SSPCA men as could be mustered, which wasn't many, and 75 Scottish coppers, some of them quite sizeable, plus another 75 police in back-up, planning, radio, command posts and so on. Everybody was issued with riot gear. We sat in a room at the police station listening to radio messages. The tension was almost visible. We were like soldiers ready to go over the top, except we very much wanted to go. The police were the same, full of adrenaline at the thought of catching half the Glasgow underworld in the act.

It was the first time that an encrypted radio system had been used on a major British police operation. Naturally, some people said it would never work, so excitement reached a peak when the message came through that a fight had happened and injured or dead dogs had been observed being put in a van. This was our signal to pack into the back of a big, race-meeting type horsebox, nearly 100 of us crushed in together, winding along country lanes to a remote farm some miles from Kirkcaldy. There was a look-out posted at the gate. Our horsebox stopped. The driver began to ask for directions while another policeman ran around, arrested the man and bundled him into the cab. Off we went down the farm track, half a mile, us in the back in pitch darkness with no sound being made. So this was what it was like being a horse.

I'd made sure I was last getting on to the horsebox so when the doors opened and the ramp went down, I was among the first off. The door to the outbuilding was locked. The two biggest coppers hit it with their shoulders and it fell open like a sheet of cardboard. Running through an area leading to another door, behind which the fight was happening, nobody noticed the 12-bore shotgun, the .45 revolver and the 9-millimetre revolver lying on the floor.

Around the ring were 30 Glasgow hardmen, against 75 Scottish police. If anyone resisted arrest, which quite a few did, he was shown the error of his ways but never gave in without a struggle. In the chaos all around, men being handcuffed and knelt on, screaming and shouting, blows being aimed and blows being taken, the fighting pit seemed like an island of calm. Two owners stood there, spattered with blood, seemingly hypnotised by the drama before them, and two pit bulls were locked together in silent determination to kill, ignoring everything else. There was a black one and a red one. Two of us prised them apart and put them back in their patent kennels ready for their trip to the vet's. Beside the pit, not noticed in the mayhem, was a pile of banknotes, several thousand pounds. Somebody had dumped their purse money rather than be caught with it. More money was found later and forfeited, along with the full paraphernalia of dog training and fighting including several treadmills.

Outside, the men were being led away one by one, two policemen to each, and were photographed leaving the place. It was an impressive sight that brought on all kinds of emotions, maybe even something of the pride in victory, and then I spotted the two dogs which had been in the previous fight. They'd been left in the back of a van to die. They'd obviously fought each other to a mutual standstill and, weak with effort and loss of blood, traumatised by their wounds and in deep shock with it all, had been ditched without a care. This was the way some owners treated their dogs after the fight, when before it they were treated like royalty. Once their purpose was fulfilled, they were so much rubbish that the dustman wouldn't take away. I was surprised they were still alive. I'd heard of owners killing their dogs with hammers if they failed to come up to scratch. They use that term, to scratch, from the old bare-knuckle boxing days when a man, having been knocked down, had to get up within a given time and come up to a line scratched on the floor, or be declared the loser.

All 30 men were charged and convicted. There was no prison sentence then for just watching a fight, so most were handed fines of a few hundred pounds. The organisers were sent to prison for six months. Additional charges were brought over the drugs found in some of the cars and all the dogs were destroyed by order of the sheriff.

Some 15 years later, we had a phone call from the Glasgow police. Remember that dog fight? Well, two of the men involved have been found murdered, probably to do with drug dealing. It's a long shot, but could we throw any extra light on their associates? Er, not really, no.

Violence must always be expected with dog fighters, and so it was in the idyllic beauty spot called Nidderdale. After several months of extremely cautious surveillance and groundwork, much of it done by my colleague Mike during which he built up a considerable file of intelligence on a Yorkshire dog fighting gang, I found myself staring through my binoculars at a small cottage on a country estate close by the quiet village of Nidd. An hour before, I'd been sneaking through fields and woods, avoiding any look-outs the gang might have posted on the quiet lanes leading to the appointed place. I got to about 300 yards away before I had to start crawling. Now I was 30 yards, lying down, motionless and as near invisible as all the very finest camouflage clothing could make me, trying not to think of what had happened in Scotland.

Over the next two hours I watched six men arrive at the cottage and go in. One of them carried a Vari-Kennel, a proprietary plastic box approved by airlines for animal transport as something strong enough to keep anything in, except possibly The Alien. When it became clear that no more invited guests would be arriving, I had to get myself into a position where I could call up some uninvited ones: 20 police officers and 10 RSPCA inspectors. This was not something I could take a guess at. If we went in too soon and the fight hadn't begun, no offence would have been committed apart from owning the dogs, if we could have proved that, and all our slow and careful intelligence gathering would have been wasted in an instant.

I'd had a case like that before. We'd had to organise the police back-up in a hurry, our tip-off had come at very short notice and the whole thing had no time for planning. Our surveillance went well, following our target from Lancashire into Staffordshire and we saw 15 men arriving at the farm, some of whom had come down from Scotland. We counted 15 minutes and called in the strike. What we found were ten or a dozen men sitting idly around having a beer and a smoke while the others supervised a mating between a local dog and a Scottish bitch. No one was in any doubt that dog fighting was on agenda but we had no evidence. Exit stage left in some embarrassment.

Trying to make sure that was a once-only mistake, I hoped this lot were all having too good a time to worry about intruders as I spent a good 30 minutes crawling in super slo-mo towards the cottage. It was dark by now but, with a fullish moon, anybody popping outside for a breather would have seen me if he'd looked. Nobody did.

With an ear to the front door, the uninitiated might have expected to hear a lot of fierce growling and barking. Not so. It's not the dogs which make all the noise, it's the spectators, especially the two owners, and they were yelling and whooping like good 'uns. Wriggling backwards into the garden where there were a few shrubs growing, I radioed the cavalry. Strike.

The cavalry had decided to exercise as much caution as possible, to keep the element of surprise, but I had to bite my lip to stop myself laughing as, helmets bobbing, 20 of the North Riding Constabulary's largest tried to creep silently down the gravel path. At the front was a very big copper indeed with a 30-pound sledgehammer. Two or three mighty blows on the door and we were in, the police shouting blue murder as they charged down the narrow stairs to the cellar, truncheons at the ready, to meet three of the dog men coming up. They were easily subdued but three were missing. Nobody had come out of doors or windows, that was sure, so where were they? One was found hiding in a wardrobe. Another lay as if asleep on a bed. He yawned and stretched and tried to look offended as the policemen disturbed his rest. Five down, one still missing.

My job, with a particular colleague, was to separate the dogs which we knew would carry on fighting after the spectators had gone. Inside the pit, constructed of old doors and bits of wood, the stronger of the two animals was dragging the other around the arena by its throat. There was blood all over the place. It must be appreciated that these dogs are killing machines and, once set in motion, unstoppable so long as they have breath. Without our intervention the fight would probably have gone on until one of the dogs was dead, and here was our immediate problem. As with most developed fights, both dogs had a hold. Although one was dominating, the other wasn't going to give up either. How do you intervene between the irresistible force and the immoveable object? With a breaking stick, is the answer and we'd brought some with us. They're pieces of broom handle about 9 inches long with one end sharpened to a flat point. Right at the back of the dog's jaw there is a small gap with no teeth. You grab the dog by the scruff and thrust your breaking stick in the aforesaid gap and twist. If you are strong enough and the stick is strong enough, you will prise the jaws apart.

This must be done in a co-ordinated way, with your colleague doing the same thing at the same time. You then turn the dog so he can't see his opponent, put him on a leash and, if he can, off he'll trot, good as gold.

The last gamester might never have been found if we hadn't known for certain that there were six of them. He'd crawled in behind a pile of old furniture and cardboard boxes in the attic, concealed himself as well as anything I could have done and stayed there for two hours. Later, with all five of his colleagues, he was concealed again for six months as a guest of Her Majesty.

Meanwhile we had to see to the dogs. The vet said if I spent half an hour stabbing an orange with a 6-inch nail I'd get an idea of the puncture wounds these dogs displayed. Even so, they recovered over some months while waiting for the death sentence from the judge who sent their owners down. What happened, and what invariably happens, is a complete denial of ownership by anyone involved in the fight. Without a court order, only the owner can have a dog destroyed and so these animals have to be looked after until such an order can be obtained, which generally comes with the hearing in court, as it did in this case. We are therefore almost always in the invidious position of having to nurse these wounded beasts through a painful and lengthy recovery, only to kill them at the end of it.

Such fights are commonplace all over Europe and the USA. For instance, one dog-rescue centre in Houston, Texas, takes in up to ten court-ordered pit bulls a year which have been put to fight. Common they may be but the chief problem we have is that, unlike most crime, this is one which cannot be detected afterwards. To be sure of getting a conviction you have to catch them at it, and success is as rare as it is difficult. One man I failed to pin down was a member of a regional crime squad. According to my regular police contacts, this chap often asks after my health.

A good informant is the key to successful discovery of a blood sport second only to badger-baiting in cruelty. You can know what a dog fighting man has for breakfast, what colour his hair is, what brand he smokes and what he bought his daughter for her birthday, but what you need to know is when and where. The word was that there would be a big fight on one of Britain's premier estates, Burton Constable in the East Riding, sometime near Christmas. This was of special interest to me because I knew the area well from my youth. The connections continued when I learned that the briefing was to be at the Tower Grange police station in Hull, where I often used to call to pick up strays when I was the RSPCA ambulance driver in those parts. One unlooked for side-effect was being 'asked' if I would 'like to' join an identity parade because they were short of tall, dark, handsome young men. I think the fee was £2, which was great except every time I did it the witness picked me out as the criminal. No further charges were brought, but it was a lesson for me about witness reliability.

At the briefing for the Burton Constable job, Operation Rosie, were about 15 police officers, me and two RSPCA colleagues Mike and Andy (Mike was the most successful dog-fighter prosecutor the RSPCA ever had), and a police dog handler called Rod who was also the local wildlife officer. Rod was ever a grumpy old sod with a beard, even when he was at primary school, and he was born to fit the larger sizes of police uniform. He would do all right for me, whatever his apparent faults, because he was an utterly straight, no-nonsense, spade's-a-spade sort of bloke who could never be turned aside from the job that needed doing. He was going to be my partner in the surveillance task to which I was appointed, as expected.

We were going to have to watch, wait and get up close, out in the open on what promised to be a very cold night, just four days before Christmas. Rod wasn't trained in observation-post work but I had no doubts we could crack it. He just wanted to know what I thought he should wear. He had quite a lot of his own insulation but I recommended thick thermals and Gor-Tex.

An unmarked car dropped us off at 5pm about half a mile from a gamekeeper's cottage on the estate, which is 5,000 acres surrounding a vast Elizabethan mansion, home to the Constable family ever since it was built. There are animal undertones, including the wildfowl lakes and the famous whale skeleton, the so-called Burton Constable Whale, a 60-foot sperm whale which was stranded on Holderness in 1825 and is said to have been the inspiration for Moby Dick. There was even a personal connection for me because, years ago, when I was still at school, my interest in animals had led me to apply for a weekend job helping the gamekeepers. I only stuck it for three or four weekends. I'm sure there must be law-abiding, wildlife-preserving gamekeepers in this country who are concerned about animal welfare; it's just that I haven't met any.

We had quite different types of constables waiting on our word, including women police constables and detective constables, as constable Rod and I set off for the place of our vigil, which had been decided for us by the police and my RSPCA colleagues. It was a clear night, thick frost everywhere, no moon but starlight reflecting off the white ground and absolutely silent. Our approach was standard stuff – keep low, move a few steps, stop, look and listen, move a few more steps. It has to be done with patience and discipline, even though your instincts and your adrenaline are screaming at you to get a move on. Wrapped up in layers of heavy clothing against the time when you will have to sit and wait, and carrying a back-pack of kit, it's easy to get a sweat on during this moving stage, which could be your undoing once you stop and start getting cold.

After half an hour we reached our post, 100 yards from Garden Cottage. I checked our radio contacts, with Bryn a couple of miles away in a nice warm car, and a police officer in a nice warm van full of keyed-up constabulary persons. A quarter of an hour went by and a red saloon car drove out from beside the cottage, onto the lane and away, quite slowly. Hammering came from somewhere near the cottage. This was last-minute reinforcements of the fighting pit, we assumed. Another quarter of an hour and the red saloon came back, its driver satisfied after scouting the district.

It's quaint, but the barbaric business of dog fighting has had its equivalents of the Marquis of Queensbury.

They agree beforehand which set of rules they're using, Old English, say, or Cajun, and one of the prerequisites is an accurate weigh-in. Inside that place would be a big Salter balance. They would weigh the animals and if one exceeded the agreed fighting weight he'd forfeit his match money. There would be pauses agreed in the fights, which might come as natural breaks when the dogs lost hold. The dogs would be taken back to their corners, turned away from their enemy, and sponged down. On the count of 30 or another agreed time, the referee would signal that battle should recommence. The dogs would be turned again so that they could see each other, and be let go at the charge.

A white van arrived and a man got out with a patent kennel. By the way he carried it, it wasn't empty. At around 6.30 we heard dogs barking, so some must have been delivered earlier. At 6.45 two more vehicles arrived, a van and a saloon car. As before, a passenger got out, opened the gate to the yard and closed it when the vehicle was in. Surely, we thought, the job was on. So many times we'd been frustrated when bad information or poor timing had led us up a cul-de-sac. More dogs barking. This was going to be a night of nights and suddenly we didn't feel the cold any more.

At some point we would have to judge when the fights had begun, then crawl forward, confirm our suspicions and call the strike. The crawl would be a bit further than I would normally have planned, our OP (observation post) being further back than I would have set it. In daylight, 100 yards to crawl would have been too far. At night, it didn't matter so much, and I thought especially so when two men came out of the cottage with powerful torches and started a search of the surroundings. Maybe they had had experience of surveillance on their activities. Maybe they knew where I would normally set an OP. Anyway, while we kept our heads down and felt the cold all over again, they confined their search to 50 yards from the house. Rod's breath was making clouds of condensation. I whispered to him to cover his face with a scarf.

Our two searchers were not the best. They didn't have a dog with them, which would have made finding us much more likely, and they didn't cover all the ground. They must have thought it was too cold to be out. I watched them through an image intensifier and saw them talking to two more men, one of whom I recognised from a badger-baiting encounter years before. That had been a job when a dog almost cost me. I was hiding in the bushes as per, camouflaged to perfection, when a chap went by with his Jack Russell on a walk. This little animal knew I was there, in that bush, and tried to tell its master so with barks and whines. I was so well camouflaged that, although the dog could sense me, it couldn't see me, and neither could the man. He concluded that his dog was making a fuss about nothing and dragged it off. Wonderful animals, dogs. We should pay them more attention when they tell us things.

The four men went indoors and I went on a fairly rapid crawl forwards, to within 50 yards of the cottage. Soon I saw all the men troop out and make for a building, a commercial type of chicken shed, and it was not long before I could hear the familiar sounds. Two dogs' preliminary low growls and snarls. Two men's loud shouts of encouragement, and the other men joining in. Go on! Get at it, you ****! Kill the ******!

More cautious fight arrangers might have had a radio or a portable stereo playing loudly to drown these noises, but not here. I was completely certain that a fight was on. I scurried back to Rod and called the strike. We were using the horsebox tactic again, now referred to as the Trojan Horse Trick. The cavalry this time was 30 riot police with all the gear, helmets, shields, batons, padded clothing, the lot. I would meet the wagon on the road, waving a small torch fitted with a red bulb. I would get into the horsebox cab, brief the officer in charge, and we would drive very, very quietly into the cottage yard. There I would point them towards the chicken shed and off they would go.

I saw the horsebox coming and waved my torch. In my earpiece I heard the senior police officer say that there was a man on the roadside waving a red torch. Did anyone know who it might be?

The horsebox pulled up quietly enough beside me and I was about to climb in when the back opened and riot police started piling out. These are not quiet people. They can't be, not wearing all that kit, and they're trained to be intimidating, not pussy-footing. Ah well, there was no option. We couldn't expect to get them back in the horsebox so it had to be Plan B. The senior officer and I set off at a jog. We had about 75 yards to go. Behind me in a phalanx, like a unit of Roman legionaries hurrying to reinforce the battle line, trotted the riot men. They never spoke, they had rubber soled boots, but they still made what to me sounded like an enormous racket. I was sure they could be heard for miles.

We turned in at the gate and headed for the chicken shed. It seemed too peaceful. I thought I could hear the dogs but there were no shouts from spectators. We burst in to an empty shed, lit by four 100-watt bulbs. At the far end was a construction, the usual kind of corral made of old doors, which was the fighting pit. Inside it were two pit bulls. One was locked on to the other's foreleg, the other was locked onto its opponent's ear. Left to themselves, as always, they would have fought on until one or both died.

Time had been against us all the way through this case and there had been insufficient of it to set up blocks on the escape routes. Normally we'd have had an aerial photograph and detailed maps so we could station police at every bolt hole, and dog handlers ready for pursuit. Now all our dogfighters were on the run in every direction, scared off by the sound of an approaching Roman legion. Calls went out, reinforcements were drafted, the net was cast as wide as possible. Whether we caught them or not, I glumly thought, we'd have one hell of a job trying to prove involvement. From an evidential point of view, we had to be able to show who was doing what, and we'd not seen anyone doing anything.

Our case against the organiser, the Burton Constable head keeper called Woodbridge, the one I recognised in my image intensifier, would not prove too much of a problem. He would not be able to explain away a pair of pit bulls locked in deadly combat, all the correct gear for a fight, half a dozen cars in his yard and a purpose-built pit in his chicken shed. The others would need to be inclined to confession or else have blood on their clothes. We rounded up about half of them, mostly local men in their late 20s. Some were run down across the fields, some were picked up on the road trying to hitch a lift.

Mike spent a year, on and off, meticulously working up the case and it came to court with three of them pleading not guilty and one, Woodbridge, pleading guilty to permitting premises to be used. One man was found guilty of possessing a pit bull without a licence, permitting the animal to be caused unnecessary suffering and permitting injury to a dog. He got six months. Two spectators were given conditional discharges and ordered to pay £350 costs. Woodbridge got six months.

Unsavouriness is a prerequisite of all dog fighting folk. Just how unsavoury I thought I knew from my RSPCA experience but, as a freelance, I was about to have my eyes opened and, as I believed from time to time, my knee-caps blown off. A certain organisation in Northern Ireland hired me to train a man called Steve who was determined to crack the dog fighting rings there. As a side issue, he was to be followed by BBC television. The man himself was an ideal subject, ex military, motivated and dedicated, already versed in basic surveillance skills although not experienced in undercover work. He would need his motivation and dedication because his targets were men who had been involved in the Troubles on both sides, who had submerged their differences and possibly compromised their own party's cause in the common cause of dog fighting.

All through that time, there had been a secret breeding facility for American pit bulls, which was also a thriving business in import and export, run by a mob called the Farmers' Boys. Customers overseas had bought Northern Ireland-bred dogs while the republicans and loyalists were shooting each other in the streets. 'No-go area' was an expression frequently used in those days, and this dog farm was certainly a no-go area for the RSPCA and any other interested parties, and nobody could blame them for that. They would get the collywobbles just filling out the risk assessment.

As more peaceful times came, there was still very little official interest in stirring things up although the Farmers' Boys were as active as ever. They were the source of the pit bull which killed the five-year-old St Helens girl, Ellie Lawrenson, on New Year's Day 2007, and were continuing to supply any number of dogs to any European country. They used the simplest of dodges. You get hold of a mongrel pup, let's say a brown one. You take it to the vet and have it chipped. The vet can't put a very detailed description of the dog in the supporting paperwork because it's a brown mongrel. You take your mongrel home, call in someone who knows what to do, in this case a crooked dog warden, and he digs the chip out of its neck and inserts same into the neck of your pit bull terrier, which also happens to be brown. You can now own and export this 'brown mongrel' legally, knowing full well that the customs will scan the dog to see if its chip matches the number on the paper but will look no further to see if it matches the description. The officer might even hand the scanner so you don't have to get out of your car. Maybe you will be unlucky and come across a customs officer who knows a Heinz 57 from a pit bull. Most likely you will sail through.

I finished my training with Steve in undercover techniques, and agreed to return and help when it came to the crunch. The BBC television people were putting on the pressure; their Panorama programme about apolitical, non-religious, non-sectarian Irish dog fighting would be no good without film of a fight. As far as I knew, nobody in Europe had ever managed to get such film before. It was an exciting challenge, possibly too exciting.

Steve got busy infiltrating the Belfast boys, and rather him than me. He must have been very good at it because he soon came up with a diamond of a story. When the message came it was short notice. In every exercise I like to have an exit strategy – what to do in case I am uncovered. I thought that in this case, such a strategy might be more important than usual but there was no time. I was working with Steve and his mate, of the same name but known as Stevie, in whom I had trust and confidence but we were new to each other, and they were new to the game.

There was also the media element, ever present. My concern is to stop the cruelty; theirs is to record it. This clash of priorities invariably leads to conflict but can usually be resolved. Then there's the legal element, which cannot be resolved to mutual satisfaction. When investigating a crime in the UK, if you find evidence you have a moral and legal obligation to go to the police with it. The TV people want to put the evidence in their programme and not wait a year or 18 months until it comes to court. Once information has been laid or charges have been made, the matter becomes sub judice and cannot be reported in the media in a way which might influence the trial.

It's a conundrum which we used to avoid in SOU by the simple expedient of not allowing the media anywhere near our investigations. We would do our work, bring charges, go to court and involve the press and TV at that point. It meant having to turn down some very good opportunities for publicity but on balance it was probably the right policy. In Belfast, with the two Steves and BBC Panorama, it was not my problem.

Trade was being regularly conducted in guns and pit bull terriers between the Farmers' Boys and a group in Finland with neo-Nazi connections. The head honcho, an American Finn amazingly called Bobby Gonzales, wanted to branch out into the winter holiday business. His summers were adequately filled with dog fighting but in the cold dark days of the Finnish winter the pit bull terriers, originally bred in warmer climes, had to put on fat to survive which made them unfit for fighting. Bobby's notion was to arrange badger-digging weekend breaks for locals and trippers, and he wanted a badger-digging consultant to help him set the job up correctly. Steve One had said he knew the very man. Me.

Before flying to Helsinki I thought I should do the proper thing and contact the Finnish equivalent of the RSPCA, a tiny underfunded organisation in a country not known for its sentimentality about animals. I gave them only the barest details but they said I was wasting my time, because there was no dog fighting in Finland.

Our first test was going to be at Tampere airport, about 100 miles from Helsinki, which is the one used by Ryanair. This was where my targets were arriving and I was due to pick them up and be filmed by the BBC doing so. Bobby Gonzales knew the men were being met so he didn't need to be there but there was still the possibility that he might take it into his head to welcome his guests. He was only an hour or so away.

It's a rule of undercover work that you must never be seen with people who might compromise you, and here was I with a British television crew, presenter, producer and all. I persuaded them to hide and I moved my car, a plush Peugeot people-carrier, BBC issue, further away so they could get plenty of footage of me walking across the airport with the bad guys.

My first arrivals were Steves One and Two plus the number three in the Farmers' Boys, a Protestant called Hami, short for Hamilton. I had no background on him at all, no information of the inside or outside variety, which is not something I would have tolerated on one of my own projects. The Steves came through the gate with hand luggage only. We had a brief word and waited for Hami, who came through after a long delay looking extremely worried, as you would if you had cocaine taped between your toes and more in your suitcase and your suitcase had been the last one to turn up on the carousel.

I drove our little party to the Eden Hotel, part of a leisure complex something like a Center Parc which was set up for family holidays. There seemed to be a hundred different sorts of sauna bath but we made straight for the bar. I had been designated as driver and therefore sober person of the weekend, but there were no such restrictions on Hami and the Steves. By the time I got up to go and meet the next flight, they were almost speaking Finnish.

My next two guests were English, from Stockton-on-Tees, both in their early 30s. Gary was a dog fighter whose name was known in the circles; Andy was primarily a terrier man with fox hunts who'd come along for a new thrill. Gary was a hard-as-nails wiry type with an assertive look in his blue eyes, and whose tattoos included a picture of a pit bull terrier. His mate had teeth whiter than an American film star's. Remember Stewart Granger? Would he have had a ring in his eyebrow? I had no problem getting accepted by these two because I knew so much about their favourite hobbies and could talk with the best about badger dogs, deer dogs and all topics connected.

On our way to the hotel, Gary told us about the difficulties he was having with an ex friend, a man who had fallen on hard times and couldn't keep up his mortgage payments. Gary, out of the goodness of his heart, agreed to take over the arrangement and the house, paying his at-the-time friend an agreed sum. This ingrate had now come back wanting more money, but was staying clear of Gary in case of physical reprisals. This was really annoying Gary, who wanted to resolve the matter in an unmistakeable way, and if the cheating so-and-so didn't appear soon, Gary would be forced to go round to the mother's house near-by and take it out on her. Yes, very annoying, that.

Once at the hotel there was no messing about with showers and changes of clothes. It was straight to the bar where a solid evening of drinking began, based on Johnny Walker Red Label, Lapin Kulta beer (made from the wild sparkling waters of Lapland, would you believe) and, of all things, Buckfast Tonic Wine which was Hami's tipple of preference. I used the well-tried device of pretending some ignorance about the finer points of dog-fighting rules and, as Gary and Hami got more and more drunk, they told me everything there was to know about the subject, several times over. This was not an entirely bad thing as it gave Steve Two several opportunities to record the conversations with his hidden camera. Gary was similarly pleased to tell us about his lifetime devotion to badger digging and his ownership of firearms. He also described his part-time career in the insurance industry, involving setting cars alight, selling the parts on eBay and claiming on the insurance.

He'd moved on from badger digging to deer poaching and thence to dog fighting, and he described in full detail a 17-minute fight his dog had had over in Ireland with a black one called Pablo, owned by a woman, Fiona, who was the one and only Farmers' Girl. Becoming rather morose under the influence of Buckfast and Johnny Walker, he bewailed the lot of his son who was bullied at school because all the other kids knew his dad was a drug dealer. At this he snorted a line of coke, right there in the bar, and said there was no justice for a working man such as himself, trying to make a living out of putting up garden fences. His pal Andy agreed and said it was the same in tree surgery. Earlier they had told me about their top-of-the-range customised Land Rover Defenders.

I was first off to bed at 2am. The others were up until five, with Gary snorting line after line of coke and taking a bottle of vodka upstairs with him. He and Andy didn't show until noon, each with the mother and father of all hangovers. Andy, bizarrely, was dressed entirely in new Realtree, the brand of choice among those who like to spend a fortune on camouflage gear. This looked rather out of place at the Eden family hotel but they checked out quickly before the management could discover the mess they'd made in their room.

It was a fairly subdued gang of dog fighters who slumped in the Peugeot as we set off for Ypäjä, about 60 miles to the south. Hami was the only brightish spark and he was soon tucking in to some vodka. The rest of us made do with fruit juice and water bought at the local convenience store. At Ypäjä, Steve One gave us directions to Bobby Gonzales' house, a bungalow with farm buildings, reached by a very narrow little bridge over a ditch. He'd been there once before as an emissary of the Farmers' Boys, to buy a dog for Hami.

Bobby himself, described later as good-looking by the BBC girl but unremarkable as far as I was concerned, was average height, average build, with brown hair, wispy little beard, blue overalls and welly boots. He gave us all a warm welcome which I have to say seemed sincere. I noticed several pit bulls tethered not far away in a bit of a wood, and two or three characters, a number later rising to eight or nine, who were anything but average for the population as a whole but were identikit replicas of each other. The shaven bullet-head, all projecting parts adorned with rings, sat squarely on a weight-lifter's neck, which was tattooed with swastikas, eagles and other emblems of the far Right, which widened into a muscular torso dressed in black leather bomber jacket and Doc Martens below army trousers.

Bobby soon took us to see his dogs in the wood and as we walked past his main shed I could see, through the doors, illuminated with spotlights and with no attempt at disguise, the dog-fighting ring. This was clear evidence for what Steve One had told me, that the Finnish police did not bother enforcing the law against dog fighting, preferring to leave rural folk to their rural ways. The dogs were tethered on running leads, each with a barrel for a kennel. Bobby proudly pointed to a fallen tree, about 18 inches in diameter, which looked like it had been felled by a beaver. Not at all. One of his dogs had done it.

The Steves and I were keen to sort our kit out so asked if we could go to our accommodation. Hami and the other two said they'd stay put. Bobby asked us if we'd be wanting a drink at our lodgings, so should we have a designated driver or all have a drink and walk back. Maybe the Finnish police were hotter on drink-driving than they were on gun running and dog fighting, or maybe Bobby was really concerned in case we got pissed and knocked somebody over. Anyway, I would drive the Peugeot with Steve Two beside me and Steve One jumped in beside Bobby in his Chevrolet pick-up. We followed him over rough tracks and narrow winding lanes. It would have been some walk back, several miles anyway. Bobby left us to ourselves at a palatial house with at least eight bedrooms and a couple of annexes, where we were shown to a bedroom each by a very nice Finnish woman who promised to return to cook our breakfasts in the morning. We were so long checking and rechecking our equipment in nervous anticipation that Bobby rang to ask where we were. The first fight was about to start.

We rushed back to join the gang at ringside, a crowd of 16 or so including us. The pit was a solid construction of marine ply and strong timbers, with a black carpet on the floor. There were chairs but nobody sat on them. The Steves and I stationed ourselves at three of the corners; Steve One and I were going to try openly using a camcorder as well as all of us filming covertly. As the first fight got underway, between two quite small black dogs which charged each other ferociously, I saw Steve One being asked to stop his filming. For some reason, perhaps because I was standing next to Bobby's wife, a petite, doll-like woman who belied her appearance by thoroughly enjoying the fighting, nobody spoke to me so I kept on recording.

The bout lasted about 15 minutes before an owner, one of the Nazi boot boys, also belying his appearance by showing a sort of kindness, pulled his badly mangled animal from the fray even though it wanted to carry on. We applauded the winner and the loser. I'd got the whole fight on tape but Hami stopped me after that, very politely, saying they didn't really want any filming so would I mind not doing it. The bottles were being passed around, whisky, vodka, as three more fights took place. All the dogs were badly injured but had shown that prime characteristic, gameness, which was their ticket to the recovery area and a continued existence. If they fell apart or lost their hold, they would be separated and taken to their respective corners. On the referee's command they would be turned to see each other again and, depending on whose turn it was, one owner would release his dog which, if game, would charge at the other.

One in particular, a big white dog, was laid in the snow outside, its red wounds on chest and neck showing up horribly. As the men began packing snow on its torn flesh, I knelt beside it so my hidden camera could record the inevitable consequences of matching one pit bull terrier with another.

We needed to recover too, from the freezing cold in the shed and the emotional draining of watching such a dismal indictment of man's inhumanity, and a welcome interval was called. Everyone went into Bobby's house where a buffet was laid out with many sorts of Scandinavian dishes based on salmon, herrings and pork and a dozen different kinds of bread. Not a lettuce leaf in sight of course but real dog-fighting men don't eat salad. I slipped outside to the car, removed the tape from my camcorder and put in a blank. If challenged I would say I'd wiped it. I could not have been more pleased with myself as I hid that tape in the car.

Back at the buffet all the guests were getting stoned on booze, cocaine and tablets which I assumed were not aspirins. I had a long conversation with Bobby about working terriers and back we went into the arena to await the next contest. I was standing next to a line of half a dozen Nazis and, as the fight didn't begin straight away, sat down on a chair for the want of something better to do. I was surprised to hear the muffled sounds of two dogs having a go at each other. They were outside. Somehow they must have slipped their tethers and got their retaliation in first.

This went on for a couple of minutes. Why was nobody stopping it? Then the truth dawned, and with it came the realisation that my new career as a freelance was about to come to a bloody end. My second camera, the one inside my shirt, had stopped, gone back to the beginning of its recording of the first fight on its hard drive, and was now playing it for everyone to hear.

I don't know what my face looked like as I realised, but one glance at Steve on the other side of the ring was enough to give me a good impression of it. This was an acutely desperate situation, and the sounds were getting louder. Steve Two could hear it as well, and he was looking at Steve One, then me, then up into the rafters, perhaps analysing how the Nazis might go about slinging a rope over them. I've been in some pretty scary predicaments but this had to be the high point so far. At such moments you pray to all the gods of the animals to give you inspiration, no matter how feeble, and the best they could come up with on this occasion was my mobile phone.

'It's my phone,' I said, to nobody in particular, patting my pockets, miming and making silly phone gestures with thumb and little finger for the benefit of non-English-speaking Finnish Nazi skinhead thugs who were looking puzzled. 'I've got terrier noises for my ringtone.' As I made a hurried exit, with the growling from under my clothes now very noticeable, I was horrified to see the two Stockton guys come in through the door. I had to walk past them, talking as loudly as I could into an imaginary phone.

What saved us was the drugs and booze. The Nazis, Gary and Andy, Hami, the lot of them, were all out of their skulls. They might well have asked themselves a question, such as 'What's that noise like dogs fighting?' but when they got no answer they were so befuddled they couldn't work out the next step.

I walked swiftly across the yard, kicking the snow up and shouting with my hand over my ear, trying to cover this superb recording of dogs which was still getting louder. Whatever faults this kit had, which wasn't my own and which I hadn't wanted to use, it had a good loudspeaker built in. I'd parked the car as near as possible to the narrow bridge in case we needed to run for it, which was as far as it was possible to get from the shed. A couple of the Nazis strolled by, smiling stupidly at me having one hell of an argument with whoever was on the other end of my call.

I was ripping the blasted equipment off me as I climbed into the car. I wanted to stamp on it, smash it up, curse it for bringing our investigation to the very teetering edge of disaster. Instead I hid it as carefully as I could, tried a confident smile in the driving mirror, gave that up immediately and reverted to panic stricken after distressing news on telephone and not feeling good after too much fictitious vodka.

Walking back across the yard, my newly revived spirits sank again as I saw the door to the shed was closed.

Everywhere was quiet. No activity. They'd obviously got the two Steves tied up and ready for dispatch and were waiting to ambush me. Don't be an idiot, I told myself, it'll be all right. Never mind idiot, scarper, I also told myself. I never thought that the sound of dogs fighting would be music to my ears but as I reached that door and heard it coming from inside, my feelings of relief were beyond description. I walked in and nobody took a blind bit of notice except the Steves, who looked pleased to see me. The possibility of a scarper on my part must have occurred to them.

The last two fights were exceptionally brutal, between well-matched pairs of big dogs which charged each other like the fearless and supremely fit gladiators they were. Both times, as they locked jaws, teeth flew across the ring. The referees picked these up and placed them in a neat row on top of the pit wall. I could not stop myself pinching one and putting it in my pocket for evidence.

The final bout ended in defeat for Bobby's champion. Hami was refereeing. It had been a very close run thing, with bones broken as both clamped teeth into the other's leg. After 20 minutes or so it became clear that they were at a standstill, not so much fighting as being too exhausted to let go, too courageous to surrender, like two heavyweight boxers in the 15th round leaning on each other, unable to act when the referee says break. The dogs were parted by their owners and taken to their corners of the pit, the walls of which were covered in blood.

Hami counted to 30 and called out 'Face your dogs'. They were turned around and it was down to Bobby to release. He did so and the dog just stood. It had nothing left to give. All its bravery, tenacity, blood and spirit had been spent for the entertainment of men. Bobby whispered in its ear, shouted at it, whispered again, but no. It was virtually dead on its feet and, no matter what its own instincts said and no matter what encouragement Bobby gave it, it could not go.

Not coming up to scratch is the unforgivable crime in dog fighting. It shames the owner as well as the dog, and the dog pays with its life. Bobby carried his defeated champion out to the treatment room at the back while the Nazi owner of the winner began wiping the blood from it. A minute later all the lights went out. Bobby came in, told us not to panic, and disappeared. In the two minutes it took to fix the lights, Steve One tried his luck at stand-up. 'Don't anybody move!' he shouted. 'Police!'.

Making a mental note to murder him with a lead balloon that very night, I made my way to the treatment room where I was greeted by one of the weirdest sights anyone could wish for. I've dreamt about it since but never could have made up a dream like it beforehand. On one of the tables was a first-aid kit more sophisticated than most vets have, with medicines including steroids and antibiotics, all kinds of surgical tackle, the full range of wound treatments. Around the room were more tables, each with an exhausted dog on it and a heat lamp hanging over it. Beside each dog was a slightly swaying Nazi holding up a saline drip in one hand and a bottle of vodka or whisky in the other.

Bobby's dog was lying flat out while one of the men tried to inject it. He couldn't find a vein. The veins had collapsed with the shock of the fight. I noticed what looked like a set of jump leads, a couple of insulated crocodile clips wired up to a two-pin plug. They should have used bulldog clips, I thought, ha ha, as I asked Bobby what they were for although I knew perfectly well. Yes, they'd sponged the dog down with water and attached one clip to its back leg and the other to its ear, and plugged in. Instead of killing the dog they'd fused the lights, so now they were trying pentobarbitone sodium, trade name Euthatol.

They still couldn't get a vein so they injected the stuff under the skin, a method which does work but only after a prolonged period of pain for the animal. This poor dog was so far gone it didn't feel anything but it wasn't dying either. With some irritation that his ex champ was wasting so much of his time, Bobby took the dog into the house with the jump leads and plugged them into the power circuit, which did the job at last.

The surviving dogs had had their wounds cleaned and anointed with antiseptic cream and had been given a broad-spectrum antibiotic. The worst wounds were stitched with a surgical staple gun. They would be given the best convalescing treatment for the next six or nine months, when they would be matched again. If they showed gameness on that occasion, they could look forward to another ride on the cycle. If not, they could be electrocuted.

The Nazis said their goodbyes and left while we, the British guests of honour, had a celebratory drink in

Bobby's house. I was concerned about the snow, now falling heavily. The way back to our lodgings would have been difficult to find in the dark anyway. With recognisable features covered in snow we'd have no chance so, with much criticism of me as a rotten old spoilsport, I got my busload of drunken dogfighters and exhausted secret agents on the road. It proved to be every bit as difficult a journey as I'd imagined, not that Hami, Gary and Andy cared, and we got lost several times. When we did arrive, the boys wanted to get stuck into the mind altering substances and I was ready for a few beers myself, so we talked dogs for hours and said what a fantastic time we'd had, and how Bobby's weekend winter breaks were going to be a surefire success if the badger digging was anything like as good as the dog fighting had been.

Steve One and I went to our rooms leaving Steve Two, who had drawn the short straw again, to stay up to babysit. Next morning we were all ready for home, even Hami. We just had to call in on Bobby to thank him for such a terrific weekend, and he gave us each a nylon jaw-strengthener, which is a sophisticated version of the car tyre from which a dog can dangle but can also be used for tug-of-war games. We dropped Hami off at Tampere airport but we had a whole day still to spend with Gary and Andy, whose flight wasn't until the evening.

Steve Two had to disappear to meet the BBC people and I couldn't stand another unnecessary minute with these types so also kept disappearing into the sauna, leaving Steve One to stay drinking with them in the bar of the Eden Hotel. Once they'd gone we celebrated with a

Chinese meal and a few bottles of Tiger beer but we were so done in, partly through the danger we'd been in, partly with the sheer emotional effort of having to watch six dog fights in one evening, that we couldn't really get ourselves in the mood. Next day we flew to Dublin and drove up to Belfast to file our reports. The rest would be up to Panorama and the police.

Conclusion

A WORLD WIDE WEB OF ANIMAL LOVERS

'There is a six weeks female white faced capuchin i want to sell. she is not having any health problem. she is bottle fed, potty and diaper raised with lots of love and attention. she will come with 12 months health guarantee, shots, worming, vaccinations and diappers. she is home and domestic raised with lots of love and attention. shipping is possible. if neccessary. get information upon request.

Where does this animal lover live? South Africa. In the same lot of classified ads, Colin of Immingham writes: 'Wawnted capuchin monkey. hi i am wantin to give a capuchin monkey a home it will be comin to a loving home we are willing to travel (but not abroad only in the uk) cash waiting for the right monkey bred in the uk … thanks.'

Pep of Bamenda, USA County, State of USA, offers a cute female baby capuchin for US$1,200. Bamenda is in

Cameroon. The gloriously named Dorris Chestnut, of the Bamenda which apparently is in the Republic of Victoria, wants US$850 for a similar animal. With a photo of a baby monkey clutching a teddy bear bigger than itself, Jack, of the newly discovered Canada County in Maryland, wants £1,000 for his:

'This is a baby capuchin monkey for sale that they are registered with there K.C, and there are of age 8weeks-12weeks old so if any want is interested he can contact me on this E mail and the prizes is 1000pounds and the are both male and female.'

SVS of Durham, UK wants £1,000:

'Family of Marmoset Monkeys, Mother aged 6 years and male and female siblings aged 2 years. Would prefer to be kept together if possible. Sorry, but for security reasons there will be no home visits by both parties, will arrange meeting place to exchange.'

Of the 24 ads offering monkeys on just one UK website, one was placed from Equatorial Guinea, one from USA, two from UK, twelve from Cameroon and eight from non-existent or deliberately misleading addresses. Mostly the advertisers offered very young capuchins as if they were human babies. Bottle fed and wearing nappies, the adverts emphasised what adorable little cutie-pies they were.

Capuchins are especially intelligent and adaptable and will take a broad range of foods, so they are the favoured monkey of organ-grinders and small-scale breeders. The majority of such breeders seem to be in Africa although the capuchin comes from South America where there are half a dozen species of Cebus and a dozen sub-species.

If the organ-grinder's monkey, with nappy or fez, isn't exotic enough, you'll probably find an animal broker offering a pair of cotton-top tamarins, Saguinus oedipus, for a lot of money. Cotton-tops are CITES Appendix I and EU Annex A, that is to say, threatened now, today, with extinction. Trade in them is only allowed under exceptional circumstances and never for a pet, and advertising them for sale is illegal.

So, what are you waiting for? Let these people know you know. Write to your MP. Penetrate chat rooms. Don't fly with airlines that carry primates and tell them why not. Start a blog.

Police can't find sufficient resources to deal with paedophilia so they're not going to assign much priority to mice. The RSPCA's position seems to be that the whole thing is just too difficult and too far away from their mainstream work. The public largely don't know anything about it. What are we talking about? Squishing. The judge ordered the destruction of the tapes in my one and only case and, without the sight of those, media coverage was scanty. We need to get some boot behind it and I've tried and tried to awaken some interest. Perhaps a politician could take a lead. Perhaps someone with intimate knowledge of the internet could do an investigation and produce evidence of how widespread this unknown activity is. Instead of wasting time designing viruses, why don't some of these whizz-kids make a name for themselves by doing something useful? Instead of attacking the easy targets, why don't animal rights activists have a go at the squishers?

Films of this perverted foot-fetishist obscenity, also called crush movies, find a ready market via the internet. For the more squeamish pervert, such scenes are also available as animated cartoons. For the even more peculiar, have a look at www.chloecreations.com or, if that's gone, just key "crush+movies" into your search engine. You can watch a substantially built lady in her bra and pants crushing underfoot a selection of snails, spiders including tarantulas, other creepy-crawlies, goldfish (one video I saw had 12 fish in it, including the lady putting one in a blender), anchovies, crabs and cheeseburgers.

As evidence of the infinite variety of the human race, someone paying US$60 to download a movie showing a half-naked woman with a cheeseburger or a snail between her toes is hard to beat. It's difficult for the unafflicted to understand, all this foot fetish business. One theory is that it's imprinted while still a baby crawling around mummy's feet; things I learned at my mother's knee and other low joints. Whatever the causes of squishing, we are equally mystified as to a cure, and we don't have a posh name for it. Altocalciphilia is a term some use to describe high-heel fetish, so how about sadobestialtocalciphilia?

If the sound of it is something quite atrocious, we now know the result, and that people are doing it, buying it and selling it. That's what's atrocious, and that in the history of justice in the United Kingdom, only one case of it has ever come to court.

The king eider duck, Somateria spectabilis, is sighted a few times a year in northern Scotland so in Britain we tend to think of it as very rare. It was among the species that The Avocet Man offered to get for me to keep in my aviary, if I'd had one. In fact there are several thousand breeding pairs of king eiders in Norway and more in Russia and in the most remote bird-favoured places like the Pribilof Islands in the Bering Sea, hundreds of miles from anywhere. No bird is safe, of course, no matter how far away it lodges, and especially so if it happens to be handsome.

'We specialize in taking Mature King Eiders for our guest's and have had a very high success rate on Island X Sea duck hunting with our guest's. Trophy Harlequin top off this truly remote hunt of a life time. The legal federal limit of Sea Ducks for nonresident hunters is 4 King Eiders & 4 Harlequin with a few Scoters and Oldsquaws thrown in for good measure. Each hunter can reasonably expect 2-4 mature Kings and limits of Harlequin for the week.'

'Island X' is the website owners' coy way of referring to the totally top-secret island of St Paul, Alaska, which has direct flights from Anchorage, a human population about 500, a bird population of anything up to 2 million and seals half a million and more. King eiders are diving ducks in sub-Arctic seas, mostly eating shellfish which their specially strong beaks can deal with. How can anyone imagine trying to keep one as a pet in a cage? And why on earth would you want to shoot them when you're not going to eat them? Why, is because they are exceptionally good looking. If you'd like to see a picture of a row of dead ones with their proud hunters, visit this very special version of the package-tour operator, www.alaskaduckhuntingguides.com.

You can see that the internet works both ways. It advertises animal abuse and makes it easier, but it also allows people who are against such things to research and expose. If, for some extraordinary reason, you won't be able to become an undercover investigator out in the field, you can become one on the net. Here's a little self-testing exercise as a qualification.

Surf the net on the subject of animals in medical research. You will find some highly emotional stuff, some sense and some rubbish, and views including:

(A) Can't do without it. If we didn't do it here, the pharmaceutical companies would be forced out to other countries where standards are lower.

(B) We can do without it. We're just not trying hard enough to find alternatives. Where there is a medically sound way other than animal testing, we can't be bothered because there's no money in it.

(C) It's not always valid in any case. For example, chimps are immune to AIDS, hepatitis B and common malaria - three big human killers. Thalidomide was tested on animals. What about the Northwick Park clinical trial, where a prototype drug tested safely on animals almost killed its human guinea pigs?

(D) The experiments themselves are not always done properly. The standard of science isn't high enough. Where animal welfare is at stake it should be of the highest, but you get low-paid technicians doing it.

(E) Bloody animal rights idiots, trashing that vet's surgery in Norfolk because he gave emergency cover to a research lab. Then it was found that one of the trashers was alive because of a heart drug which had been proved at the same lab.

Gather all the views including your own, summarise and categorise them, and next time you're at a social gathering tell everyone about your results. Will you light the blue touchpaper and retire immediately, or stay there and fight it out? Denise says I should be more tolerant and maybe she's right, but I find it very difficult.

My message is that the animals of the world must look forward to much more effective crime-fighting activity on their behalf. We need to be at least as organised as the forces seeking to exploit those animals, and we need to be free to go and get the exploiters wherever they are, in the knowledge that the authorities – the legal systems and the governments – will back us up. Currently, this does not happen in the UK. Prosecutions are few because they are so difficult under the law, the criminals are so rarely punished heavily and the crimes so hard to uncover. For instance, it is estimated that at least 5,000 badgers a year are dug up and killed for sport, and it could be twice that number, yet in that same year you might get five convictions, or two, or none.

Everywhere you look there's a law against this and that form of cruelty and legislators proudly point to such laws, as if passing them did the job. Why do they think that? They don't imagine that burglary will stop because there's a law against it. The job is almost entirely a matter of law enforcement, which means getting in among the law breakers, which in turn usually means burrowing for secrets and risking exposure to those who would take strong measures to protect their illegal activities.

The demand for investigation into organised animal crime is infinite, yet the resources are small and the necessary skills sparse. With Ken Connor I set up Ruadan (www.ruadan.co.uk), a consultancy offering the training necessary before any such risks can be taken. One day I hope Ruadan will be a registered charity with its essential work subsidised. One day, I hope there will be people everywhere, like those I've trained in Animals' Angels, who have the skills and knowledge to penetrate behind enemy lines into the camouflaged world of animal abuse, a world that's secret yet so widespread that you can see it displayed in your supermarket chill cabinet.

[section break?]Late at night in Brittany, lying in the long grass in full camouflage gear, I stared through a window at a small concrete platform set with metal railings, an animal pen raised about 6 feet from the floor. It was just a pen, an insignificant part of a much, much bigger operation in a brightly lit, huge building with state-of-the-art equipment, in business 24 hours a day.

The business was pigs, thousands of them which, at the highest possible speed in the most modern, hygienic conditions, would become joints of pork and all things made from pork on the cool shelves of Tesco and Carrefour.

Nothing wrong with that, of course, unless you happen to be a pig or, even worse, a pig with a broken leg.

What would one pig with a broken leg be to an organisation like this? Here are some public statements from the company, Cooperl-Hunaudaye, the largest pork producer in France, taken from the corporate website in early 2007.

'[We have] ultramodern factories capable of slaughtering 80,000 pigs per week … [Our sites] have complementary activities and benefit from the latest technological advances that allow them to contend in a highly competitive international market. Productivity and quality are the top priorities and serve as the foundations of their positive development.'

'Animals are received in a spacious holding area to avoid stressing them. The area has a capacity of 2,700 animals that corresponds to four hours of slaughter. A density of one cubic metre per animal along with computerised management of wait time helps to ensure animal comfort.'

Those PR-department platitudes read a little clumsily, translated from the French. Here's some more from one of Cooperl's business partners, Global Group Trading, likewise from the web in 2007.

'Specialists in both sourcing and marketing quality meat within the international marketplace having established long-standing relationships with major international producers/customers. Leaders in the sale of Brittany Pork to the UK multiple retail, manufacturing and foodservice sectors through our COOPGLOBE joint venture with Cooperl, a major French producer. Quality consistency in all operational areas ensuring customers can be confident in their purchase expectations, be they large or small. Service commitment to both producer and customer by bridging distance and cultural differences, eliminating risk and building relationships. Technical expertise thus ensuring that products continue to meet standards required in food safety, animal welfare and finished quality through production until delivery.'

Yes, once you've sourced your meat within the marketplace and bridged your cultural differences, you can computer-manage wait times to help ensure animal comfort and confidence in your purchase expectations.

Unfortunately for true animal comfort and welfare, no matter how grandiose and well intentioned the language of the press release, it all comes down to the weakest link, the worker at the bottom of the hierarchy, and how he or she is managed. Cooperl had 2,300 employees and, looking through my window, lying on the cold, cold ground, cramped and distinctly lacking in animal comfort, I was waiting for one of them: the ambulance man.

Here he came, driving a tractor with a large metal box on the rear forks. He backed up to the raised animal pen, got off his seat and walked around the back. He was medium height, heavyish build, a bit overweight if anything, middle aged, a completely normal guy. You see him all over Europe, having a coffee or a beer, maybe smoking a cigarette, reading the paper, and you take little notice of him.

I was taking notice because of what I knew was about to happen, having already seen it three times that day, and I had my video camera running for what would be my last take of the scene. He appeared in the pen and opened the gate, revealing a pig lying on its side. He kicked the pig. Through the window I could hear it squealing. He kicked it again, and again, until the pig got the idea and struggled to its feet. It carried one back leg, obviously broken, and stood on three wondering what it was doing in this world.

The man held on to the railings, put one boot against the pig's side, and kick-pushed hard, like you see policemen do on the TV breaking down a door. The pig slid over the edge of the raised pen and dropped a good 3 feet into the trailer. It gave the most God Almighty scream as it hit the trailer floor and there was no more movement. The pig was lying there, in terrible pain, and the only kind thing the ambulance man did was drive it away to be slaughtered.

I had my video evidence, so I slithered off through the grass to meet my French colleagues at our rendezvous. These two chaps, who worked with the animal welfare group Protection mondiale des animaux de ferme (PMAF), which is the French arm of Compassion In World Farming, had been filming the other end of the story, the beginning, where the pigs arrived in wagonloads.

Very efficiently, aiming to achieve 'a capacity of 2,700 animals that corresponds to 4 hours of slaughter', the pigs were ushered off their transport into the loading bays. There was a row of about 20 bays with lorries backed up to them almost continuously. From there it was a short step for the pigs to the electric stunner and the bleeding, or 'exsanguination pre-draining' as they prefer to call it. Everything would go swimmingly until they came across an injured pig which was unable to play its part in the efficiency. A pig with a broken leg was a pig that couldn't walk the walk, and that was very inconvenient. Another pig might suffer a prolapsus, its guts hanging out of its backside. These were hiccups in the system. Targets could be missed. Computerised management might ask questions about wait times.

Enter our tractor driver, without trailer. His way of dealing was to fix a chain around one of the pig's legs, maybe a broken one, maybe not, he didn't care, and drag the animal across the floor and up a ramp to the raised pen while his workmates, tolerant of his methods, got back into their stride with their own hectic, pressurised business. Well, there was no need to worry about how you handled an injured pig when it only had a short time to live anyway.

I'd trained my two French colleagues in how to use a hidden camera and rehearsed them in their cover story. They would say they were there to meet their new employer, who was driving a wagonload of pigs to the slaughterhouse but he'd phoned to say he was stuck in traffic, so they'd just hang around until he turned up. It was a busy, busy place. Nobody would pay attention to these two, provided they looked the part and not like two college boys on a holy mission.

They did well. Their film was excellent. The good folk at PMAF were very excited, partly because the results were so good and partly because it was their first ever effort at undercover work. From long-distance observation they had known that there was cruelty at the slaughterhouse but had had no idea how to prove it. They'd approached Cooperl openly and been told to go away as there was no need for them to come and inspect. So, they'd got in touch with Animals' Angels, that superb German group staffed and run entirely by women, who'd got in touch with me. In one week we'd cracked the problem and had it shown on prime-time French television news.

Cooperl were horrified. Tesco were up in arms; it was their pork we'd been filming. The tractor driver was fined and fired. Cooperl directors met PMAF, launched an internal investigation and invited Animals' Angels to check the new measures. No more cruelty to pigs, and we're very grateful for that, but we have to ask how it could happen in the first place, and where else it might be happening.

This case is typical of the work I do now: cruelty where the operation is large scale, animal welfare people wanting to stop it but not knowing how, surveillance, training, cover story, covert recording, a positive outcome and, as long as people put money before animals, no possibility of retirement for me.